Wm. J. Schaldach

PATH TO ENCHANTMENT

An Artist in the Sonoran Desert

*A coyote carries its prey, an antelope jackrabbit,
to its den across the moonlit desert*

From an aquatint by the author

William J. Schaldach

PATH TO ENCHANTMENT

*An Artist
in the
Sonoran
Desert*

THE MACMILLAN COMPANY, NEW YORK
MACMILLAN NEW YORK, LONDON

© William J. Schaldach 1963

First Printing

THE MACMILLAN COMPANY, NEW YORK
COLLIER-MACMILLAN CANADA, LTD., GALT, ONTARIO
DIVISIONS OF THE CROWELL-COLLIER PUBLISHING
COMPANY
PRINTED IN THE UNITED STATES OF AMERICA
LIBRARY OF CONGRESS CATALOG CARD NUMBER:
63–9601

Designed by Andor Braun

To Jo

HER DEEP LOVE OF THE DESERT,

AND THE WONDERS OF NATURE,

ARE MY CONSTANT SOURCE OF INSPIRATION

THE WRITTEN WORD is at best an inadequate medium to convey to one unacquainted with the great Sonoran desert more than a hint of its grandeur, wonders, and mystery. Graphic illustration helps, but it still falls short of the mark. Writers and artists are confronted with a difficult task in attempting it. It is simpler to use the shopworn expression "It must be seen to be believed," yet to the totally uninitiated a brief preview can be of some help.

This book was done with that thought in mind. Written from more than a dozen years' experience in painting, fishing, camping, fieldwork, and observation, and mingling with the people in many parts of the desert, it is popular in concept and presentation. I am not a scientist— just an amateur naturalist—and I have purposely avoided the use of technical names throughout, even though at times this may lead to difficulties.

It is my hope that the brief sample of the several fascinating subjects presented in these pages may serve to whet the appetite and that this condensation may lead to further pursuit of the various subjects through the medium of the titles suggested in the Bibliography. And, best of all, that the reader may be tempted in person to visit *La Tierra Encantada*—The Enchanted Land.

For help in the preparation of text and illustration I am indebted to the following, whose kind and willing assistance is hereby gratefully acknowledged and greatly appreciated:

Dr. Frederick J. Dockstader, Director of the Museum of the American Indian, Heye Foundation, New York, for help with certain problems concerning the pre-Seri people. Also to the above Institution for permission to make drawings from its collection of figurines for reproduction.

Mr. P. Huber Hanes, Jr., for permission to reproduce several watercolors from his collection.

Natural History Magazine for permission to use material that originally appeared in that publication.

My son, William, Jr., who has been of great assistance because of his more than a decade of fieldwork in Mexico, in ornithology and mammalogy.

And finally to my son, Robert, who shares our love of the desert, who has accompanied us on many camping trips, and who has given me some valuable suggestions in the preparation of this work.

Sequence of Chapters

PATH TO ENCHANTMENT

An Artist in the Sonoran Desert

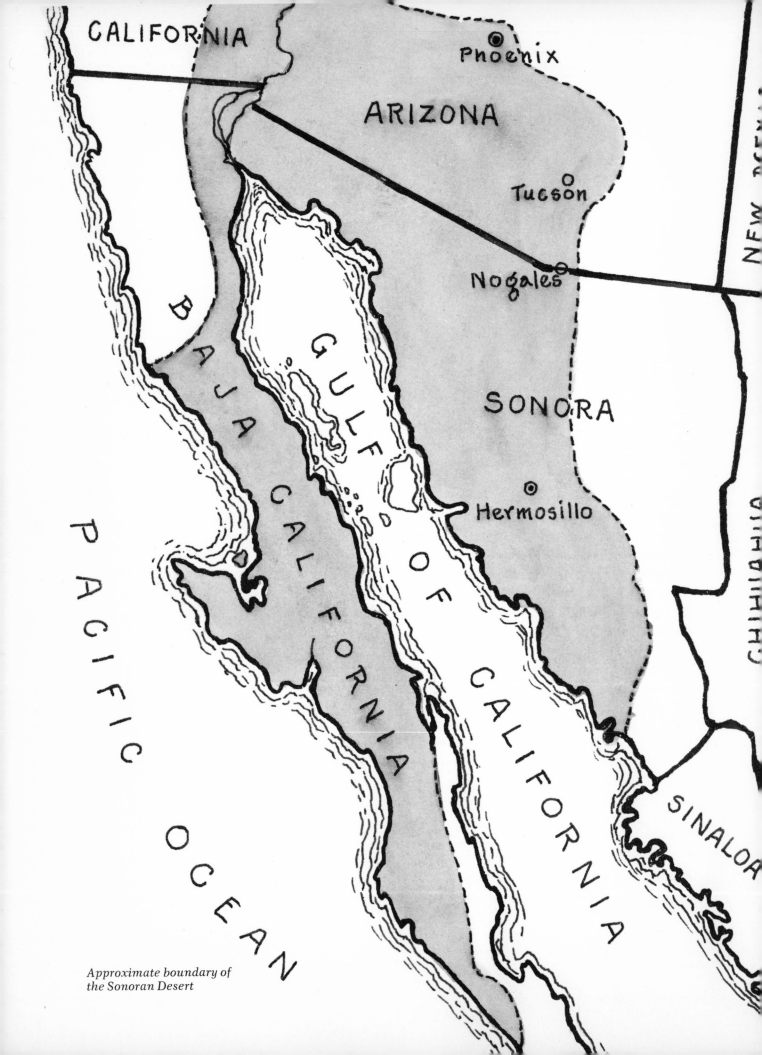

CALIFORNIA

Phoenix

ARIZONA

Tucson

NEW MEXICO

Nogales

BAJA CALIFORNIA

GULF OF CALIFORNIA

SONORA

Hermosillo

CHIHUAHUA

PACIFIC OCEAN

SINALOA

Approximate boundary of the Sonoran Desert

ONE

THE SONORAN DESERT

What it is—and is not

THE DESERT! The word has an electrifying effect. It conjures up visions of weird and strange things. To the uninitiated a procession of images passes across the mind's eye, bearing impressions that range from the thrilling to the chilling. Mirages like pleasant dreams: giant cactus—distant mesas and mountains that flame hotly, and cool to the color of wine in the sunset before donning the ashy-blue coat of evening—carpets of poppies, verbena, penstemon, covering the earth solidly; the desert in bloom. Romance! But then—

Snakes. Huge rattlers and coral snakes—Gila monsters—tarantulas and black widow spiders—unbearable heat—great wastelands of burning sand—thirst, even death. Horror!

Any region, the very name of which alone has the power to evoke such violently conflicting impressions upon the minds of those who have never seen it, must possess a powerful and unexplainable appeal.

The desert! A compelling word that one may come to love—or hate—but never to ignore. For the desert is a compelling place, unique in every aspect and in all its moods. Sunrise, midday, sunset, shifting cloud patterns, rain—all combine to create the very essence of the desert—mystery.

Since a mystery can never be solved (which is a blessing), the desert leaves much to the imagination. "I wonder . . ." is the beginning of a phrase often heard with respect to many things. It comes to the

1

"Cathedral Rocks," Santa Catalina Mountains

beholder naturally, because the place is filled with wonderment. The futility of imagination at a distance becomes obvious when the reality is faced. One must see the desert to believe. The reactions of visitors are varied—and often amusing. I think of an incident that occurred some years ago when my wife and I were taking a leisurely pleasure drive on a sun-bathed day in late March.

The spot we chose for a picnic lunch embodied all the elements that delight the true desert lover. Gently rolling land stretched from our position under the shade of a large old mesquite tree across sufficient miles to paint the distant mountains a gray-blue. Adobe red and ocher earth tones of the desert floor contrasted brilliantly with the olive-green foliage of the creosote bush, the grayer green of the giant Sahuaro cactus, and many large colonies of both purple and light yellow-green opuntia, commonly called prickly pear. Aside from a windmill and water tank some ten miles distant, no evidence of the hand of man was apparent—provided you kept your back turned on the hard road that brought you there, and the comfortable picnic table and benches that the Road Department had thoughtfully installed for your pleasure. Midway through lunch a large shining car pulled up and parked near us. Two men got out and stood looking at the view. They were dressed in eastern clothes, and looked prosperous and well fed. Their faces and arms were bronzed and reddened, the mark of an outdoor life. They looked intently and silently at the vast expanse for a full five minutes; then one turned to the other and said:

"Well, what do you think of it?"

"It don't look like corn country to me," he replied with a slow shake of his head.

2

Without further comment they got in the car and drove off. The rear bumper bore a license plate marked IOWA.

Several years ago a couple who live in a New Jersey suburb drove across the country to visit us. On numerous semiannual trips back in the days when my wife and I "commuted" between Vermont and Arizona, prior to our taking residence in the West, we used to stop over with them for a day or so. Our descriptions of the desert, together with color slides and landscapes in watercolor, fired their imaginations to the point where they agreed to make the long drive. Being city people who had never driven west of New York State, their timidity was understandable. But we were totally unprepared for their initial reaction. Herb, who had done the driving, was pretty badly shaken.

"My God, those roads!" he said with genuine agitation.

"What's the matter with the roads?" I asked. "You took the route I suggested, didn't you?"

"Nothing's the matter with them. That's the trouble. They're perfect—too perfect. Straight as an arrow, without a curve anywhere. You drive across that plains country, and there is that strip of road ahead of you, on and on, without a twist or bend until it meets the horizon. And when you get there—wherever *there* is—it's the same thing all over again. Once I drove 150 miles without seeing a gas station or even a hot-dog stand; and I was hungry too. A fellow could starve out here; or run out of gas and be in a hell of a fix. Now, in the East where the roads curve and you go through forests and—"

I explained to him gently that motorists out here always see to it that their gas tanks are well up, carry a jug of drinking water, and pretty well plan on where they are going to fetch up for lunch. Also, I told him that after he was out here a while the great open spaces wouldn't scare him so much; in fact, if he stayed long enough the land he lived in might even seem to choke him a bit.

The term "desert" frightens many people. A desert is a sandy parched waste of limitless area. Under the influence of a burning sun that broils the earth mercilessly, there is no vegetation except a few sorry clumps of burroweed scattered at intervals of hundreds of yards. Many perils beset the traveler who is foolhardy enough to venture into this infernal land. At intervals convenient to the horror writer (who incidentally has never been in a desert) grinning skulls and bleached bones of unfortunate souls may be found. It makes good background material for lurid western fiction, but it "jist ain't so." The dictionary may have something to do with the commonly accepted idea of a desert. Webster's New Collegiate says:

"Desert—1. A deserted region; a region left unoccupied.

2. An arid region lacking moisture to support vegetation."

3

In places the statement may be true. It certainly applies to great arid lands like the Sahara and even to certain very limited areas of our own American deserts. But that leaves vast expanses of land in the United States and Mexico alone to which neither definition applies. Among them are the Great Basin Desert in Nevada and Utah, the Mojave Desert, principally in California; the Chihuahuan Desert in southern New Mexico, and the State of Chihuahua in Old Mexico, and our great Sonoran desert.

All the American deserts have vegetation. The amount and varieties depend largely upon the annual rainfall and the variation in temperature. Through countless generations, in the process of evolution, desert species have been able to adapt themselves to a bare minimum of moisture and still thrive. In regions where rainfall averages as little as three inches in a year, the number and variety of plant species are a source of never ending wonderment.

The Sonoran desert has been blessed with a multitude of floral riches. It is the delight, and at the same time the dismay, of the visiting amateur botanist. Leaving aside for the time the many species of cactus, all of which bear blossoms at the proper season, small flowering plants occur in such numbers as to baffle anyone but a plant student. Then there are trees and shrubs that seem endless when one tries to identify them. Now, the miracle of all this is that this many-faceted blanket of vegetation, which transforms an otherwise sere land into a patterned design of greenery, is able to thrive on a minimum of precipitation. It is this startling fact, more than anything else, that strikes the visitor with force. This is the desert? Why, it's green; there are trees, shrubs, even great expanses of real green pasture grass in the summer. It is not a sandy waste, after all.

Love of the desert may come slowly, or may never come at all. It all depends on how one's feelings have been conditioned by environment and tastes. I had an uncle who went from Minnesota to live in California. After a residence of thirty years amid palm trees, avocados, bougainvillaea, and hibiscus, he still mourned the loss of the maple trees of his native Midwest. I have often wondered about the Iowa farmers who passed snap judgment on the desert. It certainly isn't corn country, if you except the rich bottomlands along the rivers where everything will grow when irrigated; and that's a boon. Those who are unable to tear away from corn and maple trees, and look with unprejudiced eyes upon the things of another land, will never like the desert—or any place but home.

Our friend Herb was different. In less than a week he was having the time of his life. His spirit expanded in direct ratio to the loss of his fear of what he had imagined the desert might be like. I almost had to restrain him, at the end of his visit, from dashing down to the Chamber

4

Superstition Mountains from the south

of Commerce to tell them about some of the wonders he had "discovered" that they might have overlooked and that should be included in their literature. Herb's trouble was that he was confusing the Sonoran desert country with the West in general. Admittedly there are some long stretches of monotonous wheeling in several of the states between the Eastern Seaboard and Arizona. The drive across the Great Plains is an ordeal at best, and by the time one's destination is reached nerves can be frazzled. Before we settled in Arizona, my wife and I drove across the country twenty-one times, so we are in a position to know! Unless one is fond of long grinds, it is better to fly, or go by train and relax.

Our own introduction to the desert dates back to the winter of 1937. During the previous summer we had bought an abandoned farm with a rather run-down house in the Pomfret Hills of Vermont. My wife and our two pre-teen-age boys had lived in Weston, Connecticut, in a small colony of artists and writers. One of these was the painter Ray Strang, noted for his fine oils of the desert. Before we moved to Vermont, Ray, his wife Gladys, and their son Dick settled in Arizona. They bought a place near Cortaro, consisting of forty acres of desert land containing many sahuaros and having a fine view of the Santa Catalina Mountains. There was a small cottage on the place, and they lived in it until their new house was completed.

We hadn't succeeded in getting our Vermont house fit for winter occupancy during the summer and fall, so the Strangs suggested that we go to Arizona and spend the winter in the little cottage on their place. Travel conditions were rugged more than a quarter of a century ago. Until you crossed the Pecos in Texas, motels were scarce and of poor quality. And even main-artery roads were pitifully inadequate, narrow and poorly surfaced. Our car was a 1933 Plymouth, tough and dependable, but not exactly comfortable for a long cross-country trip. We slipped on icy roads in the Cumberland Mountains, fought through a heavy rain-

Desert yesterday

storm in Tennessee, shivered in a Texas norther, and finally entered Arizona. It was early December, and the weather had remained cloudy and cold all across the country. We were still wearing overcoats when we stopped in Benson, a few miles out of Tucson, for lunch. The sun was shining brightly, and the air felt like spring. Winter, as we had known it for many years, was left behind, and with no regrets.

We had contracted colds on the long trip, but we shed them rapidly under the influence of the welcome sun. The radical change from the eastern flora to which we were accustomed—none of us had been west of Minnesota before—to the strange and fascinating plant forms of the desert, together with the sense of space and the grandeur of the mountains, enchanted us almost from the beginning. Before we had been in the desert a month, we felt that this was our country. At the end of our five-month stay we were sure of it.

I had arrived loaded with commitments, so for me the stay was not entirely a vacation. After a week the daily task seemed to lighten, and I ended the day without the feeling of exhaustion I had experienced at   6 home. The clarity of the air and constant sunlight had a benign effect on my spirits. I felt a strange sense of exhilaration I had not known before. Something else struck me forcibly. From the time I was ten years old I had been plagued with headaches, as many as two or three in a week. They did not incapacitate me; they simply nagged, and made work a chore. At the end of a month of daily work, the confining occupation of drawing in black and white, I suddenly realized one day that I hadn't had a headache. It must be temporary, I thought, and I waited for the blow to strike; but it never did, and I have been free of that malady ever since.

Between work and play the winter passed quickly. By the first of April I had made a complete set of pencil drawings for our good friend Dorothy, wife of the noted etcher John Taylor Arms, to illustrate her charming book *Fishing Memories* (Macmillan, 1938); I had also written two short stories for magazines, had done two sets of drawings for another magazine, and had made many pencil studies of the desert, besides a series of watercolor landscapes. Painting outdoors proved to be a delight. The great variation in color in the mountains, desert floor, and always the wonderful skies were sources of never ending inspiration, and a relief from the too green landscape of the East. Here, I felt, is real painter's country.

We left the desert with regrets, knowing that it would be a long time before we could return. There would be high school and college for the boys, and, though we did not of course then know it, a war that would keep us in the East.

A decade later, in 1948, we felt free to go back. The late Ernest Miller, who, with his wife, Grace, operated the Elkhorn Ranch, found a small house for us to rent in the little Mexican border village of Sasabe. Time had increased the lure of the desert, and we settled in contentedly, as though we had never left. But for several years it had to be winters only. We would leave regretfully in May and fret through the Vermont summer, undeniably beautiful as it is, impatiently awaiting September and the westward migration. Each spring when we arrived home the countryside seemed a little smaller. The hills seemed to have shrunk; the foliage on the trees seemed twice as thick as before. Then there were those gloomy days, days of semilight when it didn't rain, but when the sun failed to come out. They seemed endless. It was fatal for a painter.

One day my wife said to me, pointing to a huge old maple near the house, "Do those branches seem to be reaching down to grab you?"

She had hit it right on the nose! It was what had been bothering me right along, but I hadn't put it in words. Of course the New England hills hadn't shrunk; it was just that our outlook had expanded.

"They sure do, honey," I replied. "Let's face it: we're just desert rats at heart. Let's sell out and move."

We settled our affairs in June of 1956, and on an early morning pointed the nose of the car toward the desert. When we saw the first sahuaros, and a roadrunner darted in front of us, we felt that we were truly home.

If anything in the foregoing account of our move to the desert seems to read like a plug for the desert, let me say that it is not intended that way. I am not in any way connected with the Chamber of Commerce or the Sunshine Club. Goodness knows, they don't need help. The drift of population to this area in the last two decades has been astonishing, sometimes even a little appalling. As an example, in 1937 Tucson was just a quiet little cow town of some 40,000 people. Today the population is something like 220,000! It has several industries that sprawl over acres of ground, the Hughes Plant, to mention only one. Tucson is the seat of the University of Arizona, with its fine museum of archaeology, and a few miles out of town the unique Arizona-Sonora Desert Museum is located (a description will be found in another section of the book). The new Kitt Peak Astronomical Observatory is situated in the Quinlan Mountains, about forty miles west of town.

The climate is not a panacea for all ills known to the flesh, though this quaint idea seems difficult to shake off, especially among the miracle seekers. My headaches left me, and Ray Strang got rid of the severe ones that were slowly killing him, though his chronic sinus condition never completely cleared up. In general, bronchiatrics are benefited, provided they live outside of the dust area of the large cities. Many arthritics derive help, but others report no gain whatever, depending upon the type of arthritis with which they are afflicted. As one old lady said, "I came to Arizona for arthritis—and I got it."

The term "Sonoran desert" covers a lot of territory, and a statement about one part of it may not be true of another. So far I have referred only to the area around Tucson. This city is the principal gateway to Mexico, through Nogales, on Route 15, the western highway to Mexico City. It leads through the heart of the Sonoran desert in Mexico, and is the one used by the great majority of tourists. Much of interest in the way of typical desert flora and fauna may be seen along the route, but the full flavor of the land may be sampled only by allowing sufficient time for side trips off the main highway.

Desert zones are determined by the flora of the region, and that in turn is dependent on several factors. Among them are precipitation, temperature, and elevation. Because there may be a rather wide variation of these factors within a comparatively small range, the stated boundaries of a desert zone must necessarily be flexible rather than

8

Sabino Cañon, a fascinating recreational area near
Tucson, in the Santa Catalina Mountains

arbitrary. Often there will be small extensions that may stretch for
several miles, owing to topographical conditions.

Roughly, then, the Sonoran desert might be described as occupying
the country bounded on the east, in Arizona, by the San Pedro River; on
the west somewhat beyond Ajo, and on the north to a line running
northwest a few miles beyond Phoenix to the Mojave Desert. Below the
Mexican border the western extension of the desert takes in much of the
plains land of Baja California, a great deal of it being on the Pacific
slope, and the area east of the Gulf of California from the United
States line to the border of Sinaloa. The eastern boundary is irregular,

being determined more or less by the Sierra Madre Mountains. (See map.)

Since elevations in this vast area range from sea level to several thousand feet, it can readily be seen that there would be a considerable difference in temperature between two points, even relatively close together, at the same season of the year. And that brings us to a matter of perpetual interest to everyone from the Eskimo to the Hottentot; for after all, we must live with the weather and be governed by its whims. Next to the horrors of having to live in a land overrun with deadly, crawly creatures like snakes, scorpions, and Gila monsters, the stifling, shriveling heat takes only second place.

"Why, I hear that the temperature gets way up over a *hundred* and *stays* there for weeks at a time. My dear, how can you *stand* it?" said a gushing lady at a cocktail party in Vermont.

It does.

"And I understand that people pass out by the *dozens*," she continued, "and even have to go to the hospital."

They don't.

I don't know where the lady got her information, but it certainly was wrong; cases of heat prostration in the desert are far fewer than in the land east of the Great Plains. The reason is lack of humidity, except near the sea.

As a general thing, the hottest months in the desert are June and September. These are the dry months of summer. Heat builds up, but 10 humidity reaches an unbelievably low point. Not uncommonly it will drop to 4, or even 2 per cent. Now, humid heat is much harder to bear than dry heat. This is not to say that a temperature of 110 is comfortable, but when the humidity level is well below 10, the combination is a lot more bearable than a temperature of 90 and a humidity of 95, as is so often the case in the East.

The highest temperature I can recall occurred one day in the summer of 1956 when the weather bureau at the University in Tucson recorded 117 degrees. It touched that briefly, then descended to a cool (?) 110. We didn't play any baseball or hoe weeds in the garden. We stayed in our house with the cooler on, and weren't aware of the record until we read about it in the paper next day.

Every degree over 100 can be felt—no use kidding yourself about it, but extreme heat rarely lasts more than a few days, and it is invariably accompanied by low humidity. We have been through a few hot spells in the desert, but strangely enough the highest temperature we ever encountered occurred in Glasgow, Montana, in July of 1948. We were traveling the northern route to the Canadian Rockies, just ahead of a violent storm that later struck us with full fury soon after we were safely bedded down in a motel. The heat buildup had been terrific, though we didn't fully realize it while we were running with windows open. Upon stopping the car, the hot blast that rose from the ground almost knocked us off our feet. The local paper stated that the official high, recorded by the weather bureau, was 129! We haven't encountered anything like that in Arizona, though it may come close to it on rare occasions in Yuma, which is situated only a little above sea level in the desert of the Colorado River.

Elevation is the great temperature regulator. In Arizona, Yuma and Gila Bend are hot spots. Phoenix (1,100 feet) is hotter than Tucson (2,400 feet). Nogales at 3,800 is definitely cooler than Tucson. Going

south into Mexico on Route 15, we find that after crossing the height of land a short distance south of Nogales the gradual drop in altitude heats things up again. Magdalena, a small town some sixty miles south of Nogales, warms up, and by the time we reach Hermosillo, about 175 miles down and in, we are sweating. It is only 800 feet above sea level.

All of the above applies to summer temperatures—and not all summer at that. Nature has thoughtfully supplied a built-in air-conditioning service for us when the rains come. Then temperatures rarely go above the 90's, and evenings are delightfully cool. In general the season of real heat extends from about late May until early October. I have gone into the matter of hot weather a little for the benefit of those who are considering the Southwest as a permanent home. The majority of visitors come here in the fall and winter months and stay until early spring.

Barring periods of rains, which may last two or three days and occur from late November to early February, the winter climate in the desert is about as delightful as can be desired. But it gets cold in the deep part of the winter, and the air can chill you to the bone if you don't dress properly. Frost occurs frequently at night during December through mid-February, and the temperature sometimes drops to the low 20's. At noon it often reaches the 70's. Two or three times during winter a rainstorm coming up from the Gulf of California may turn into snow and leave a cover of as much as six inches. It is usually gone by noon of the next day. This applies to the low country in the vicinity of Tucson. The mountain areas gather and keep snow for long periods. Mount Lemmon (elevation 9,185 feet) just outside of Tucson, has a ski tow that usually is able to operate for several weeks each season. Skiing in the desert! Ridiculous, but true.

Arizona is noted for its fine guest establishments, popularly known as dude ranches. Here the business of entertaining visitors has been developed into a fine art. The many ranches in the area visited by people who take their vacations in the winter are located in excellent riding country. There is always some comparatively level terrain for beginners (one doesn't have to know the starboard from the port side of a horse at first), and there are more interesting mountain trails for experienced riders.

The three most important industries throughout practically all of the Sonoran desert are cattle raising, agriculture, and mining. Cattle "spreads" vary in size and importance from the five-hectare holding—complete with two cows—which is the pride and joy of José, to vast tracts of more than 200 sections. The Buenos Aires Ranch lying along the Sasabe Road in Pima County, southern Arizona, is one of these. In 12

Sonora cattle brands

case you are hazy about the extent of a section, as I was when I first came to the West, it consists of 640 acres, or one square mile. This, as an old-timer put it, is quite a "passel" of land.

It is impossible to drive far in the desert without seeing cows; they are everywhere, even in towns and villages that have not yet got around to employing fenced range. Many of the roads in both Arizona and Sonora, Mexico, still traverse open range country, and this constitutes a hazard to motorists. The law states that if a driver hits a cow and kills or injures it, he is responsible, not the cow. He not only pays for the cow but also has to foot the bill for repairs to his car, as well as to himself if he is so unfortunate as to have a bad crash. An unfair law? Many of us think so, but it is still on the books. Public sentiment, however, is rapidly changing the situation, and the day is not far off when there will be no more open range. In the meantime, when driving through cattle country be on the alert. Signs are posted at regular intervals warning the motorists. They read: OPEN RANGE or WATCH FOR STOCK. In Mexico the signs are worded: CUIDADO CON LOS GANADOS.

The traditional cow of the West is the white-faced Hereford, and it still predominates on the ranges in most of the cow country from the Great Plains to the Pacific. But there has been a drift in recent years to other breeds. Brahmas are seen in increasing numbers on many of the desert ranges, as well as Black Angus and the breed developed by the King Ranch in Texas, the Santa Gertrudis. There are many crosses, and this sometimes results in weird effects. Coming suddenly upon a black cow with a white face in the eerie light of dusk is apt to give one a start. Such a creature results from crossing a Hereford with a Black Angus. It is being done a great deal on the Buenos Aires Ranch.

The rancher's life does not consist entirely in high living through profits from beefsteaks. There are good times and lean ones, depending wholly on how nature has seen fit to treat the rangelands. In years of bountiful rainfall the grasses—gramma, crowfoot, love grass, and many other varieties—grow up almost to a horse's belly, and there is joy in the land. But at other times, often for several years in a row, the searing hand of drought scorches the earch, and grass will not grow. During such periods the rancher must buy expensive feed for the cattle he decides to keep. Animals on the range ate mesquite leaves, various weeds, prickly pear, and cholla. The cholla is a cactus having very succulent flesh, but unfortunately it is covered with vicious spines. When a cow's belly begins to burn with hunger, she will tackle anything, and it is a common sight to see animals with their lips and noses festooned with cholla.

The common conception of a cow is that of an animal developed by man to supply such useful commodities as milk and T-bone steaks,

13

Sonora cattle brands

but with a brain not much above the level of that possessed by a chicken. However, cows sometimes do things that make you wonder. It is a common sight to see an animal gingerly holding the edge of a large prickly pear leaf in her mouth and methodically beating it on a rock to pound off the spines, then calmly munching it. Now how did she learn that?

During dry periods cattle will eat off every available blade of grass in a pasture until nothing but dry earth remains. There is a story current among the ranchers about the owner of a big spread who was riding range with one of his cowmen. Everywhere the earth was brown and sere; even the weeds had dried up. In the midst of his dejection he spotted something that made him sit bolt upright in the saddle.

"My God," he exclaimed, "a blade of grass! Hurry up, go fetch a cow!"

Rivaling the cattle industry in importance, agriculture employs a great proportion of the arable land in the Sonoran desert from Phoenix in Arizona to below Ciudad Obregón in Mexico, and gives employment to many thousands of people. Here again the term "desert" is a misnomer. While the soil may look like a gravel pit to the uninformed, actually most of it is extremely fertile. Many of the big farming projects are situated in the valleys along watercourses, but this is not necessarily true of all of them. Some of the finest farms, producing wheat, cotton, chiles, frijoles (beans), sorghum, tomatoes, and other products, are to be found on flatlands far from a stream. This is particularly true in Sonora. As one example only, the visitor driving from Hermosillo to Kino Bay will be amazed to see fields of wheat that billow in the wind to the distant horizon without a break. It reminds one of the Dakotas.

The reason for this, of course, is water. Irrigation (the Spanish word is *riego*) is necessary. Given sufficient water, any plant suited to temperature conditions will grow profitably. The big problem is to get water, and therein lies one of the greatest dilemmas facing not only the people of the Sonoran desert but also of the entire Southwest. To get to the bottom of the problem it is necessary to understand where available water may be found and how to obtain it. Since the average rainfall varies in the desert from as little as 3 inches to an approximate maximum of 20 inches, in most areas, with an average of about 12 inches, it can readily be seen that natural, or "dry," farming is out of the question. Dependence must be placed wholly upon ground water. The problem is very complex, and nothing but the sketchiest explanation can be given here.

Ground water is present in areas along the rivers, washes, and creeks in most sections of the desert. The term "river" or "creek" is puz- 14

Arizona cattle brands

zling to most strangers. It is natural to expect water in a river, but during most of the year what they see is a dry, gravelly stream bed. When the rains come, the parched ground is transformed into a muddy, raging torrent of churning water. Draining the watershed, the flood may come suddenly and sweep everything before it. Many motorists have been caught and lives have been lost in such a sudden rush of water. Where a road crosses even an insignificant-looking wash there may be a sign: DANGER IN FLOOD SEASON. If you come upon such a place during a heavy rain, stop, look, and listen before crossing.

The surface water that flows in rivers and washes isn't very useful as such, except as it is diverted into cattle tanks (*represas*) and ponds. During the runoff, much of it sinks into the earth to replenish the natural underground reservoirs. All such areas along the important rivers are known and mapped. The water may lie from a depth of a few yards to several hundred feet below the surface. For irrigation purposes, wells with large-diameter metal casings are sunk, and the water is pumped out.

Some of the principal rivers in the Arizona desert supplying water for farming are the San Pedro, the Santa Cruz, the Gila, and the Salt River. Some important streams in Sonora are the San Miguel, the Altar (farther down it is called the Magdalena and, before it reaches the Gulf of California, the Concepción), the Sonora, and the Río Yaqui. All these streams are called upon to yield more and more water from their underground reservoirs as the years go by. The water table, as a consequence, sinks lower, and wells must be drilled deeper in order to produce.

The farmer has been profiting for many years. He makes money in spite of ever increasing restrictions being placed on acreage and number of wells. On the whole he does very well. He might be completely happy except that he lives under the shadow of a cloud cast by two factions that are somewhat less than pleased with things as they are.

One of these groups is composed of the industrialists whose large plants have been increasing yearly, especially in the vicinity of Tucson. They require great quantities of water daily in order to operate. The other faction is made up of cities and towns whose outskirts spread like dandelions in a lawn and grow with the rapidity of mushrooms. Their constant cry is Water! Give us more water!

The City of Tucson derives its water from underground storage reservoirs filled by washes and rivers and from subterranean sources in the Rincon Mountains. A number of private companies have been pumping water from the earth and supplying it to residences throughout the sprawling area of the city. They are gradually being taken over by the

Arizona cattle brands

city, and are being consolidated. But the supply is inadequate even now, and it grows more so yearly. Under these conditions something must give, and it looks as if that something might be a limiting of agriculture. Agitation is increasing to restrict drastically farming for commercial crops such as cotton, which requires large quantities of water, resulting in the lowering of the water table.

In Mexico the problem may not be so serious, owing to the dispersal of most farm areas away from populated centers. Cities in Sonora are few. Hermosillo, the most important one, is fortunate in having the Sonora River, which fills a large lake just outside town. It also seeps into the ground and affords a bountiful supply of deep water for pumping. Most of the agriculture in the vicinity of Hermosillo is carried on far enough away so that the city's water supply is not affected. The large area of flatland lying between Hermosillo and Kino Bay, previously mentioned, is well supplied with underground water because of topographical conditions.

The third large industry, mining, is an extensive industry throughout the mountain areas of most of the Sonoran desert. The region is rich in minerals of many kinds, and mine operations, from the little one-man diggings of the prospector to the huge operation of corporations like Anaconda, may be found in every range of mountains and mineral-bearing locality. The subject will be taken up in another chapter.

Much of what has been written concerns the part of the Sonoran desert lying in Arizona, and particularly in the area around Tucson. In visiting a region we must start somewhere, and Tucson, via Nogales—the port of entry to Mexico—is the point of arrival of the majority of tourists. The easternmost port of entry to Sonora is at Douglas, through the Mexican town of Agua Prieta. The next port to the west is Naco, Arizona. Both have roads leading through the mining and cattle town of Cananea to Imuris, where Route 15 to Mexico City is picked up. It is possible to enter Sonora through the Port of Sasabe, reached by taking the Ajo Way from South Tucson to Robles Ranch (popularly called Three Points) and then dropping south some forty-five miles to the border. This strip of sixty-two miles to Altar, where the main paved highway to Santa Ana is joined, is scraped periodically and is passable most of the year by driving slowly. A new paved road is being planned. The last practicable entry to Sonora is at Lukeville, on the American side, to Sonoyta. There one may go to Punto Peñasco (Rocky Point) on the Gulf of California, or take the road east through Caborca and Altar to Santa Ana and connect with Route 15.

Entering Mexico is a simple matter for United States citizens. Proof of citizenship must be provided in the form of a birth or baptismal certificate in order to obtain the necessary *permiso*. This may be   16 got at the Mexican Consul in Tucson or Nogales, or at any port of entry. It is necessary only to answer a few simple questions. Visitors are permitted to enter Mexico only for purposes of health or pleasure, not business. When one is going into the country with a car, two papers are issued, an immigration form (*migración*) and a customs paper (*aduana*). The latter is issued only to the driver of the car and is marked *"Entró con automóvil."* The ordinary form of *permiso* is valid for a stay of six months in Mexico, but must be surrendered at a port of return even if used for a day. The current price of this *permiso* is $3.00.

Another form of *permiso* is provided for visitors who wish to make a number of trips back and forth during a six-month period. It is known as the *"Viajes múltiples"* form. To obtain this paper two small passport photographs are required. A customs permit is issued, as in the case of the single entry, but it is valid for only three months. It must then be renewed (without charge) for the remaining three months of the life of the immigration paper. Currently, the price of this *permiso* is $5.00.

When entering Mexico through Nogales, one drives to the first checking station a short way out of town. There, customs and immigration officers examine papers and check the contents of the car. No firearms are allowed without special permits, and there may be questions about articles like phonographs and radios that might be disposed of without paying duty. But aside from these considerations there will be no difficulty. It is customary to offer the porter a little tip (*propina*). A dollar will do. He will paste a sticker marked *revisado* (inspected) on your baggage, and you will have no further examination at the several inspection stations you will stop at on the way to Hermosillo.

Route 15 is a well-maintained blacktop road traversing interesting country. It is well posted with signs for the guidance of the motorist,

but since the information is in Spanish it will take time to get used to them. Here are some typical examples:

PUENTE ANGOSTO—Narrow bridge
CAMINO SINUOSO—Winding road
CONSERVE SU DERECHA—Keep to the right
NO DEJE PIEDRAS EN EL CAMINO—Do not leave rocks in the road
ZONA ESCOLAR—School zone
CURVA PELIGROSA—Dangerous curve
PELIGRO, DERRUMBES—Danger, falling rocks
NO CRUCE LA LINEA CENTRAL—Do not cross the center line

Another thing to remember is that distances are marked in kilometers, not miles. This, of course, also governs speed. The sign VELOCIDAD 100 K means that the motorist is entitled to drive the United States equivalent, which is about 62 miles an hour. He should resist the urge to push the pedal down to the floorboard!

Mexico has recently been adopting the sensible European system of marking warning signs with symbols. The figures are black silhouettes against a yellow background. A child carrying books means school zone; a cow, open range, and so on.

The brief sample of the Sonoran desert presented in the foregoing pages was designed for two purposes: to correct some misconceptions concerning certain phases of the land; and, like the anchovy on the cracker, perhaps to whet the appetite of those who have wanted to visit the desert but have hesitated for lack of anything more concrete than hearsay. The following chapters are intended to convey in more detail the things that, taken together, truly make the great Sonoran desert *La Tierra Encantada,* the Enchanted Land.

Mine tipple, Tucson Mountains, Arizona
From a watercolor by the author

TWO

MOUNTAINS AND MYTHS

*Reality and fantasy blend naturally
in the mysterious desert ranges*

TO PEOPLE who have never visited the desert, the mental picture usually envisioned is one of a great expanse of flat or perhaps gently rolling country. For some reason, mountains are not associated with the arid country; or if they are, they are thought of as something apart from the true desert. Now this may be true of some deserts in various parts of the world, but it does not apply to the Sonoran desert, nor to the great arid regions of North America. In any of these areas, mountain ranges are always in sight, surrounding them and a part of them.

Many of the mountains in Arizona and Sonora are high, and all are impressive. The rugged and bulky mass of the Santa Catalina Mountains looms up against the sky north of Tucson, and is one of the most spectacular ranges in Arizona. A serrated outline on the western ridge is known as "Cathedral Rocks," and the highest point is Mount Lemmon, altitude 9,185 feet. A hard road leads up to a fine recreation area,

Santa Rita Mountains from Tubac

around 8,000 feet in elevation. There, within the compass of a few miles, one may change from low desert heat to the necessity of using a blanket at night, in mid-August. There, also, the snow lover may satisfy his yearning for skiing and winter sports, in January and February, and even have the convenience of a ski tow. The area is clothed in pines and firs, and the handsome tufted-ear Abert's squirrel—a northern form that has been introduced—scampers happily about. Incredible as it may seem, this is still the desert.

20

Probably the most fabulous of all the mountains rimming the desert is the range known as the Superstitions, which lies about midway between Phoenix and Globe. This is an exceedingly wild and rugged region—the very name is eerie—which has never been completely explored. The area is steeped in romance—and tragedy. It is the land of bloody feuds where prospectors have been shot from ambush by rivals, and still are. A number of incidents have taken place in 1960 and 1961, not to mention a long list of dire happenings since the earliest times. In the interminable maze of canyons and rough eroded land, venturesome souls are continually getting lost and many of them never return. Sometimes their remains are found months or years later, often never. This is the land of old mines of fabulous richness—the famous "Lost Dutchman" is just one of them, the existence of which is positively known, but the exact location . . . ? Ah, that is the enigma. It is the will-o'-the-wisp that sends men out into this desolate region, knowing that they are risking their lives in pursuit of a phantom. Desire overbalances reason. Someday, somehow—

When driving from Tucson to Phoenix the Superstitions will be seen from the right of the road (north) about midway between Florence Junction and Mesa. Several roadside signs indicate them. The range is a fine and impressive sight to see—but as good a place to keep out of as one could name!

Mountains make a powerful appeal to the imagination. From an esthetic standpoint, few natural features of the landscape surpass them. They are cloaked in mystery; they are ever changing and ever the same. They flame in the sunset with tones of wine and accents of deepest blue: they partly conceal themselves in clouds of mist and driving rain in the fury of the storm; they stand firm against the sky

Baboquivari Peak from the south

like giant grotesque figures in the moonlight. They are a challenge to the young and vigorous to climb their rugged escarpments and sloping faces, and a consolation and source of serene contemplation to the aged, who can do no more than admire them from afar.

In the mountains there is always something to do. The bird watcher will delight in looking for rare species, some of which have been noted in another chapter; and the amateur botanist will find plants that will surprise him—ferns, rare cactus not found at lower altitudes, and many variants of shrubs and trees, belonging to families with which he may be familiar.

And here the "rock hound" will find much to delight him. Minerals of many kinds are present in all mountainous areas. Some must be loosened from their matrix with a geologist's pick; others may be found as "floats" in washes, on the talus slopes of eroding mountain faces, and in the heaps of detritus found in many areas. Common minerals are agate, quartz (sometimes fine crystals in geodes), jasper, chalcedony, azurite, malachite, garnets, rhyolite, calcite and tourmaline crystals; obsidian, iron pyrite, in cubical crystal form; chert, and a long list of rocks known to most hunters, besides several rarities.

Old abandoned mining workings usually are fertile fields for the rock hound, and often beautiful and rare specimens are found in the discards in dumps. One such old mine north and west of Tucson yielded some excellent crystals of tangerine-colored vanadinite. In roaming over mountains one never knows where treasures will turn up. One day in March, my wife and I climbed one of the lower slopes of the southern end of the Cerro Colorado Mountains. Near a pass, which overlooked a vast area of country on two sides, we were delighted to find a ledge of pure reddish chert. Underneath it was a huge pile of chips that had been hacked off the main mass. We had found an ancient quarry, undoubtedly made by the Hohokam centuries ago. They went there to collect "stockpile" chunks of the fine chert from which they later made arrowheads, scrapers, and knives.

All mountain areas are cloaked in legend that reaches back to the earliest of recorded times. Tales are handed down from one generation to the other—of buried treasure, of mysterious incidents that are unexplainable, of intrigue and foul play. They become magnified with time, and many of them are accepted as true, among the uneducated, even to this day.

Many of the mountains in the Sonoran desert, as well as elsewhere, are said to contain buried treasures of great value. And it is not all legend or hearsay, for a number of caches have been found. But the huge booty, the one that contains millions of dollars' worth of gold and silver bullion, besides a king's fortune in precious gems, remains yet 22 to be unearthed. Everyone knows that several such treasures exist, both in Arizona and in Mexico. The Conquistadores buried booty on their northward march, and the early padres did also, when pressed by the Indians and forced to evacuate an area. Many people have dug up ancient maps—somewhere—giving the "exact location" of fabulous wealth, and the excavation that has gone on would put a colony of prairie dogs to shame—with at least 99 percent failure.

There are many explanations of why treasures are not found, none of them very logical, but the one I particularly like is current in much of Mexico. It is usually told in different versions, but the theme is that buried treasure is guarded by sinister forces that will not permit its discovery by mortals. A cave in the side of a mountain is a favorite locale. Someone finds a large loose rock that looks suspicious, rolls it back, and enters a vaultlike chamber. There in great piles are bars of gold and silver, and sacks of coins. He rubs his hands in avaricious anticipation, fills his pockets with gold coins, gathers as many of the bars of bullion as he can stagger with, and turns to leave. But it is dark now; no light comes through the opening where he entered. He takes a step; then a sonorous voice booms out in sepulchral tones—*Todo, o nada! Todo—o—na—da!* All, or nothing! Since it is obviously impossible for a man to carry the whole load, which amounts to tons, the treasure is still there.

Another tale, having nothing to do with treasure, is current near Pozo Verde, a few miles south of the border; it seems to be a curious mixture of Mexican and Papago lore. A long time ago a wicked witch lived in a cave in the mountains near a settlement. Strange things happened: cows got sick and died, horses broke their legs, and crops withered. But worst of all, little children began to disappear, one by one. Then, one day one of the men found the bones of a child in the ashes of a campfire. The witch was a cannibal! But what to do? Her spells were so strong that no one dared lay a hand on her. A council was held and a plan agreed upon.The people prepared a great feast, and obtained a large quantity of mescal (or sahuaro wine, if you follow the Papago version) and, pretending friendship, invited the witch to the party. Drinking began early, and while it was going on a number of men went to the cave and piled a great heap of firewood on the old hag's bed. Then they gathered a lot of stones and placed them near the entrance of the cave.

The old gal was pretty hardheaded, and it took a lot of mescal to knock her out; but she finally collapsed in a stupor and was carried to the cave. They put her on the pile of wood, touched it off, and quickly sealed up the entrance. And that was that. Now, should anyone doubt the authenticity of this harrowing saga, he has only to go to the cave, which to this very day is blackened with smoke from the fire that sent the wicked old witch to her doom. The place is easily reached. I have seen it myself, and it is sooted up pretty badly. I don't want to spoil a good story, but I personally know of at least a dozen other caves, the roofs and sides of which are smoke-blackened.

As is true in every part of the country, the desert has its share of quaint and colorful characters. Take, for example, the prospector. The typical "desert rat," as he is sometimes called, has no use for civilization, or the comforts thereof. Establish him in a modern house in town, with all its conveniences, and he would soon choke to death. All he asks from life is a stock of sowbelly and beans, his pick, shovel, and rifle, his blanket and his burro (more recently, an old pickup truck), and he will be off to roam the back country for months at a time.

There are several types of so-called prospectors—the term is a loose one. Some are equipped with Geiger counters and all sorts of modern mineral detectors. Theirs is a grim business; they are out to make a killing—to discover a rich lode, sell the rights to a company, and get out, to live in luxury the rest of their lives. They are interested only in end results, and the sooner they achieve the goal, the better. The true prospector, on the other hand, pursues his occupation from an urgency that lies deep within him, an unexplainable force that might be termed "the pull of the desert." He is starry-eyed, always anticipating making a big strike, yet secretly hoping he never will. When, as sometimes happens, he does really hit pay dirt, he spends the money as quickly as possible, gets an outfit, and takes to roaming the desert again. The real prospector wants only the hunt, not the gain.

Old mine entrance

In an age when traditions are rapidly passing, the old-time prospector is just another piece of flotsam, to be swept away on the current of progress. Mining has become big business, and crews of experts take the place of the colorful characters who used to locate valuable deposits of ore, and deal directly with the companies. The operations of the old-time prospectors nowadays are chiefly limited to panning washes and streams for the small amount of gold they can find, seeking surface "floats" of silver ore, or perhaps locating a small vein of gold- or silver-bearing ore in the side of a mountain, and patiently pecking out a living. These metals can always be sold in small quantities. Some of the old boys still hang on, preferring their occupation to one that might be far more remunerative, but, to their restless spirits, deadly boring. They invariably have a sunny disposition and a rare sense of humor. Here is a typical example:

In a mountainous area near the border, in southern Arizona, a grizzled old fellow had located a small vein of silver ore, staked a claim, built a shack, and settled down to tunneling in, following the vein with pick and shovel—the hard way. His diggings were situated on a ledge above a wash, which was dry except in the rainy season. One day he saw an old Mexican some distance below him, busily digging in the sand. Looking up, the Mexican saw the miner. *"Buenos días,"* he said, waving. *"Buenos días,"* replied the other, returning to his work with a puzzled look. The next day the same thing happened: *"Buenos días"* and *"Buenos días"* were the extent of the conversation. It went on for a couple of weeks; then one morning the Mexican failed to show up. A week passed, and there was no sign of him. The miner's curiosity kept mounting until he could no longer bear it. He had to make a trip to the assay office, anyhow, and while there he gently eased the conversation around to the subject that was puzzling him. He thought he might find the answer there; and he was right.

"Say," he started out, "you wouldn't know anything about a li'l' ol' stooped-shoulder' Mexican—mebbe seventy years old or so—with a big white moustache and a kinda gimpy left leg, would you?"

"Sounds like old José Ortega. Why?"

"Well, he's been working the wash near my diggin's for a coupla weeks, throwin' sand out with his shovel somethin' scandalous; you'd think a mess o' badgers had been in there. I coulda told him there ain't nothin' there, only I don't palaver Mexican good. Figgered it wa'n't none of my business, anyhow. But just the same I'd like to know what he was doin'. The old guy must be nuts."

"Yes, I guess he's nuts all right," replied the assayer. "Last week we handed him a check for a little over $6,ooo. He had silver chloride floats, the richest we've seen in a long time."

The best part of this story is that the old miner took it as a great joke, even though it was on himself. He delights in telling it again and again, and laughingly quotes the old proverb, "There's no fool like an old fool."

The lonely life of the prospector, or solitary miner, tends to develop a sense of calmness and philosophy. He lives with nature and is a part of it, not merely a spectator, as is the average town dweller, who occasionally takes time out from his daily grind to gobble down a hasty picnic lunch, or engage in a breakneck drive through a beautiful country he has neither time nor understanding eyes to see. A perfect example of the prospector-philosopher was old Jess, who has become a legend in a little village in southern Arizona, located on the Mexican border.

I never knew Jess—we arrived a year or so after he had died—but everyone in town had a good word to say for him. To them he was something much more than just another "desert rat." He was described as being tall and lean, with a great beard and kindly eyes—a Whitman-like character. He was soft-spoken and friendly with everyone. Dogs, even the most aloof ones, flocked to him with wagging tails, and children listened in rapt silence to his wondrous stories; such was his personality.

Jess lived in a little cabin near a sizable wash, some ten miles from town, in a rough country, about a mile from the border. He panned a little gold here and there, visiting washes in the area by riding the saddle horse that was his only companion. When he needed provisions he would sell the few small nuggets and dust that had taken him weeks to get. Sometimes he would ride into town with a haunch of venison thrown over the saddle. It was a "gift" to the local storekeeper, who in turn reciprocated with canned tomatoes, crackers, bacon, and other staples. It was all very dignified, and could not even be considered barter. Whether the deer that produced the venison was shot in season or out is a matter that does not concern us here. Jess was an honorable man, and everyone knew it, including the game warden.

The International Boundary runs right through the middle of a tall, rounded hill, separating Mexico from the United States. It is a barbed-wire cow fence, mostly in a bad state of repair. Were you to look at a survey map, you would find it marked *Cerro Fresnal* (Hill of the Ash Trees). But if you mentioned it to any of the villagers they wouldn't know what you meant. To them it always has been "Jess's Mountain," and it always will be. The old man never possessed much of the world's goods, in the popular sense, but he did achieve a degree of immortality not granted to everyone. Very few people have a mountain, even an insignificant little one, named after them.

We had heard that the cabin in which Jess spent so many years was still intact, a few months after we went to the little village to live, so we made a trip over there. It was a one-room affair, snug and well built, still sound and weathertight. On the gentle slope back of the place a cactus garden, containing some rare items that Jess had transplanted with loving care, still thrived. Inside, over the bed, a long shelf contained some magazines and a few books. The magazines were the *National Geographic,* dating back to the 1920's. Among the books, we found: *The Odyssey,* Plato's *Republic,* a complete set of the plays of Shakespeare, and the Bible.

No, Jess never possessed much of the world's goods—or did he?

Mining claim boundary marker

THREE

CACTI, YUCCA,

AND OTHER ODDITIES

Many lovely things have their thorny side

WHEN THE NEWCOMER to the desert recovers from his initial surprise at finding the country rich in flora, instead of the desolate sandy waste that he had imagined, he immediately becomes interested in the many exotic forms of plant life that occur abundantly in much of the area.

Almost everyone has heard of the sahuaro (also spelled saguaro), or giant cactus. Because of its size and grotesque form, it appeals so strongly to the imagination that publicity men and motion-picture script-writers have placed it liberally throughout the Southwest, in areas where it has no business being. It is a common motif in advertising signs in Texas and New Mexico. I once saw a sahuaro, made of concrete and painted a garish off-color green, in a little prairie town in Texas. Actually, the distribution of this giant form is very limited in comparison with many other species of cactus.

It occurs only in Arizona—in the central, southern, and southwestern parts—in a small area in southeastern California, and it extends into much of Sonora, Mexico.

Regardless of what mental picture the visitor to the desert may have formed, from pictures and oral descriptions, his first reaction upon encountering a sahuaro growing in its native state is one of surprise and wonderment. Sahuaros average from 10 to 35 feet, occasionally 40 feet, in height, and the largest known specimen grows in Sahuaro National

29

All these desert plants have thorns or prickles in some form.
From left to right and up: sotol, hedgehog cactus, rainbow cactus,
agave, and ocotillo.

Monument, about fourteen miles east of Tucson. It is 52 feet in height, has 52 arms, and is estimated to be about 240 years old. It is believed to weigh about 10 tons! Sahuaro National Monument has one of the finest stands of giant cactus in the state and it is a place well worth visiting.

The trunk of the sahuaro is fluted, yellow-green in color, and is covered with sharp woody spines. In the early days of the phonograph sahuaro thorns were often used for needles to play the shellac discs. This big cactus may bear from two or three to as many as twenty or more branching arms. Often they are erect, and parallel the main trunk at a distance of two or three feet. Many sahuaros have curved twisting arms that sweep toward the ground in grotesque fashion. The effect in the dusk or moonlight is weird. One of my friends who used to winter at a dude ranch never joined the moonlight rides because the route lay through sahuaro country. "Darned things might reach out and snatch me off my horse," he said. I think he really meant it!

The flesh of the sahuaro is supported by an ingenious framework of hard woody ribs, vertical and somewhat basketlike, that constitutes the skeleton. When the plants die their weathered ribs are gathered and used as covering for *remadas*, which are Spanish-style arbors. And in many of the little Mexican houses called *jacales*, the ceilings are made of sahuaro ribs, covered with palm thatch and coated heavily on top with adobe mud, which bakes hard in the sun.

In May and June, according to location in the desert, the sahuaro bears white blooms in circles around the ends of its branches. They are roughly cone-shaped, about four inches across, and have a fragrance like that of a melon. The product of the blossom is a red egg-shaped fruit, from two to three-and a-half inches long. It is sweet and edible, and when it matures, in late June or July, there is joy among the dwellers of the desert. Sahuaro fruit is consumed by many creatures, from insects to man, and the crop disappears in a short time after ripening.

The fruit is important to the Pima and Papago Indians. From the earliest recorded times even to the present they have held festivals, during the sahuaro harvest, in which all members of the family join. The fruit is gathered by means of long poles—often several sahuaro ribs lashed together—to the ends of which are bound forked twigs of greasewood. The fruit is wrenched loose by working the fork into place at its base and twisting.

The sahuaro festivals formerly had a religious significance, and probably still do among some of the old people. They still prepare a wine by fermenting the juice in large earthenware jars called *ollas*. It is ready to drink in two days (!) and is said to be very potent. Fiestas are an intoxicating time, and regardless of their original purpose, they

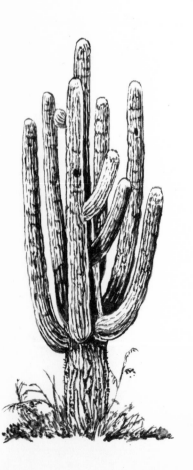

Sahuaro, or giant cactus
(typical form)

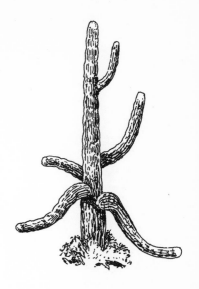

still furnish an excellent excuse for a good many members of the tribe to get drunk. Judging from the short period allowed for the brew to mature, it can be assumed that inebriation results from quantity and not quality.

These sociable drinking parties, though, have never been the main purpose of gathering the fruits. The bountiful supply of food furnished by the giant cactus forms an important part of the native diet, eaten raw, during the season when it is ripening, and a large part of the crop is boiled down into a heavy rich syrup which keeps very well for future use. The black seeds are strained from the boiled product, and are ground in *metates* with *manos* to form a buttery substance said to be very palatable and nourishing.

The sahuaro is a splendid example of the adaptability of a desert plant to its environment. It has the ability, as do most cacti, of storing water in its pulpy flesh and utilizing it slowly during periods of drought. In seasons of heavy rain the giant cactus takes in water like a dry sponge. It can almost be seen to swell from day to day, until it becomes fat and prosperous as the proverbial alderman. Then, when the drought comes, it is prepared. Week after week, month after month, it continues to live when plants of less hardy design wither and die. It lives on its stored water and slowly shrinks in diameter—but it lives. One can tell to an extent what the moisture situation has been by noting the condition of the big cactus.

Besides its wonderful sweet fruits, the sahuaro serves as a natural shelter. Lizards find sanctuary on its spiny arms, and several species of birds—among them crows, Audubon's caracara, vultures, and hawks—build their nests of twigs in the space between the arm and trunk. One rarely sees a sahuaro without several sizable holes pecked in it. These are made by woodpeckers and flickers who shelter in the spiny cactus that stands like a tree and resists the storm. A little pecking with an awl-like bill, and an aperture is formed that has only to be filled with nesting material. The sahuaro is not permanently damaged. It soon grows a parchment-like sac that seals off the wound and prevents the escape of fluid. When, eventually, a giant dies (which is very much less seldom than one might think, judging from the few dead cacti seen), the sacs, or "boots," are gathered and used for decorative purposes. Abandoned woodpecker nests are utilized by the elf owl, who lacks the engineering ability of the sharp-beaked woodpecker but who takes advantage of the latter's labor.

Contrary to popular belief, sahuaros are not found everywhere in the desert. They are choosy concerning temperature conditions, type of soil, and altitude, as many people have found out who have tried to transplant them to unsuitable sites. In general the giant cactus thrives best in well-drained rocky or gravelly soil, and it likes foothills and slopes

31

Some variations in sahuaro growth habit

better than valleys. It is an amazing sight to see sahuaros growing out of what appears to be solid rock, with a bare minimum of visible surface soil, and thriving like corn-fed hogs. An extensive colony of them growing under these conditions may be found covering the Pozo Verde Mountains in Mexico, a few miles from Sasabe on the road to Altar.

The giant cactus is found mostly at elevations of from 700 to 3,500 feet. Occasionally it will grow as high as 4,500 feet in altitude, but it is never stable at such heights, and a prolonged spell of cold, with the temperature dropping well below freezing, will kill the plants. The heaviest growths occur on slopes of hills and mountains that face south.

Next in importance to the sahuaro, from the spectacular standpoint, is the cactus popularly known as the organpipe. Its proper name is pitahaya. Casual tourists see little of it because its range is restricted to a few places in Arizona. But in Sonora, Mexico, the pitahaya occupies a much more important place in the landscape, and occurs in many localities. In Arizona the northernmost area in which it may be found is situated in parts of the Picacho Mountains in southern Pinal County. It occurs in the Roskruge Range in Pima County and west to the Growler Mountains in the southwestern part of the state. The largest stand of this cactus in Arizona is located at the Organpipe National Monument, a huge tract of land that, like the Sahuaro National Monument, has been set aside for the preservation of this remarkable species.

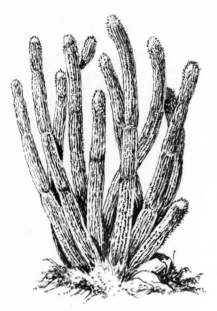

Organpipe, or pitahaya cactus

One reaches the monument by the Ajo Way leading west from Tucson. At a point a few miles from the town of Ajo, a road branches off to the south. It goes to Lukeville, the port of entry to Sonoyta, Mexico, and thence to Punto Peñasco (Rocky Point) or to Santa Ana, to join Route 15. The monument begins a few miles from the breakoff on the Ajo Road, and extends, on both sides of the road, to the border. The area embraced is more than 5,000 square miles.

The headquarters building is situated several miles south of the northern boundary of the monument, and from it roads lead into the surrounding hilly country where the heaviest stands of cactus may be found. Visitors often express disappointment at not being able to see many organpipes from the main road. To get the most out of this unique and wonderful area one should plan on spending at least a day or two. Long drives over well-maintained gravel roads, one of them over a distance of some forty miles, lead through magnificent stands of organpipes. There is a good campground, with facilities to make the visitor comfortable, near the headquarters building.

The organpipe cactus differs from the sahuaro in having its branches grow directly from the ground, instead of branching out from the main trunk. They are spiny, light green, cylindrical, and from five to eight inches in diameter, and ridged or fluted somewhat like the giant

32

Cholla with fruits

cactus. The usual height of the plant is from 10 to 15 feet, but some specimens attain a height of 25 feet. There may be 5 or 6 to as many as 20 or more branches. A large plant covers a considerable area of ground.

While the above description covers the pitahaya found in Arizona, it is interesting to note that a change takes place in some—not all—of the pitahayas found in Sonora, Mexico. In these irregular specimens the branches rise from a central trunk that is short and thick and extends only a few feet above the ground. Such a cactus resembles more closely the sahuaro. I have seen many such specimens in the vicinity of Kïno Bay, mixed in with the more conventional type having individual branches rising directly from the ground. The trunk organpipe also occurs freely in the Sonoran desert part of Baja California.

The flowers of the organpipe grow near the tops of the branches and average from two-and-a-half to three inches in length, and are about two inches across. In color they vary from purple to light green, or green mixed with purple. The fruits are almost round, and average from two or three inches in diameter. They are sweet, juicy, and luscious, and are eagerly gathered by the Indians, who in former days, held festivals at harvest time. They are also gathered at the present time by many people who make jam, jelly, and syrup from them. It is claimed by some that the fruit of the pitahaya is superior to that of the sahuaro.

The third big cactus belonging to the genus *Cereus* is a spectacular plant known as the senita. Unfortunately, it is very rare in Arizona. Only a few specimens, perhaps less than one hundred, are to be found in the state, and these are in the Organpipe National Monument.

The senita cannot bear cold, and an elevation of fifteen hundred feet is about the limit at which it will thrive. It is extremely plentiful in Sonora and in Baja California. When driving south into Sonora from Sasabe, the first senitas are found near the little village of Los Molinos, about thirty miles from the Arizona border. A few clumps may be seen along the road on the way south, and they increase in number until they are a common sight by the time Altar is reached. It too is a treelike cactus, as much as 20 feet in height, composed of many branches that —as in the case of the pitahaya—rise from the ground without a central trunk. Individual examples may vary from a dozen or even fewer branches to as many as 50 or 60, a truly impressive sight. A large senita may occupy an area almost equal to that needed for a small house, and it affords shelter, and a safe haven from attack, to many species of small birds and animals.

The branches of the senita are angular rather than round, and are as much as eight inches in diameter. The fleshy green arms are grooved with five to seven vertical ridges. The first four or five feet of the branches are almost spineless, but above that, clusters of gray, twisted, bristlelike spines occur. They look like matted hair. It is from this characteristic that the name "old man" cactus was derived. Unfortunately, there is a small very hairy cactus that bears the same name— another example of the confusion resulting from the haphazard use of common names.

Descending the scale in size, but certainly not in distribution and quantity, is the cholla (pronounced chō-ya). This ubiquitous cactus occurs throughout the length and breadth of the entire Sonoran desert, and may number from a few scattered plants in some areas to many square miles so completely covered by it that practically nothing else can grow. These are the regions termed "cactus forests."

Prickly pear, or opuntia

There are several species of cholla, the most representative being the jumping cholla. The name is derived from the mistaken idea that the clumps of vicious barbed spines actually jump out and impale you if you get near the plant. It is not true, of course, but sometimes I think it comes pretty close to it! The slightest touch of clothing or flesh will cause a spine-covered tubercle to detach itself from the parent plant and embed half a dozen or more red-hot needles in the skin. It is not a pleasant experience.

The cholla is usually under six feet in height, but occasionally grows to as much as twelve feet or more. The trunk is woody, up to six inches or more in diameter, cylindrical, covered with a scaly dark bark. The wood of the trunk forms a curious network formation, with many large perforations. It is light, but very hard when dry, and is used a great deal in making stands for lamps and furniture. These are sold in curio shops and are eagerly bought by people having a taste for knickknacks.

The trunk is much branched. The joints of the branches are round and about six to eight inches in length, and up to two inches in diameter. While the flesh of the plant is light green, as in so many of the cacti, the general appearance is yellowish, owing to the straw-colored spines.

Other varieties of cholla are the *tasajo,* or cane cactus; the staghorn, and the buckhorn cholla. All species of cholla bear attractive blossoms in the spring, the colors varying from red to yellow and sometimes greenish-white.

From the standpoint of propagation, the cholla is undoubtedly one of the most successful of all plants. Animals brushing against it carry its spiny tubercles long distances before shedding them. Left on the surface of the ground these soon root and form new plants. The tubercles that drop on the ground underneath the parent plant are all potential youngsters, waiting for some animal to scuff along so they can hook a ride and be carried off to start new colonies.

Economically, the cholla is a serious detriment to the desert. Once started, it takes over vast areas of otherwise good rangeland, choking out grass and forage plants. There isn't a rancher who doesn't wish that he could close his eyes, open them again, and find the cholla gone. But it is not so easy. Bulldozing and firing have been tried, but with little success in ratio to the effort expended.

A few people seem to like cholla, but they are in the minority. True, a stand of big plants, particularly when in bloom, does have a certain decorative quality—especially the type known as the Teddy bear having great clusters of straw-colored spines. But to me it is a sinister rather than an esthetic sight. However, for the opinion of man the cholla cares not a hoot. It continues to thrive and spread, providing impregnable nesting spots for the cactus wren and thrashers, who love its spiny shelter.

One of the most interesting of the large cacti is the barrel cactus, or *bisnaga*. It is eagerly sought by photographers who want atmosphere in desert photographs, and is often introduced into landscapes by painters.

The barrel is a thick and heavy cactus, spherical when young, and growing into an elongated round form as it develops. The average height is perhaps two feet, but the plant may grow to as much as eight feet. Older plants have a tendency to twist and develop scaly bark toward the bottom. This cactus is light green in color and is covered with verticle ridges from two to two-and-a-half inches apart. Each ridge bears rosettes of strong sharp spines, some awl-like and others hooked at the ends. The shed spines of the bisnaga, cholla, and mesquite can be a source of misery to the motorist who drives across desert land without benefit of roads. The ability of a thorn to work through a tire tread and puncture the shoe is uncanny. I speak from experience, having had it happen oftener than I care to think about.

In midsummer the barrel cactus produces a ring of exquisite flowers, yellowish pink to red in color, and a couple of inches wide. These later produce bright yellow fruits, which are eaten by birds and small mammals.

When the barrel reaches a considerable height, it has an interesting habit of sometimes leaning over toward the south. The reason is that it grows faster on the shaded side. Because of this trait it is sometimes called "compass cactus." Though this big cactus should not be depended upon as a reliable guide to the points of the compass, it can prove a real friend to the traveler who is so unfortunate as to become stranded in the desert without water; it may even save his life. Inside its spiny hide, the bisnaga is filled with a spongy pulp, saturated with a sweetish and quite potable juice. If you hack off the top of the cactus, the pulp becomes accessible. When wrung out, the tissues yield a surprising amount of liquid.

Another use for the barrel cactus has long been known, but plant lovers consider it a doubtful blessing. This is the making of cactus candy, which may be found on sale in every curio store in desert towns. The pulp is cooked in sugar, allowed to harden, and cut into little cubes. To my taste it is rather insipid. It certainly does not seem to justify the destruction of great numbers of these interesting cacti.

Widely distributed throughout much of the temperate regions of North America, the prickly pear is familiar to almost everyone. There are many varieties, ranging in size from the plants found in the Midwest, having leaves not much larger than the top of a tin can, to the huge, 36

Hedgehog cactus with blossoms

almost treelike Mexican forms known as *nopales*. The prickly pear is a member of the genus *Opuntia,* and is closely related to the cholla. It attains its maximum size and most luxuriant growth in the desert.

Not only is the prickly pear one of the most characteristic features of the desert landscape; it is also one of the most decorative. A large plant spreads over a considerable area of ground; it may be as much as 15 feet or more in length, with a height of 5 or 6 feet. The leaves of the plants in different species vary in form from round to elongated; sometimes they are squared off at the top. Some of them may be as large as dinner plates. A handsome variety bears leaves of a deep purple color, with clumps of bright yellow spicules. These innocent-looking little tufts are composed of many minute spines that smart and burn like fire when embedded in the flesh. In addition, the prickly pear is liberally covered with long sharp needles. Some species have more than others. Never fool around with the opuntia unless your hands are encased in heavy leather gloves!

Pincushion cactus

In the spring the prickly pear bears many lovely blossoms, which grow on the upper edges of the leaves. The color varies from a bright yellow to purple, depending on the species. Leaf buds also form at the same time, and rapidly develop, adding greatly to the size of the plant each season. The blossoms produce reddish to purple fruits which mature late in the season. The fruit of the large Mexican *nopal* is called *tuna,* and is edible.

Like the cholla, the prickly pear is a tough and durable plant. It withstands much abuse from the weather, and multiplies at an amazing rate, often encroaching dangerously on rangelands. But it is easier to control than the cholla, having fewer spines. It may be bull-dozed out fairly readily. The flesh of the prickly pear is succulent and very nutritious as a food for cattle. In times of drought ranchers some-times employ a flame-throwing device to burn off the spines, much like singeing a chicken.

The fleshy roots of this cactus are relished by the javelina, or peccary, and a band of the animals working on a plant soon destroys it. It will regenerate, however, as leaves lying on the ground send out roots and form new plants.

One more species of opuntia should be briefly described before going on to some of the small cacti that are greatly esteemed for decorative purposes in the garden. This is the plant commonly called Christmas cactus. It fits into the "beautiful but damned" department.

This handsome small cholla has slender jointed branches, heavily covered with spicules and perfectly villainous spines. It usually grows to a height of less than two feet. The flowers are inconspicuous, but they produce a tremendous crop of magnificently elongated, bright scar-

37

Rainbow cactus

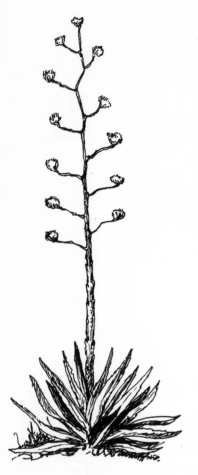

A type of agave in bloom

let fruits. The effect is so enchanting that one has a desire to pluck a branch. Don't do it!

On one well-remembered trip in Sonora my wife and I were camping in a lonely spot situated in a grove of old mesquite and paloverde trees. We arrived just before dusk, and while I pumped up the air mattresses my wife volunteered to do the squaw job (gather dead branches) for the evening campfire. In a few minutes the air was filled with an agonized wail. I rushed over in the direction of the sound and found her badly messed up in the treacherous branches of a Christmas cactus. She had been working along a little wash with steep banks and had not noticed the cactus that slightly overhung one bank. Having stooped to pick up a branch she straightened up suddenly and struck the cactus squarely with her back and shoulder.

She was wearing a cloth jacket that was so covered with spines and spicules that it had to be burned. By the light of the gasoline lantern I worked for an hour with tweezers, removing all the visible spines. But a few were missed, and they kept popping up for months. One formed a small tumor and finally worked out almost a year later. Useful suggestion: Admire the Christmas cactus, but keep away from it!

There are many kinds of the small decorative cacti previously mentioned, and they are among the most interesting and attractive features of the desert flora. One of the commonest is the hedgehog, a cactus averaging from six inches to more than a foot in height. It grows in clumps of several elongated tapering stalks, three to four inches in diameter, bearing rosettes of small spines with larger and stouter ones protruding at an angle from the stalk. It is a veritable floral porcupine. It is the first of the small cacti to bloom in the spring, the flowers usually appearing in March or even in late February in the more temperate parts of the Sonoran desert. This plant is very abundant, and widely distributed.

The handsome little pincushion cactus is greatly admired and is much transplanted into gardens, where it will thrive if the soil is sandy and if it is not subjected to much cold and water. It is a round elongated plant, usually growing in clumps, and from three to eight or ten inches in height. Rosettes of small spines that lie horizontally along the sides cover the plant completely. From the center of each whorl longer and thicker spines protrude at an angle. These spines are curved at the ends, giving the plant the additional name of fishhook cactus. The general color of the cactus is gray-green because of the local color of the spines. Fruits are small and bright red.

One other small cactus is worthy of note, though it is not widely distributed and must be sought in rather out-of-the-way places. It is the rainbow, perhaps the most colorful of all small cacti. It is covered with close-lying bands of spines, alternately ruby red, white, or ivory and sometimes pale light green. The greenish flesh shows through the bands of spines, giving the plant an almost iridescent look. The rainbow is slightly more chunky than the hedgehog, but has the same general cylindrical tapering shape. It usually grows singly, but twins are sometimes found. Size varies from three or four inches in height to as much as a foot. I have seen several specimens in the Pozo Verde Mountains that were an estimated fifteen inches tall.

The rainbow cactus is very choosy about where it will live, and while it may last a year or two when transplanted into an unfavorable location, it never really thrives. This is strictly a foothill and mountain species, and it occurs normally at elevations of between 3,500 and 6,000 feet. It prefers dry, well-drained soil, and seems to thrive best in rocky terrain. Some of the finest examples I have found were growing out of crevices in rock ledges, with practically no dirt apparent.

All the smaller species of cacti, in common with their larger relatives, bear beautiful blossoms. Their blooming season is usually early, occurring from late March to mid-May. Flowers average from less than an inch in diameter on the smaller varieties to slightly more than two inches on the larger ones. The colors range from light yellow through pink to red and, in some varieties, rich purple. They are the photographer's delight.

Aside from the cacti, interesting and often spectacular plant forms are so numerous and of such widespread distribution in the desert as to fill the newcomer with confusion. Only a few can be mentioned here, those that will be seen in many places commonly throughout the length and breadth of the Sonoran desert.

Of these, one of the most attention-compelling is the agave, commonly called century plant, with reference to the larger species, and *lechugilla* as descriptive of the smaller ones. There are many species of agave in desert areas, and they vary in size and character markedly. The most spectacular is the giant form often cultivated in landscaping homes and estates. The gray-green leaves grow from the ground in a curving lanceolate shape. Broad at the base, often six to eight inches across, they taper upward as they spread out. They are serrated on the edges with sharp spines, and the top of the leaf terminates in a wicked brown needle-sharp thorn that can play the very devil with you if you are so unfortunate as to bump into it. A few years ago, while transplanting a "pup" (young agave) that grew under an adult plant, my hand slipped and I drove an agave thorn deep into the palm. It broke off and soon formed a tumor that all but crippled my hand. I had to be "put out" with sodium pentothal while the surgeon removed it. Since then my admiration for the big agave has been somewhat dampened.

39

Yucca

The smaller agaves vary greatly in size. Some are no larger at the base than a dinner plate, while others would fill a bushel basket. A species of agave is specially cultivated in Mexico, particularly in Jalisco, for the manufacture of tequila. It is called *maguey*.

The agave yields leaf fibers that the Mexicans use to weave a kind of coarse cloth. This cloth has many uses, one of them being the making of shopping bags that can be purchased in any little *tienda*. They are often gayly dyed with bands of clashing colors—cerise, sky blue, fire-engine red, and howling purple.

The glory of the agave is its spectacular and beautiful blossom, but the price of glory—as in many spheres of life—is death. The plant may spend from ten to fifteen years building food to throw into the grand climax, the production of a huge stalk bearing many flowers that branch off the main stem to afford a most exotic sight. The big agave often produces a stalk twenty feet or more in height, covered with large

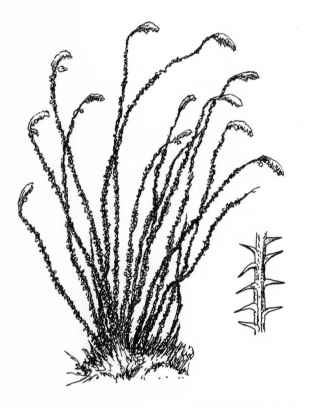

Ocotillo with leaves and flowers

Thorny stalk without leaves

flowers of varying shades of yellow. The stalk, green at first and somewhat resembling a gigantic asparagus spear, turns brownish yellow after the seed pods are formed and the plant dies.

An interesting and commonly encountered species similar to the agave is the sotol. The leaves are smaller and narrower than those of the 40 giant agave, but the plant produces an impressive stalk, bearing numerous small flowers, sometimes well over twelve feet in height. Flowers are creamy in color, and may be produced from May to August, according to elevation and location.

We again refer to the ubiquitous curio shop, where "desert spoons" are sold. These are the rounded bases of the leaves that grow close to the ground. The leaves are stripped from the plant and come loose as yellowish spoons. The serrated leaf is trimmed to a length of a foot or so, and "spoon" and leaf are allowed to dry. Since the plant must be destroyed to yield a supply of these novelties, traffic in this commodity is generally frowned upon by conservationists.

A sight that never fails to delight the visitor to the desert is the yucca. This shaggy, rather grotesque plant is common in many areas, and in some ways has become almost as much a symbol of the desert as the sahuaro.

The yuccas are of two varieties, broad-leaf and narrow-leaf, with several species of each. The narrow-leaf yucca is typical of the genus, and is widely distributed. It is sometimes confused with the agave because of its rather similar leaves. This is the plant known as Spanish dagger and, in Spanish, *candelario de Dios* (The Lord's candlestick) because of the growth habit of its flowers. Yuccas grow in clumps, in height from six to twelve feet. The characteristic shaggy brownish trunk of the plant is formed by layers of leaves that have died and dried up as. the yucca grows. New leaves at the top form a thick clump. The flower stalk grows from the center of the leaves at the top when the blooming season arrives. In southern Arizona this is usually in early May; farther south, in Mexico, yuccas may bloom much sooner.

The flowers of the yucca are ivory or slightly off-white, and are produced in the form of a large plume. A stand of yucca in full bloom on a gently rolling hillside, or the steep slope of a canyon where the plant often grows, is a thrilling sight. When intermixed with the brilliant scarlet blossoms of the ocotillo, the effect is lovely indeed.

The ripened stalk of the yucca makes a very light, porous, but stiff and hard wood. It takes a high polish, and is used for canes and sometimes as struts in rustic furniture.

The ocotillo is certainly one of the weirdest of plants. Strictly confined to desert areas, it is widespread over most of the dry regions. Because of its thorn-covered stalks it is sometimes thought to belong to the cactus family, but this mistaken idea is another case of appearance being deceptive. The stems are long, up to twelve feet or more, and are covered with a greenish scaly bark. They expand, fan-shaped, from a common point in the ground, and in mature specimens the top of the

41   plant covers a considerable area.

One of the peculiarities of this plant is its ability to send out small rounded green leaves in profusion along the stalks, so that they are almost completely covered. This takes place in periods of rain. When the earth dries out the leaves turn yellow and are rapidly shed. This process takes place several times a year, regardless of season. If there have been late rains extending into the spring, the ocotillo may be covered with leaves and blossoms at the same time. But if blossom time arrives during the normally dry weather, the plant will bloom without leaves.

The ocotillo in bloom is a spectacular floral wonder. Individual blossoms are borne on the ends of stalks. They are composite and several inches in length, and two to three inches in thickness near the base. Each plant bears many blossoms. The color is brilliant scarlet or vermilion. A single ocotillo plant is wonderful in itself, but the sight of acres of close-growing plants reaching fiery-red spears into the azure sky must be seen to be believed. The blossoming season extends through April and May in most of the desert.

The ocotillo has the obliging habit of rooting stalks that are cut and planted in the ground, when kept well watered for a few weeks. Unique fences are made of stalks cut to the proper length and laced together with wire or cord. During wet weather most of the stalks will make up leaves; some will even bloom.

The diamondback is the largest and most formidable of the desert rattlesnakes, and is one of the commonest species. Of all the poisonous reptiles of the United States, it is exceeded in size only by the Florida diamondback.

FOUR

SNAKE!

Don't let the thought scare you—know the facts

OF ALL the crawly creatures on earth, snakes undoubtedly take first place in engendering fear and loathing in the great majority of people. Ignorance of what snakes really are, and the role they play, lies at the base of this difficulty. It is suggested that one who is obsessed with this fear should obtain a good work on herpetology, and study it. Knowledge, not hearsay, will not only allay groundless fear, but will open up an entirely new and fascinating field.

Among people who have even a slight acquaintance with natural history it is pretty generally known that in the entire United States only two types of snakes may be considered dangerous to man. This also applies to Sonora. They are the pit vipers—rattlesnakes, copperheads, and water moccasins—and a small, brilliantly colored snake that is closely related to the cobra, the coral snake. Visitors to the Sonoran desert will have to consider only two of these: the coral snake, in a very limited way, and the more abundant rattlesnake. The problem is further simplified by the interesting fact that, no matter how much a reptile may look like a rattler in color markings—the bull snake is a good example—*it isn't one unless it has rattles on the end of its tail.*

Serpents in some form occur in practically every temperate and tropical climate throughout the world. In places they are plentiful and of many species, in others both numbers and species are severely limited. The Sonoran desert, in common with much of the associated arid lands, is inhabited by a very large number of species of both poisonous and harmless snakes.

But many other areas have larger populations of snakes, both venomous and harmless, than the Sonoran desert. I recall once reading a statement by Raymond Ditmars, the noted authority on reptiles, that one of the heaviest populations of poisonous snakes—timber rattlers and copperheads—anywhere in the world occurs in the Appalachian Mountains. Years ago land was offered at fifty cents an acre in Pike County, Pennsylvania. There were no takers because the area was heavily infested with timber rattlers. We once lived in rural Connecticut, some fifty miles from New York City, and one summer we killed, or found dead on the road, a dozen copperheads. None of this is written to controvert the fact that there are poisonous snakes in the desert, many of them; but here conditions are different and in a way that makes a solution to the problem simple.

Visitors to the desert who have a knowledge of the varieties of nonpoisonous snakes occurring in the Midwest and East will recognize some old acquaintances. Some of these will be variants or subspecies, but essentially there is little difference. Among them are the garter snake, hog-nosed snake, greensnake, and small striped snake. Racers of

44

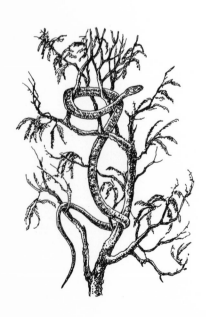

Red racer

several species are common, and may frequently be seen crawling across a road.

One of this group—which probably contains the swiftest reptiles known—is the red racer. It reaches a length of about six feet, is very slim and extremely active. In common with all the nonpoisonous snakes of the desert, the red racer is highly beneficial. Its diet consists largely of small mammals, mice, shrews, and voles, which, most people agree, can be dispensed with around the house. It does occasionally rob nests of birds, having a taste for poultry as a change from red meat; but because of the great amount of good it does in general this whim seems justified. Going out to our carport one time, we found a red racer plastered against a wall and partly wrapped around a stud. In its jaws was a small bat, fluttering wildly. The snake had seized it by the lower part of its body. Too occupied with the bat to notice me, the racer remained motionless until I touched it. What followed was one of the most incredible exhibitions of pure speed I have ever witnessed. Dropping the bat, which fluttered away, the racer was off through the length of the port and through an opening at the end so quickly that it was out of sight before I could reach the door.

Tail

Gopher or bull snake
Harmless and beneficial

One of the commonest and most valuable of desert reptiles is the bullsnake or gopher snake. It is a handsome serpent, sometimes reaching a length of eight feet, but more commonly averaging under six feet. It feeds almost entirely on small mammals, and is hell on wood rats and cotton rats. Farmers and agriculturists welcome it; it is a veritable living rat trap. Unfortunately, like several other species of harmless and beneficial snakes, the bullsnake has markings—tan blotches on a yellow background—that immediately label it as "deadly poisonous" to uninformed people. So the needless and regrettable slaughter of this valuable species continues year after year.

The bullsnake is one of the constrictors, snakes that kill their prey by crushing. Another valuable member of this group is the king snake. Though gentle toward man—it is one of the most favored species with people who keep snakes for pets—it is a perfect terror in the reptilian world. While it feeds on small mammals and lizards, its diet includes many species of snakes. It has the peculiar property of being immune to the venom of the rattlesnake which it attacks, crushes, and eats, in spite of the bites it undoubtedly receives. The king snake averages three to four feet in length, and is black, with irregular white or creamy bands.

A curious reptile belonging to the constrictor group is the rubber boa. It is found rarely throughout the Sonoran desert, probably because of its secretive habits. It is ordinarily under three feet in length, and the tail is so blunt that one may have to look twice to determine which end is the head. The rubber boa is occasionally found in southern Arizona, and specimens have been reported from the foothills of the Baboquivari Mountains. This little reptile is a rodent eater and is very gentle.

In the southern part of the United States and in Mexico and other warm countries, several reptiles of a unique type occur. These are the rear-fanged snakes, and two species are found in the desert, although they are very rare. A typical example is the lyre snake. It is a handsome serpent, marked with a broad diamond-shaped pattern, and the few people who encounter it—it is strictly nocturnal—are sure it is a rattler. One certain identification is the tail, which is long and slimly tapering, and of course bears no rattles.

Rear-fanged snakes, as the name implies, have their venom-administering equipment located in the back of the mouth rather than in the two forward large fangs present in the pit vipers. This is in the form of small grooved teeth. The snake chews its prey, and the toxin soon takes effect on the victim. It is powerful enough to kill small rodents, but not dangerous to man. A bite from a lyre snake under normal natural conditions is practically inconceivable, but if a careless handler should be bitten and sufficiently chewed he would probably suffer nothing more serious than some slight swelling, according to authorities. The lyre snake and related species are not therefore rated among the deadly reptiles.

Rattler! The very sound of the word is enough to make one jump.

Every person who has lived in the desert, or other parts of the country where this malevolent snake occurs—and that covers some areas of most of the United States and all of Mexico—knows that here is a creature that demands the greatest respect from both man and beast.

The publicity this snake receives, through word and picture, is so widespread that there is hardly a child who has reached the age of reason who wouldn't be able to come up with a pretty accurate description of a rattler, even though he had never seen one.

The distinctive thing about a rattlesnake, of course, is the rattle, which is found on no other serpent anywhere. This unique device, which terminates the tail end of rattlers of all species, is composed of a series of interlocking horny, hollow segments and ends with a solid "button." When vibrated rapidly by the motion of the serpent's tail, a dry raspy sound is emitted. It is hard to describe, but once heard it will never be forgotten. Some people say it sounds similar to the tone produced by a grasshopper's wings when the insect is hovering in the air. It never quite struck me that way. The best imitation I have run across was suggested by a naturalist friend, who is known to temper his serious research work with an occasional practical joke. It goes like this:

Take a box of safety matches (the type known as Swedish matches) and remove about half the contents. Keep this handy, and when a group is gathered around the campfire at night direct the conversation to rattlers. When things have progressed far enough so that everyone is in an edgy mood, surreptitiously remove the box from your pocket and, with hand concealed, shake it violently from side to side. The explosive departure of the listeners can best be compared to a flushed covey of quail. It never fails. Perhaps one other point should be mentioned: the performer should be prepared to depart rapidly in the opposite direction, once the hoax is discovered.

As with so many other phases of wildlife, unnatural history plays a big role in weaving false tales around the rattlesnake. One of these concerns the growth of rattles. You will be told that the age of a snake can be determined by the number of its rattles—one rattle for every year. This is simply not true. A new segment is added each time the snake moults, but this may be several times in a year, depending on the climate, especially in southern regions where the reptiles do not hibernate. Then too, rattles are continually breaking off, and many individual snakes with imperfect rattles are found. The average number of rattles may be about six or seven to perhaps ten. More than that number would be considered exceptional. It depends on the species and size of the snake, too.

Once, while traveling through New Mexico, I stopped at a gas station in a lonely little burg. The proprietor, who gave the impression of being a sort of shifty character, ran a small curio shop. On display with other things and mounted on a card was an enormous rattle composed of thirty-six segments.

"Whew!" I said, "Must have been *some* snake. Did you kill him?"

"No, feller up the draw did. Eight feet long. I'd sure like to uv got him."

"I sure would too, podnah," I replied, dropping into the vernacular and looking at him real hard. He glanced away, knowing that I hadn't swallowed the story. Stunts like this are often pulled to confound the "tenderfoot." Segments of rattles coming from snakes about the same size can be fitted together and, with the aid of a little glue, be extended theoretically to infinity.

It has been stated previously that the acid test of whether a snake is a rattler or something else depends on one question—does it have rattles? This is a reliable rule, but in rare instances it may not be infallible. Cases have been noted where, owing to an accident, a rattlesnake has lost its warning equipment. An amusing one occurred some years ago on the property of friends near Cortaro.

It was a year when there was a heavy buildup of snakes, and my

47

Harmless Arizona king snake

friends, the Strang family, had killed several near a shed with an open foundation that furnished protection from the sun. Dick Strang, then in his teens, spotted a diamondback coiled at the edge of the shed. He ran up to the house and got his .22 caliber rifle. Returning, he took aim and shot at the viper's head, but being excited he missed and hit the snake squarely in the tail at the base of the rattles, clipping them off as neatly as though it had been done by a knife. The rifle was a single shot, and before Dick could reload, the rattler had crawled away to safety. His father, Ray, said: "Now look what you did. This is a hell of a note— a rattler without rattles." But a few days later Ray found the snake out in the open and finished him off with a shovel.

There is a common belief that a rattlesnake will always give warning of its presence by buzzing. This is a fallacy, as people who have had experience with the vipers know. On two occasions I have encountered rattlers on the desert, one coiled, the other stretched out, that made no attempt to rattle. Unless cornered, most species of rattlesnakes are docile and will attempt to escape whenever possible. Tales of rattlers pursuing and attacking people are just that—tales and nothing more. The tiger rattlesnake is reputed to have a more pugnacious disposition than most other species, but it definitely will not chase you.

In the United States close to thirty species of rattlesnakes occur. Of these, some fifteen are found in the Sonoran desert, in both Arizona and Mexico. The largest and, because of its size, the most dangerous of 48 the desert rattlers is the diamondback. Some other species include the sidewinder or horned rattler, tiger rattler, and green and pigmy rattlers. A few species are found in higher elevations, among them the black-tail rattler—while others, like the sidewinder, inhabit sandy areas.

The diamondback is perhaps the most plentiful species, and it is the snake most frequently seen. It has a thick, powerful body and a definite pattern of diamond markings of dark brownish color on a background that varies from cream to greenish gray. The head is roundedly triangular and massive, and the mouth is equipped with two vicious fangs like hypodermic needles. In a large specimen they may be close to an inch long. A distinctive thing about the diamondback that occurs in no other rattler, and is a positive means of identification, is the tail. It is encircled by several alternating bands of black and white, giving the snake the name "coontail."

With the exception of the Florida diamondback, which exceeds it in size, the western diamondback is the largest venomous snake found in the United States and northern Mexico. It reaches a length of six feet, in exceptional cases even more, is heavy and massive, and packs a terrific dose of very lethal venom. Most of the bites from rattlers are caused by this snake, though with prompt treatment surprisingly few deaths occur. The average diamondback is usually much smaller, running from two and a half to three feet. A four-footer is considered a walloper.

An interesting little rattlesnake with habits different from its relatives is the horned rattler, commonly called "sidewinder." This name stems from its habit of throwing loops sideways as it crawls, in order to get traction in the sand where it lives. Sidewinders are found only in limited areas of sandy country. They are sometimes seen along the dunes bordering the Gulf of California, and also in some of the sparsely vegetated and arenose country in the lower desert near the Colorado River. The scaly plates resembling horns that protrude from the side of the snake's head toward the mouth are distinctive with this species.

Green rattlesnake

Early one morning, before the sun had heated the earth, I came upon a sidewinder curled up in a tight ball and partly buried in the loose sand, at Tastiota, a little fishing village on an estuary of the Gulf of California between Guaymas and Kino Bay. The snake was indifferent to my presence until I gently prodded him with a stick. He became alert and vibrated his tail rapidly. Although he had fully developed but tiny rattles, no sound was detectable. There was a light wind blowing, which may have interfered somewhat, but I had the feeling that the eyes would be a better guide to safety in sidewinder country than the ears. The little viper, probably less than eighteen inches long, looped away with surprising rapidity, and soon disappeared.

The statement that a rattler will always sound a warning, formerly mentioned, has been thoroughly disproved by many people who have had much experience with the vipers. But another story that makes the rounds regularly wherever snakes are discussed needs correction. It is frequently said that you don't have to worry about a rattler that is stretched out at full length, or resting in loose loops; he can't strike unless he is coiled. Don't believe a word of it! A snake can strike by simply twisting its head ever so slightly, and it will when under restraint and when it has the opportunity. Several cases of bites through a burlap bag containing snakes, to careless handlers, have been recorded. Remember, a pit viper is always dangerous until it is dead!

Now that we've had a look at the sinister side of the snakes, the question naturally arises: What chance has a person of encountering poisonous snakes, and how can they be avoided?

A good way to provide an answer is to cite my own personal experiences.

My wife and I, alone and in company with various friends on trips too numerous to be recounted, have wandered over vast areas of the desert from its northern limits to the region deep down into Sonora. We have camped in many isolated places, hiked through the low desert, climbed into mountainous country, and roamed as fancy dictated. In all this area many rattlesnakes of several species occur. Our wanderings have covered a period of more than a dozen years. During some of this time, in the winter months, snakes were in hibernation. They usually hole up after the first frost, in late October or November, and don't emerge until late February, March, or even early April, depending on the season. But much of our experience took place during the hot periods of spring and early fall, when snakes were abroad in full force.

In all that time we have seen less than half a dozen rattlers, either coiled or crawling over the desert. This is not to say there were not plenty of snakes in the terrain over which we hiked. There undoubtedly were, but we are abroad in the daylight hours, usually when the 50

Sidewinder, or horned rattlesnake

sun is shining full blast, and though the temperature may be comparatively low snakes do not then roam at large.

Of the rattlers actually seen, we killed only two. One was an unidentified species (it is not easy to ascertain the exact kind unless one is an expert) about three feet long. Since it was near a ranch where there were children, we decided it best to eliminate it. The other was a diamondback, about forty inches long, which I discovered stretched out at full length in a little wash. This was near Pitiquito in Sonora, and a Mexican friend who was with us insisted on killing it, even though it was far from a habitation. Neither of these snakes rattled. This incident took place in April, and the other one, involving a snake coiled on a gopher mound, happened in October. In both instances the weather was warm enough for us to be comfortable in a shirt without a jacket. Since snakes are very sensitive to extreme heat and even moderate cold, the temperature may have been responsible for their not sounding a warning.

Our experience in encountering so few rattlers on the desert is not unusual. There are several reasons for it. The most important is that snakes are cold-blooded creatures; unlike mammals and birds, they do not possess a built-in temperature that enables these higher forms to withstand heat and cold. A snake's temperature is the degree of heat or cold present in the air and on the ground. This, of course, is what necessitates its hibernating below frost level in the winter. On the other hand,

its tolerance of heat is amazingly low. Rattlers seem particularly susceptible. Exposure of only a few minutes of direct sunlight generating heat
of over 90 degrees (F.) will kill the snake as surely as though it were
struck by a bullet.

On overcast days when the temperature is cool rattlers will occasionally be abroad, but even this is rare. Sometimes they may lie in cool
glades near water in thick brush. But almost invariably snakes crawl
into holes and other underground shelter to await the night.

The desert hiker, then, is reasonably safe in open areas during
sunny hours. It is certainly wise to watch where one is going at any
time, but the incidence of finding a rattler is so rare as to be notable.
The real danger lies in roaming about at night. Since rattlers are nocturnal, they may be encountered anywhere. They are apt to be particularly numerous near gardens and dwellings, and often rest on the sun-
heated brick or flagstones of patios. These are danger spots. A rule that
absolutely must be followed at all times is never to venture out in the
dark, even for a few yards, without using a strong light. Give bushes
and other lurking places a wide berth. The great majority of cases of
snakebite have occurred at night to people who have walked blindly
into situations where they had no business being without a light.

Ledges and other concealed hiding places in mountainous country
are dangerous. Unthinking persons have been struck in the hands, even
in the face, through carelessness in climbing up ledges with concealed
crevices.

A question that often is debated is the advisability, even the necessity, of wearing snakeproof boots or leggings in the desert. Most bites
occur low on the leg; a rattler rarely strikes higher than a foot above
ground level, usually much lower. Stout boots certainly afford a degree
of assurance and confidence of safety to the wearer. But they are hot,
cumbersome, and ill-suited to long hikes. They may also instill a false
sense of safety, so that the wearer becomes careless, feeling he is fully
protected. In that way he could easily become incautious, and receive a
bite in an unprotected part of the body.

My wife and I travel overland in ordinary stout, low, desert-type
boots, which we find to be both comfortable and nontiring after a long
hike. *But,* through long force of habit we subconsciously watch the
ground ahead. This soon becomes second nature. If I were traveling
much in rocky mountainous country where there are many concealed
crevices and a known large population of rattlers, I should probably
choose to wear high tough boots. But for ordinary desert field trips the
low boots are adequate.

The population of rattlesnakes in all inhabited areas has rapidly
decreased in the past few decades, and the decline continues each year. 52

"Coontail"

*Tail of diamondback, showing
rattles and rings*

Everywhere the hand of man is against this creature. Because it is poisonous and therefore dangerous, it is thought that it must be killed wherever found. The motto seems to be, Get rid of the varmints! Unthinking people, and that unfortunately includes the bulk of ranchers, farmers, and persons whose work lies in the outdoors, lose sight of the fact that the food of the rattlesnake consists almost entirely of the small mammals that plague the very people who insist on exterminating it. These are the gophers, mice, rats, and other pests that run up a costly toll in destroyed crops, harvested grain, damaged equipment, and other ills.

We have a rule that we consider a good one to follow. If a rattler is found near the house or in the yard, where it might be a menace, we kill it. But any snake encountered in the open desert away from habitation is allowed to go unmolested. There is no sentiment attached to this whatever; it simply makes sense from the economic standpoint.

Every year in all parts of the country where poisonous snakes occur a few people are struck. Some of them are made quite ill for a short period, but surprisingly enough an unbelievably small number die. Those who succumb do so because of treatment administered too late, or oftener, no treatment at all.

Measures to be taken in case of a bite are the application of a tourniquet between the wound and the heart whenever possible and the employment of suction by means of the cup supplied with a snakebite kit. The tourniquet should be loosened for a few seconds at the end of twenty-minute periods. The latest technique employs ice in a pad at the point of puncture. No alcohol is allowed, regardless of tradition, and no potassium permanganate. It has been proved harmful rather than beneficial. Get the patient to a doctor as soon as possible. He will administer an antivenin that will probably clear up the case in a very short time.

Three types of venomous snakes belonging to the pit viper family occur in the northern part of Mexico and the southern United States. They are the water moccasin, copperhead, and rattlesnake. Only the rattlesnake, however, is found in the Sonoran desert.

Totally different in physical structure, color, and habits is another venomous serpent—the coral snake. It is small, averaging perhaps sixteen to eighteen inches, and is brilliantly colored with bands of red, cream, and black that *completely encircle the snake's body.* There are several other species of reptiles that closely resemble the coral snake, among them the Arizona king snake and other small banded serpents, but these are all harmless. Bands on the coral snake repeat the color sequence red, cream; black, cream. Its nose and the greater part of its head are black. Color sequence of bands and head color distinguish the coral from similar snakes.

While the rattlesnake is a pit viper (the term coming from a small depression located halfway between the eye and nostril), the coral snake belongs to the elapine group of reptiles, closely related to the cobras and kraits of Asia and other parts of the Old World. It is unique in being the only cobralike snake in the Western Hemisphere. In the United States and northern Mexico the coral snakes are represented by two species. The larger of these is found in the Gulf States, and the other is the Sonoran coral snake.

Elapine snakes differ from pit vipers not only in appearance but, most importantly, in the type of venom they possess. The poison of the rattlesnake is haematoxic, reacting on the blood, while that of the coral snake is neurotoxic, affecting the nervous system. Symptoms of this toxin are paralysis, convulsions, loss of breathing, and cyanosis. It is a quick-acting poison, difficult to counteract unless the specific antivenin is administered almost immediately after a bite.

Now, all of this sounds very ominous and grim, but if you had planned a trip to the desert please don't cancel it for fear of a fatal meeting with a coral snake. It is almost impossible to happen for at least two good reasons. The first of these is that this handsome little brightly colored reptile is one of the gentlest of all snakes, and possesses no belligerence of spirit whatever, as do some species of rattlesnakes. One might spend many years in the desert and never see one. Because of its retiring habits—it spends practically all its time underground—the sighting of a coral snake on the open desert would be a matter of exceptional note. Most of the few reported cases of finding one involve digging in a garden, or perhaps rummaging around among piles of boards or firewood.

The other good reason why the coral snake is not considered dangerous—despite the formidable character of its venom, which, drop for drop, is said to be many times more potent than that of the pit vipers—is that the little serpent, fortunately for man, lacks an efficient means of administering it. Its head is tiny, about the size of the nail of a woman's ring finger, and the extent of its mouth opening is so small that biting anything but the finger or toe of a child or very small person would be all but impossible. Furthermore, the arrangement of the fangs plays an important part in reducing danger from a bite. The fangs of the rattler are long and curved, and are located in the front of the mouth. It has a tremendous mouth, and strikes by making a lightning-like lunge at its prey, embedding the fangs in flesh, and at the same time squeezing venom into the wound by muscular action on the poison glands.

Sonoran coral snake

But the fangs of the coral snake are small and rigid, and are located at the back of the very small mouth. In order effectively to administer poison, it must get a firm grip on the victim and chew for some time.

The Sonoran coral snake is small and very slim. Any similar reptile that the desert hiker might see having a length of two feet or more would most likely be one of the group of snakes closely resembling the coral. W. H. Woodin, director of the Arizona-Sonora Desert Museum, has kept careful records of this species, and he has noted that, up to July of 1961, the largest specimen reported from Arizona measured 20¼ inches. The record was broken that month by a coral snake that was dug up during road repair work in the Organpipe National Forest. It measured an even 21 inches.

The statement is repeatedly made that there has never been a case of a fatality resulting from the bite of a coral snake in Arizona. This may also be true of the region of the Sonoran desert in northern Mexico, though there records are probably not so carefully kept. The danger to natives living in the country, the *campesinos* working in the fields, and particularly to children, would be greater, as many of them travel barefooted.

Throughout the entire range of the species of coral snakes occurring in the Gulf regions, there have been very few recorded cases of deaths from bites. But some have been noted. An item in a newspaper datelined Green Cove Springs, Florida, July 22, 1961, told of the death of a lad, thirteen years of age, who picked up a coral snake when he was mowing a lawn. It retained its grip for a minute, administering a large dose of venom. Though antivenin was administered, the toxin paralyzed the boy's respiratory system rapidly, and it had no effect. It must be remembered that the Gulf region coral snake is larger than the Sonoran species, has a correspondingly bigger head, and is therefore more dangerous.

The coral snake is a mysterious creature because of its furtive habits. Since it is seldom seen unless dug up or, rarely, encountered on the surface at night when traveling, there is no way of telling what the population may be in a given area. In a good many years of living in the desert I have come across just one specimen. It was dead, stretched across a lonely section of sandy road in northern Sonora. A car had run over it at night. Since I had no ruler, I estimated its length at about 17 or 18 inches. My experience extends to another example, this one alive.

One day several years ago I was having the car lubricated at a gas station in the northern part of Tucson. A pickup truck drove up and a quaint old character emerged. He was grizzled and sun-baked to the color of burnt adobe, and he carried a Mason fruit jar in one hand. 55 After a pleasant greeting he deposited the jar on a workbench. Some-

SNAKE!

thing was squirming around inside, and I stepped over for a look. It was a coral snake—the real thing—about 15 inches long, I judged.

"Real purty, ain't he?" the owner said, seeing my interest. "Here, I'll show you," he continued. He unscrewed the top, which had been perforated to admit air, and in a flash the snake slithered out, hit the floor, and started crawling away.

"No you don't," the old fellow said, reaching out a huge horny hand and seizing the snake by the back of the neck. "Back in the jar, baby." He popped him in and screwed on the lid.

"What are you going to do with him?" I asked.

"Give 'im to the Desert Museum. I gives 'em all my snakes."

"Are you a snake collector?" I asked.

"Well, not 'zactly. You see, I caught this un in my bedroom."

"Your *bedroom!*" I exclaimed. "For heaven's sake, man, you must have a leak somewhere!"

"Come to think of it, I guess I must. I got a small rattler in there last week. I'll have t' look into it."

The Gila monster is the only poisonous lizard in North America. It is the subject of many erroneous tales, and its numbers have been greatly reduced in recent years by indiscriminate killing and collecting for roadside "zoos." It is now protected by law in most states of the Southwest.

FIVE

MORE CRAWLY CREATURES

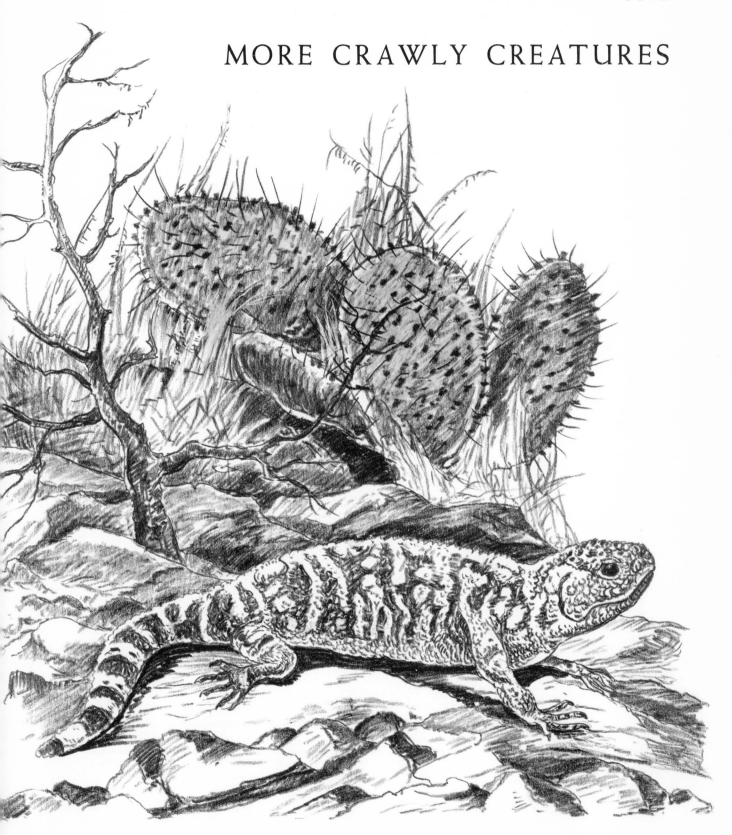

A few are poisonous—all are interesting

SCORPIONS, centipedes, Gila monsters, tarantulas. Creatures of horror! How dangerous are they? How frequently does one meet them?

The tarantula makes a good starting point. It has acquired a perfectly villainous reputation. It supposedly follows people around like a sleuth, lies in ambush, leaps from a distance of several feet, and pounces on the unwary victim to bite viciously. If this were to happen to you, or so the horror tales go, you would have had it. It is also cried out that there is no known cure for the poison of the tarantula. Finally, you are advised to see that your will is in order, then to settle down calmly and die.

Actually, this big hairy spider is not only one of the most interesting of desert creatures but also among the most harmless, to man, on the whole list. In addition, it is of great value because it eats insects. Tarantulas living in a garden may be considered an asset; they eliminate many grasshoppers, squash bugs, harmful beetles, and other pests. Their presence should be encouraged. If they intrude in the house, as they occasionally will, don't kill them. Simply sweep them out with a broom and tell them to go play somewhere else.

The tarantula, belonging to the arachnid, or spider, order, has eight long fuzzy legs that support an incredibly large, mouselike body. The head is big, too, but it doesn't have much in it in the way of brains. In addition, the poor creature is said to be nearsighted, and can see only a few inches away. Its jumping ability is limited to what is directly in front of it, and it secures its food by making short leaps and pouncing on the prey. Since this is by far the largest spider in the desert, it is easily identified. The tarantula has sharp jaws and could undoubtedly inflict a painful wound, but if any inflammation resulted it would be due to bacterial infection, not poison, because the toxin present is not effective on man.

As is true in all parts of the land, there are many species of spiders in the desert. They range in size from little things to the large long-legged wolf spiders. All are harmless to man, and beneficial in the role of helping to control harmful insects—with one exception: the black widow.

This venomous creature is not limited to the desert. It has spread to all parts of the United States, and much has been written about it, in newspapers and magazines. The distinguishing characteristics are a shiny black body, often described as a "shoe button," and an orange hourglass design on the belly.

Years ago when my older son was a student in Dartmouth College in New Hampshire, we lived nearby, in Vermont. At that time the black widow had not spread its range so extensively as it has in recent years. One day while cleaning the woodshed I came upon a shiny black spider 58 under a pile of boards. Though I had not seen a black widow up to that time, I became suspicious, got a fruit jar, and bottled it up. When my son came home I asked him what it was. "Black widow, gee!" he replied without hesitation. The next day he told his zoology professor about it, and got the reply, "Impossible, this is way out of range. They don't occur here." Bill wasn't convinced, so he took the specimen in and asked the professor what it was. A puzzled look came over his face; then, in a tone of amazement, he said, "Yes, it *is* a black widow!"

While black widows are widely distributed, populations in warm climates are larger because there is no necessity of their hibernating in the winter. But these creatures do not infest the desert in droves, as is sometimes believed. In fact, one may look a long time without finding a single specimen unless the search is made in the right location. This is not a creature that wanders at large; it settles down in shady hidden spots, under logs, stones, and often in the corners of eaves. It may even elect to set up housekeeping in a kitchen drawer, as one did in a house in which we once lived in Sasabe.

Tarantula

Fortunately, the black widow has a gentle and retiring disposition. It is not aggressive, and will flee at the first sign of intrusion. It will bite only if constrained, or if it feels itself in danger of being crushed. The rare cases of bites from this spider have been occasioned in this way, and the method of avoiding trouble is simple: Never put your fingers under anything—board, rock, branch—that you wish to lift or turn over. Use your boot or a pry. On several occasions I have found black widows under various objects of cover in the field, one of them being a broken *metate,* turned upside down, in an ancient Indian village.

The poison of the black widow is reported to be much more virulent, in ratio of amount, than the venom of the rattlesnake. Effects of a bite are not only local, but also systemic, with nausea and muscle rigidity present in addition to other symptoms. The condition may last a few days, but generally wears off without permanent injury. A very few deaths are on record, mostly involving young children and feeble old persons.

Another creature that is the subject of tall horror tales is the centipede. This is a familiar form to everyone, for centipedes of some kind live everywhere. They are commonly found crawling under boards and in shady places. Some fairly sizable ones, three inches or slightly more in length, may be seen in colder northern regions, but the giant desert centipede tops them all in size and formidable appearance. It is enough to give anyone, especially a sensitive person, the creeps. But it is not so bad as it appears to be.

Roughly described, the centipede seems to be a creature composed of a long series of interlocking movable segments, propelled by rows of legs, some twenty on each side. It has a rounded head with a pair of vicious hooked jaws and long antennae. The color is usually a dull yellow, with brownish black markings. Nothing else in the world looks like a centipede, not even its close relative, the millipede. This is merely an elongated, ambulatory blackish tube, propelled by myriads of hairy legs. A large form of this curious creature is also found in the desert, but it is harmless.

The desert centipede has a definite poison, and while its bite can be painful and cause swelling that may take a long time to subside, it is not dangerous and certainly not fatal, as is so often erroneously reported. In addition to the bite the centipede is equipped with another feature not exactly an asset to anyone coming in contact with it. Each leg ends in a very sharp, needlelike claw that can cause an irritation like that produced by a nettle, if the beast crawls on one. One evening my wife and I were sitting in a patio talking, and she suddenly yelped. Something had crawled over the instep of her foot and left a sharp stinging sensation. I got a flashlight and soon discovered a giant centipede crawling near the barbecue. It measured about eight inches, and was a tough-looking customer. The itch lasted for a day, but did not cause an infection.

The centipede is a critter to avoid, but this is not difficult, because it is nowhere plentiful. Sometimes several seasons will pass without our seeing one. The instructions that apply to all sorts of crawly things— not putting your hands where you can't see—will keep you out of trouble in all but extraordinary cases. A centipede might just drop on you from the roof of a remada, or crawl up the leg of your pants, but lightning might hit you, too, if you're unlucky.

Scorpions occur in all hot climates, and their evil reputation is as widespread as their distribution. Much of it is justified, but not all. There seems to be a common impression that any scorpion is deadly; if you get stung you are in grave danger. While there is nothing to commend the scorpion, from the human standpoint, the supposition, as a general statement, is not true.

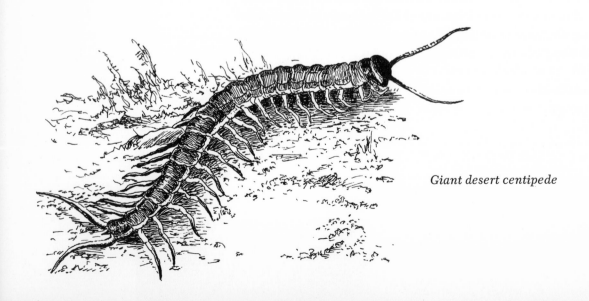

Giant desert centipede

In Arizona about twenty species occur, and of these only two are classified as deadly. A few more are found in Mexico as a whole, with several others being added to the dangerous list. The term "deadly" does not mean that everyone who is so unfortunate as to be stung by a scorpion will die. Persons standing in the greatest danger are children, particularly those under four years of age, and aged or infirm adults. While the seriousness of the scorpion problem should not be underestimated, neither should it be a source of undue fear or panic. An understanding of the situation with regard to dangerous species, control measures, and remedial action in case of emergency all contribute to a sensible approach to the problem. People in hot countries throughout the world have always lived amid scorpions, and they have done pretty well.

It is natural that persons unacquainted with this weird and sinister creature do not have a very clear idea of how it actually looks or how it behaves. Scorpions are arachnids, having eight legs, and are therefore related to the spiders. Their bodies are segmented and equipped with long tails that terminate in barbed stingers attached to a poison gland. They have sharp and powerful jaws, and a set of two pincers that resemble lobster or crab claws growing from the body near the front of the head. This equipment looks formidable enough to make one believe that it is here the danger lies.

This, of course, is not true. The scorpion seizes its prey, which consists of insects, in its claws and crushes it with its powerful mandibles in the act of dining. The danger to animals and humans lies at the rear end of the beast. It raises its tail in an arc and with a quick thrust drives the stinger into the flesh. Muscular action at the same moment sends poison into the wound, as it does in the case of a snakebite.

All species of scorpions are poisonous, but the important difference is that the venom of the nondeadly varieties is local in effect, much like that of a bee sting. There may be swelling, and some inflammation which persists for a day or so and then subsides without any particular treatment. Many people who have been stung by nondeadly scorpions report that the results have not been so bad as a bee or wasp sting.

But the venom of the deadly species acts very differently. The effect is general, not local; in fact, the wound may not swell at all. The poison spreads rapidly throughout the system and affects the muscles of legs and arms, causing them to become rigid. Temperature rises to 103 or 104 degrees. Breathing becomes labored, and in extreme cases cyanosis may set in. None of this is a light matter.

It is important to know the treatment for scorpion stings and to apply it promptly. Of great importance also is, if at all possible, to kill the scorpion that stung and have it identified promptly. The chances in the great majority of cases are that it will be one of a nondeadly species. But

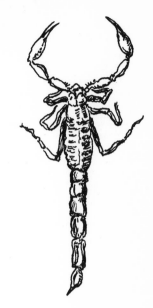

Scorpions

Deadly (long slender tail)

if it should turn out to be otherwise, much ground will be gained in the treatment.

In the case of any scorpion sting, we are advised to apply a tourniquet between the wound and the heart, wherever possible, the procedure used in snakebite incidents. Crushed ice wrapped in a thin pack of cloth should be placed on the wound and the surrounding area for a period of ten or twelve minutes; then the tourniquet may be removed. If no systemic symptoms appear within a very short time, in cases where the scorpion was not positively identified there should be no serious trouble. But in the case of a sting from a deadly species, the patient should be taken to a doctor immediately. A very effective scorpion antivenin, perfected in Mexico, is available in the Southwest. In the event of a sting by any scorpion, it is wise to see a physician, after first applying the tourniquet and ice treatment.

The identification of the various species of scorpions is not an easy matter, even for experts. There are, however, a few general rules that will guide the layman. If you see a huge, heavy-bodied crawling creature over four inches long, it will be the giant hairy scorpion, not a deadly species. Other scorpions of the nondeadly type vary greatly in size, but have quite thick chunky tails. The real villains, constituting two species in the northern part of the range, are pallid or straw-colored and have extremely slender tails. One has no distinctive markings. The other has two blackish marks on the body. A technical description refers to a tiny notch, called a subaculear tooth, just in front of the stinging spine. Now, this is fine, and probably perfectly clear to specialists, but I shouldn't want to go on record as recommending it as a means of identification to be depended on by nontrained folk. In case of doubt, take the beast to someone who knows about them.

Various poisons and scorpicides are very effective in controlling scorpions around the house. They should be used regularly during the hot part of the year around baseboards and in corners where the creatures harbor. No one in the Southwest puts on shoes in the morning without first shaking them out. And the same precaution applies to bedding; strip it down and look carefully before crawling in for the night.

While an occasional scorpion may be found in the house, most of them will be encountered outdoors, especially when camping. Again, never put your hand into places where you cannot see what is there. Kick over stones or chunks of wood first before picking them up. One time at Kino Bay I lifted a stone with the toe of my boot and found a scorpion that looked as though it were glued to the underside. It had a

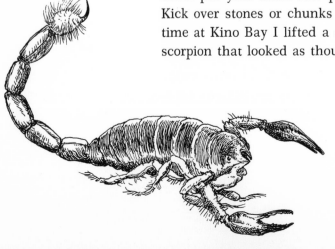

Giant hairy scorpion.
Not deadly

flat and dry appearance, and I thought it was dead. I experimented—but with a stick. It instantly arched its tail and was ready for business.

Good advice about all desert critters:

Never tech the piz'nus things;
They pack a heap o' bites and stings
—CACTUS PETE

A poisonous insect found throughout the Southwest and in other hot climates is the kissing bug, sometimes called the assassin bug. Since it is not deadly it has not received the publicity that attaches to scorpions and venomous snakes, but the bite of one of these insects can prove to be serious enough to put one out of the running for a period of time.

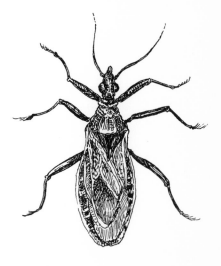

Kissing bug

The kissing bug closely resembles a squash bug and is about the same size, but there is a species that reaches an inch in length. It has eyes that stick out of the side of the head, and a beak, or proboscis, that hooks downward. Unlike scorpions and snakes this creature is sneaky and furtive in habit. It attacks animals and humans when they are asleep, and is able to bite and draw blood without awakening the victim. It lives entirely on blood.

The first indication of trouble a person has upon awakening is a severe burning and itching sensation at the seat of the bite, followed by swelling, and inflammation that rapidly spreads in the afflicted area, sometimes to the diameter of a foot. Occasionally the bite is followed by systemic symptoms such as abdominal pains, nausea, headache, and a lethargic feeling. No specific remedy has been found for the bite of the kissing bug, but relief may be obtained, according to doctors who have treated cases, by the application of a pad containing hot epsom salts, used as soon as possible after a bite. Later, the use of ice at the point of puncture helps to localize the poison.

The best way to avoid bites from this malignant insect is to prevent their occurrence. It is well known in the Southwest that the pack rat (wood rat) is the most desirable victim of the kissing bug, and a colony of these rodents near a house is a sure invitation to trouble. By eliminating these little animals, the incidence of kissing bugs in the home will be reduced to practically nothing.

In contrast to the several poisonous creatures described, there are, in desert areas, other things that have a villainous look, but are harmless. A glance is enough to convince the observer that the beast is not only poisonous but probably very dangerous as well. But appearance does not always disclose fact. A good example of this is the sun spider, or solpugid.

After having lived in the desert for a number of years, I still can't resist calling out, "Scorpion!" at the first quick glance at a sun spider.

The resemblance is only superficial, and close examination will show even a relatively inexperienced person the difference. The sun spider may reach a length of two inches, stretched out, has eight legs and a segmented body—an arachnid—but no tail and *no stinger*. It has strong jaws, and might nip you if you handled it, but it is definitely not poisonous, in spite of its rather fearsome appearance.

The sun spider is not only an interesting desert creature, but also a most valuable one. It lives entirely on insects, and is an asset both in the house and outside. Many people balk at the idea of harboring any kind of "pet" insect inside, but we never kill a sun spider. They industriously hunt through the cracks and crannies present in even the most well-built house, and ferret out all sorts of obnoxious insects that, in spite of screens and other precautions, are bound to find their way in. Recently I watched a sun spider eat a sizable moth it had captured on a screen. Starting at the rear end it worked through the body to the wings, and then consumed them deliberately for dessert, with apparent gusto.

One other weird and horrible-looking creature is the source of many false and unfounded tales. This is the whip-tail scorpion, commonly called the vinegarone. The name is derived from the body juices, which give off a strong acid odor like vinegar, if the creature is stepped on. The vinegarone has very strong and large claws or pincers and a segmented lower body that is decorated with a long whiplike tail. This appendage is straight and almost hairlike. It has no stinger and there is no poison gland.

The vinegarone, like the sun spider, is not only harmless but is an asset as well, helping to control many pestiferous insects.

The Jerusalem cricket is another in the list of weirdies that has spawned many horror tales, all false. It is a shy and retiring little insect with a head out of all proportion to the rest of it. Being nocturnal in habit, it is seldom seen unless dug up in the ground. Mexicans call it *niña de la tierra*—earth child.

Among the most interesting creatures of the desert are the lizards. They are reptiles that occur in several forms and species. Practically everyone has at least a rough idea of the appearance of a lizard, even though he has never actually seen one. This strange long-tailed, scaly creature is much used as a motif in designs on fabrics and other materials because of its graceful appearance. The standard type for this use is the long slim-bodied lizard, with tapering tail that twists itself into decorative shapes. But there is a thick pudgy form, with rounded, slightly oval body thickly covered with spiny scales, that enjoys wide recognition, even if only through illustrations.

Again, almost everyone knows what a horned "toad" looks like, but many are not aware that this strange creature is not a toad at all, but a 64

true lizard. "Horny toads," as they are called locally, occur in quantities throughout desert lands. Of different species, they come in many sizes and colors. Some are not much larger than a quarter, while others are as much as five inches long, and correspondingly obese. With armored body and head crowned with pointed scaly plates, the horned toad is a fearsome-looking creature. But its looks belie its disposition. Actually, it is gentle, and may be handled with impunity. While it will squirm in the hand and attempt to escape, it never bites.

The horned toad buries itself in the sand so that only its head, with its small beady eyes, protrudes. The camouflage is so perfect that it is difficult to spot one. Touch it and it will explode a shower of sand and be off like a flash. Color of the various forms varies from light sand through gray almost to black. One species is a dark bluish purple with gray patterned patches.

Because of their popularity as pets, horned toads have been greatly reduced in areas where dealers in curios have collected them for sale. Some of the Southwestern states have made it illegal to capture them for commercial purposes.

Some species of horned toads have a curious habit that is often commented on but not always seen. When picked up, probably under the stress of excitement, they shoot drops of blood from their eyes. It does the creature no harm.

Visitors to the desert will be delighted by the antics of the many species of lizards to be seen in all but the coldest months. Among the most active of creatures, they are abroad during the sunny hours, and spend much time in pursuit of insects. The rapidity with which a lizard can move is a never-ending source of amazement. It can close in on its prey with a flashing movement that the eye can scarcely follow. Because
65 of their insectivorous nature, lizards are a definite asset in the garden

and patio. The quantity of insects that one lizard alone will eat in a day is impressive.

There are so many species of lizards that it is impossible to cover more than a few that will be commonly seen by the visitor. The spiny lizard is a big fellow, sometimes twelve inches long, completely covered with large spiny scales. It is to be seen frequently resting on the sides of patio walls or houses, sometimes in an upside-down position. Apparently it spends much time contemplating the problems of the universe, but when it makes up its mind to move it can really go!

A handsome form is the collared lizard. About a foot in length, it is covered with small scales. It is yellowish in tone, with markings that range from dark brown to a gray-blue tone. A light band around the lower part of the neck is bordered by two dark lines. The head of this lizard is very large, and though the creature is not poisonous, unlike most small lizards it is apt to bite, if handled.

Most smaller species are docile, and make no use of their jaws in defense. While a person with quick reflexes can sometimes capture lizards, it is better not to—for the lizard's sake. If roughly handled, this strange creature has the ability to drop most of its tail and leave it squirming on the ground through reflex action. A lizard thus de-tailed will soon grow a new one, though it will probably be stubby and never reach its original length.

A real oddball in the lizard group is the chuckawalla. It is often fifteen inches or more long and has loose baggy skin, with a fat chunky body. The tail is long and fleshy, and thick at the base. The legs are thick and strong, and the head is somewhat pointed, with two scaly horns and, behind them, a loose collar of small scales.

Next to the Gila monster this is the largest lizard in the desert. It is perhaps not so scarce as secretive, for it lives in rocky situations and is seldom seen. If an attempt is made to drag a partly concealed chuckawalla from a position in rocks, it will inflate its body and wedge itself in.

Collared lizard

Should the would-be captor succeed in freeing the creature, let him beware, unless he wears very heavy leather gloves, for this lizard can bite like the very devil. It is a sport better left to collectors. Unlike other species, the chuckawalla is herbivorous.

One of the commonest, and at the same time handsomest, of all species is the zebra lizard. It is small in body, but has a very long tail encircled with dark bands on a creamy white background. This is one of the swiftest of all lizards, running with unbelievable rapidity, and stopping abruptly. It arches its tail high in the air and waves it slowly sideways, as though it were signaling. At the same time it engages in a series of push-ups, a habit common to many of the smaller lizards. It is a rather ludicrous sight, and undoubtedly has some meaning—for the lizard.

A handsome lizard of small to medium size is the banded gecko. Of a light tan to pinkish background color, the skin is banded with dark markings on the tail that run up irregularly on the body and form blotches. The head is large. This lizard is nocturnal, and is seldom seen unless one is found under a board that is turned up, or some other hiding place.

For some reason not readily apparent, the gecko is often thought by uninformed people to be a young Gila monster. A close examination will show that the similarity is very superficial, mostly a matter of ground color and markings, certainly not form. This pretty little lizard is entirely harmless, from the standpoint of being poisonous. A fact that should be known and remembered is that *all* lizards occurring in the Sonoran desert are nonvenomous, with one exception. This is the Gila monster of the northern area, and its closely related variant, the Mexican beaded lizard.

While some confusion in identifying serpents, especially at a quick glance, is understandable—several species have markings not unlike those of the rattler—it is impossible to mistake a Gila monster. Nothing else even remotely resembles it in size, color, or markings.

Once seen, a Gila monster will never be forgotten. To say that it would be out of the running in a beauty contest would be to understate the facts. It does, however, have one redeeming quality. Its color is a fascinating pattern of irregular bands and blotches, warm brownish-black in tone, on a background that is essentially a grayed coral red. This tone may vary considerably; some specimens are quite bright, while others are rather dull.

The hide of the Gila monster is covered with small "warts" or tubercles, giving it a rough appearance. In shape, it is long and tapering at both ends from a thick chunky body. The tail, though usually thick, slims down in the spring when the creature first comes out of

67

hibernation. It is there that fat is stored, and this is utilized for food during the long inactive period.

The Gila monster is by far the largest lizard found in the northern part of the Sonoran desert. The iguana, a tropical form, though occurring in the lower regions of this desert, does not ordinarily reach maximum size much north of the Tropic of Cancer. This lizard is not only non-poisonous but also edible, and is much esteemed as food by the Mexicans and Indians living in the tropics.

In length, the Gila monster averages about fifteen to eighteen inches, but it occasionally is seen as long as twenty-four inches. No matter what its size, this lizard is always an impressive sight. It is slow in movement, and it ambles over the desert in a very deliberate manner. Owing to its striking color pattern and lumbering gait, it can be seen and recognized at a considerable distance. When approached closely it is apt to turn and eye the intruder, but generally it makes no hasty attempt to escape. If plagued by a tossed pebble, it will open its jaws menacingly and hiss loudly.

One might think that such a ponderous creature would be slow in all its reactions, but this is certainly not true. One time I came upon a large monster that had crawled out of a gopher hole and was sunning itself on the warm gravel. Small animal burrows are the favorite dens of this creature. I found a long mesquite branch and prodded it gently in the side. With a movement that the eye could scarcely follow, the beast whipped around and seized the stick in its powerful jaws. It seemed to be fully as fast as the strike of a rattler.

Many misconceptions surround the life of the Gila monster. It is commonly stated that it has no elimination system; that food which is swallowed and not utilized is later regurgitated, after becoming putrid, and that a bite from a Gila monster produces poison that is the result of putrefaction. This is nothing more than a fable, spawned by ignorance. The creature has definite poison glands. They are located in the lower jaw, and do not connect directly with teeth or fangs. In order to poison a victim, the Gila monster must get a firm and deep grip, and then chew for a considerable period. The poison from the glands can then enter wounds made by the teeth.

How poisonous the venom is has long been another subject of controversy. In concentrated doses it undoubtedly is very virulent and could cause death, especially to a child or infirm person. But even in cases of a severe and prolonged bite, it is stated, the venom is much diluted by saliva that reduces its efficacy. The symptoms of a bite are similar to those of a rattlesnake bite. Victims may have a very bad time, with high temperature, respiratory trouble, and nausea, but very few deaths have ever been reported.

68

From the foregoing it will be seen that, in a broad sense, the Gila monster is not one of the desert's great perils. Because of its habits it can be seen and avoided. The cases of bites from the creatures almost invariably stem from undue familiarity. Overconfident collectors, or people who have a yen for handling reptiles, pick one up, lose their grip, and in a flash are clamped down on by a set of viselike jaws that may require precious time to remove—unless help is at hand. The safest way to avoid trouble is to keep away from the critters.

The Gila monster is largely carnivorous, and it has a habit roundly denounced by ornithologists; it is excessively fond of eggs. During the nesting season this might be a serious matter, except for the fact that these big lizards are nowhere numerous enough to make an impression on the future generation of birds. Other creatures—notably snakes, skunks, and other mammals—are avid egg hunters, and are far more numerous.

The Gila monster, in common with some other desert creatures, seems to suffer from myopia—or else it displays a flagrant indifference to intrusion. By walking slowly one may approach the big lizard to within a few feet before it will display alarm. Several years ago a visitor from the East expressed a desire to see, among other desert creatures, a Gila monster. I said that I couldn't guarantee it, because they are far from common, but that we could try. I drove to a ridge that I knew to contain a large colony of gophers that made many mounds with burrows, in the midst of a thinly covered mesquite area.

After parking the car and walking a few hundred yards, we saw a motion a short distance ahead. It seemed to be a continuous weaving, seesawing movement. Approaching slowly and carefully we came upon the amazing, and probably very rare, sight of two Gila monsters engaging in an exotic mating performance. They seemed to slither and roll back and forth in an area of about a yard, rubbing against each other, and sometimes turning on their backs. These weird antics were accompanied by intermittent hisses. In their preoccupation they were unaware of any intrusion, and we were able to stand within a yard and watch the performance. My friend took many color shots, and neither movement nor the click of the shutter disturbed the performers in the least. We watched the show for a full ten minutes, then tiring of the thing, they slowly lumbered off towards a mound and crawled into different gopher holes.

Banded gecko

The Gila monster has long been a major attraction in the ubiquitous —and many think—all too numerous roadside, so-called "zoos" that advertise *ad nauseam* for miles along the approach in sinister and marrow-chilling phrases. DEN OF DEATH! SEE THE DEADLY GILA MONSTER, THE SCOURGE OF THE DESERT! Fortunately this sort of thing is gradually being done away with, in the case of the Gila monster, for the law now protects this interesting and fast-disappearing lizard—a traditional and worthy living symbol of the desert.

South of the border the Gila monster is replaced by a relative known as the Mexican beaded lizard. The difference is largely a matter of color; in habit the two forms are alike, and their occurrence in numbers is about equal. Although more may often be found in one area than in another, probably because of the availability of food, neither the Gila monster of the northern area of the desert nor its more southerly cousin is numerous.

The newcomer to the desert may be surprised to see a medium-sized turtle lumbering through the sand or gravel, along a road or during one of his hikes. After a sufficiently long stay in this arid land he will be surprised at nothing; but the initial meeting with this antediluvian creature, whose ancestry dates back almost to the beginnings of what might be considered well-developed forms, is apt to cause him to wonder. Turtles and tortoises are among the oldest of living animate forms, and are commonly thought of as being aquatic on the one hand, or living on land in cool climates, as is true with the box tortoises and other purely terrestrial species.

The desert tortoise, however, has either never heard of this theory or he simply disregards it as something not worthy of consideration. So he goes on ambling about the desert, apparently enjoying it. Tortoises are usually seen after rainy periods, when they come out of estivation and wander abroad to feed on prickly pear blossoms and tender succulent plants.

This strange creature is really an ambulatory fortress, living between thick shell carapace and plastron, and having the ability, possessed by most turtles and tortoises, of retracting its thick and heavy scaly legs and claws, and its beaked head, into safe cover under the shell when danger threatens. As a consequence it has few enemies. The carapace is composed of a series of plates, welded into a mass that forms an interesting design. It is usually a dull brown.

The reputation for longevity enjoyed by the various turtles and tortoises is well merited and seems to apply also to the desert tortoise. Individuals that have been marked by letters or dates carved on the carapace have been seen twenty years or more later. Since the tortoise is a great rover, it may cover a lot of territory, and may not reappear in a location where it was first seen for several years. Some friends of mine carved a name on a tortoise they found in their garden, and released it. It stayed around a few days and then disappeared. About three years later it came ambling leisurely into the garden, stayed a day or so, and then left. They expect to see it again someday, if it isn't run over on the road by a car. This is the fate of a great many tortoises—a fate shared by an appalling number of wild creatures, ranging from chipmunks to deer.

Besides coming on a tortoise in the desert, there is the surprise of seeing a toad. These amphibians are thought of as inhabiting damp and shady places, seeking the shelter of ferns and mucky places along streams and ponds and the cool moisture of dewy lawns in the evening. The desert toad, however, of which there are several species, is just as different, and—from the human standpoint—just as mixed up in his philosophy of what we would consider the good life, as is the tortoise.

After a heavy rain in the spring and summer, even into the fall when the weather remains warm, toads will appear literally in swarms. They are little things, perhaps an inch and a half long or even smaller. They hop along ludicrously with short jumps, and head for the nearest water. If it is a reservoir the toads will be able to complete the breeding act and to lay eggs. The tadpoles will then have a chance to hatch and develop. But if the toads chance on a *charco,* which is Spanish for a puddle, it will soon dry up, and that particular future generation of toads will die.

The toad must get on with things in a hurry, for rains may come at widely spaced intervals, with a long dry spell in between. The toad is faced with the necessity of digging in while the ground is still damp. If forced to remain out long, it will perish from drought.

In periods of dryness between summer rains, toads probably stay close to the surface in damp soil. A little while ago I was watering a plant, and suddenly a little head with two beady eyes emerged from the wet soil. It was followed by a pudgy little toad who blinked and hopped down a bank. The ground was completely dry, as it had not rained in several days. The toad soon lost itself in some acacia and mimosa brush where the ground was as hard as flint. It had mistaken the watering for a rain.

A much larger toad, a *Bufo,* frequently appears after heavy rains. Normally it lives near streams and dams, but it also spends much of its life estivating. The skin of this toad is poisonous, and dogs mouthing one in play, as they sometimes do, are made very ill. Small dogs may even die. The bufo reaches a length of about six inches, and is very heavy and chunky.

Paloverde, the unique tree that is "green all over" and that gets along with tiny leaves that last for short periods only. There are several varieties that are common to all parts of the lower desert. The paloverde is the state tree of Arizona.

SIX

TREES AND SHRUBS

*They have learned to adapt
to an arid land, and thrive*

"WELL, I suppose cactus and yucca and those other funny things on the desert you talk about are all right to look at. But I just couldn't live in a land without trees. I was brought up in the East, where there are lots of fine trees, and I intend to stay here. Got to have them to be happy. You don't have trees on the desert, except maybe a few little scrubby ones."

This arbitrary statement, made with finality, came from an old New England friend of mine who knew nothing about the desert, and wasn't interested enough to find out. The idea seemed to be: in order to grow, trees—large important ones like oaks, sycamores, poplars—must have water. There is no water on the desert, or very little—therefore there are no trees. Now, the most enthusiastic desert lover will grant that trees do not grow everywhere in the arid lands, but trees there most certainly are; and many of them will match, in size and beauty, examples of the same species found in wet regions.

The difference is that one may have to travel a little to find them. One may have to make short trips to canyons, rivers, or benchlands, always a pleasant diversion. If trees are wanted around the home they may be grown readily, and often faster than in cooler regions, as long as they are watered about twice a week. Indeed trees of almost every variety will thrive if given comparatively small amounts of water during the dry season.

Trees growing naturally in the wild state often astonish visitors who have had no foreknowledge of the desert. The sycamores in Pepper-sauce Canyon in the Santa Catalina Mountains, for example, are as fine and large as any seen in more obvious localities. Willows along many rivers that are dry for the majority of the year are large and thrifty, with thick trunks and large sweeping branches that spread over a considerable area, furnishing gracious shade to cattle. The cottonwood, or alamo, is notable for its ability to grow to impressive proportions on a bare minimum of surface water—moisture in the form of rain.

In a climate so arid, a natural question is, How do trees grow and thrive in the desert? By adaptation. Water is always present in the ground to some degree, and trees have learned to alter their root systems, some of them quite remarkably. They have obeyed the law of the desert: Adapt or die. As a result, they thrive.

The mesquite is a stunning example.

The mesquite is one of the commonest trees of the desert, varying from a few isolated specimens to thick forests covering many acres. It may occur as a small bush shrub, or an impressive many-branched tree thirty-five or forty feet tall, with a trunk diameter up to four feet. The difference in size is accounted for by the nature of the terrain. One can guess the water-holding content of the ground by observing the size of the mesquite. Dry benches and hills grow small, unthrifty, shrublike trees. They may be old, but they never develop because there is not enough water under the ground. Bottomlands along creeks and rivers, even though the latter are dry most of the year, produce the largest and finest specimens. The roots of the mesquite have been known to spread more than fifty feet in search of water. Mesquites belong to the legume family, and produce long beans that provide food for many wild creatures. They are closely related to the various acacias and mimosas. All have compound fernlike leaves. Most of the smaller branches are well covered with sharp spines, but some are almost lacking in them. The wood is very hard, heavy, reddish brown in color with creamy sapwood. It is probably the most important wood growing in the desert, and is much used as firewood, as the main source of charcoal, and as fuel for adobe brick kilns, of which there are many in northern Sonora. It also serves for fenceposts and decorative woodwork. Large old mesquites are now rare, having been cut long ago for their valuable lumber. The doors of the Mission of San Xavier del Bac, a few miles south of Tucson, are made of panels of mesquite wood more than thirty inches wide.

A tree unique in several ways is the ironwood, or *palofierro*. True to its name, the ironwood tree possesses wood so tough that it dulls an ax and soon exhausts the woodcutter. The Mexican *leñeros* shudder when you mention ironwood. These able workers will chop mesquite, which is a very hard and tough wood, all day long and never complain, but *palo-* 74

The mesquite is found abundantly throughout most of the desert. It is an important source of firewood, and cattle feed upon the tender new leaves in the spring. This is a drawing of an old specimen that has shed its leaves in winter.

Ironwood, or palofierro

fierro—ah, no, *señor, por favór!* In addition to being tough the wood is extremely heavy. It is second only in weight to the leadwood of southern Florida, among all the native trees of the United States. The wood takes a beautiful polish because of its hardness, and is sometimes used in the making of small bowls and boxes.

Mature ironwood trees grow to a height of about thirty feet, and assume interesting shapes, with branches that spread at an upright angle from the trunk. Very old trees may attain a trunk diameter of as much as three feet, though such specimens are rare. The tree is evergreen in most of its range, and the foliage is a gray-green. While the ironwood is found throughout the Sonoran desert, unfortunately it is limited to low elevations, and therefore its distribution is much restricted. It will not grow well above 2,500 feet. Being very susceptible to frosts it can suffer foliage damage during severe cold spells, even in 76 its normal range. In a recent winter I observed browned-off foliage on *palofierros* along the main highway to Mexico City some hundred miles south of the border. In general, the ironwood does not like hill or mountain country, but grows thriftily along sandy washes and bottomlands. It grows to almost forest density near Florence, Arizona, and along the Mexican highway from Nogales between Benjamin Hill and Hermosillo. In May, the ironwood develops smoky lavender blossoms that completely envelop the trees. A stand of ironwoods in full bloom is an enchanting sight. The flowers grow in short clusters, are about one-half inch long, and are pealike in form.

In a land of strange and exotic trees the paloverde is outstanding. Its trunk, branches, twigs are covered with a green smooth bark, varying in hue from bright yellow-green to blue-green. The chlorophyll in the bark takes the place of that in normal leaves on less specialized trees. Each species of paloverde has very small leaves, but only in the wet season of summer, which normally lasts a few weeks. On the Mexican paloverde, tiny leaves less than a quarter of an inch long are formed on long drooping streamers. These may have a length of from eight to twenty inches. The green, or foothill, paloverde and the blue paloverde are sparsely clad with small leaflets barely an eighth of an inch long. The leaves on all species dry up and fall shortly after the rains cease; then the bark takes over and continues manufacturing plant food. Paloverdes vary greatly in size. Some mature trees may be thirty feet high, with trunks a foot or more in diameter. Sweeping branches form irregular masses that give the trees a rather careless and uncontrived shape. Bark on the lower trunk and larger branches of old trees takes on a brownish hue; otherwise the trees are completly green or blue. Paloverdes are often found growing in forests, in association with the sahuaro cactus. The range of the paloverde is extensive, covering most of the Sonoran desert in Arizona and Mexico, in localities favorable to it. It thrives and reaches its most typical form in altitudes below 4,000 feet. While the paloverde is always a fine sight at any season of the year, it achieves grandeur when it blooms from mid-April through May. It is asking almost too much of the imagination to try to visualize a single green tree covered with a shower of blossoms of purest yellow gold. Multiply this by fifty, one hundred, a thousand trees carpeting a gently rolling hillside, their blossom-laden boughs flashing sheets of brilliant color as they sway in the breeze. It is a sight that can never be forgotten, and it has brought many fortunate pilgrims back to the desert. The paloverde is the official state tree of Arizona.

The cottonwood, or alamo, in Arizona and Sonora thrive in bottomlands along creeks and rivers and furnish dense shade to cattle, horses and picknickers. It is a tree that requires water, but it will send out long roots to find it. It is often planted around ranches and haciendas. A mature old cottonwood may reach a height of one hundred feet with a trunk diameter of as much as four feet. Unfortunately the wood is brittle, and branches suffer damage during windstorms. While occasionally used as fuel, the wood is not very desirable, owing to its softness. The cottonwood produces catkins in the spring that are covered with a cottonlike material. They drift in the air and make a mess of things around the house. But the short-lived nuisance is well worth putting up with, when the good qualities of the tree are considered. The leaves of the cottonwood are a glossy deep green, turning to a magnificent cadmium yellow late in the year. In most of the Sonoran desert this occurs in December. The alamo is a restless tree, anxious to get on with it. It sleeps only a short time after shedding its leaves. Sometime in February the branches are covered with a gray-green haze of awakening buds. Spring has come to the desert.

On a par with, or even surpassing, the cottonwood from the standpoint of utility and beauty is the sycamore. The species found in the Sonoran desert is popularly known as the Arizona sycamore. It occurs commonly along streams and canyons in the mountains and foothills of the higher desert having a water supply. It often grows in the oak country, and it thrives at elevations of from about 2,000 to 6,000 feet. Its large somewhat star-shaped leaves are decorative, and form a marked contrast to most of the other tree and shrub foliage ordinarily found on deciduous desert plants. The most attractive feature of the sycamore is its handsome bark, which dresses the tree in a cloak of warm white, accented by brown patches in a decorative pattern where the bark has peeled off on larger limbs and the trunk. The flowers form in small ball-like clusters, two to four in number, and later ripen into fruits of the same shape. The wood is hard, and the grain has brownish veins. It is often used for inlay work. While sycamores do not ordinarily attain the height of the largest cottonwoods, they can be impressive. Individuals of about seventy-five feet may have a trunk diameter of four feet. There are fine examples of the sycamore in Sabino Canyon near Tucson. A nice group along a little stream some thirty miles south of Nogales, on the Mexican highway, at a pleasant spot named Agua Caliente grows in company with a stand of large old willows, making an ideal place to picnic.

The willow is one of the most widely distributed of all trees, being found practically everywhere in the world. It is said to be the last tree with the courage to penetrate into the far Arctic, where it finally peters out in a small, miserable, but still brave, brushlike thing. Practically every wash, creek, and river in the desert having a reasonable amount of water not too far underground is clothed with willows. The larger 78

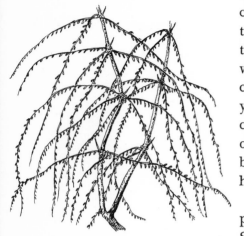

Tendrils and leaves of Mexican paloverde

varieties reach a height of fifty feet, while smaller species are little more than shrubs. Cattle feed on the leaves of willows during periods of scant range grass, and there is no better plant to hold banks of *represas* and prevent erosion.

The ash requires about the same conditions as the willow, and is often found growing in association with the latter. Perhaps the commonest species is the velvet ash, also known as the Arizona ash. It is a handsome tree, growing to a height of about forty feet, and its dense foliage provides considerable shade. In late autumn the compound leaves of the ash turn a beautiful tone of yellowish bronze.

All the trees previously described may be seen by the tourist, driving through various areas of the desert, without leaving his car. To make close acquaintance with a very unusual and interesting tree, the piñon pine, he must leave the low desert, and climb. He may even have to park his car and hike, for the best groves of piñons are usually off the highway in scattered areas in the Arizona and Sonora mountains at elevations from 5,000 to 7,500 feet. The tree itself is rather small and bushy, and it is not particularly attractive. Its value lies in its product— the pine nut or "Indian nut." Pine "nuts" are the seeds of this species of

Cottonwood, or Alamo

Palo santo, or morning-glory tree

conifer, and are widely gathered and sold in the markets as far away as New York City. The shells are thin and may be cracked by the teeth, freeing the sweet rich meat. It is eaten raw, or roasted.

Oaks also grow in the Sonoran desert but only in mountainous country, at elevations from 3,500 feet to about 7,000 feet. The Mexicans refer to them loosely as *encina*, *roble*, or *bellota*. The *bellota* is the most abundant oak of the mountain regions of the Mexican border and northern Sonora, much of the high benchland and rugged canyons in areas being well clothed with them. The term *bellota* refers to the fruit of the oak, the acorn. This tree bears small sweet acorns, having a minimum of tannin, which are gathered and sold much the same as piñon nuts. A small community south of Arivaca, on the border, is whimsically named *Tres Bellotas (Three Oaks)*. The *bellota* is a black oak, properly termed Emory oak in honor of Lieutenant Colonel William Hemsley Emory who led an expedition in the Southwest in 1846-1847. It reaches 80 a height of fifty feet or more, has a wide spread, and affords good shade. The leaves are roughly lance-shaped, and bear several short points or serrations along the edges. They are thick and leathery and a shiny olive green in color. As with all oaks, the *bellota* is a tough and very durable tree, resisting winds and adverse weather. The wood is very hard and heavy, reddish in color, and ranks along with mesquite as top-quality firewood. The tree might be said to be evergreen, since the shedding process is gradual, the new leaves replacing the old ones in the spring as they fall.

The desert willow is a splendid example of misnaming a thing. While this graceful little tree greatly resembles a true willow, it really is a member of the catalpa family. The desert willow may often be found growing profusely along the banks of washes and creeks, and thinly covered damp bottomlands. It is very valuable in controlling erosion and is often planted for this purpose. It sometimes reaches a height of twenty-five feet, but it is usually smaller. In growth habit it is slender and graceful, thin rather than bushy. The leaves are narrow and taper-ing, from three to six inches in length, and light green in color. Seed capsules are four to eight inches long and very narrow, reminding one somewhat of the "Indian cigars" produced by the catalpa tree. One of the pleasures afforded by the desert to which we look forward in late winter is the spring blooming period of the desert willow. From mid-April to late May, according to locality, the tree sends forth lovely little blossoms that scent the air with a subtle fragrance. The flowers grow in small clusters, and are an inch or slightly more in length. They re-semble small orchids, being white with purple and pink markings inside their bell-shaped form. This unspectacular and modest little tree is truly one of the assets of the desert, both economically and esthetically.

Tree tobacco, a nicotiana

The *palo santo* (holy tree) or morning glory tree may equal or run a close second to the paloverde as a desert exotic. The range of this re-markable form is severely restricted, and it has always been a matter of regret to me that it will not grow in Arizona. Even in Sonora it is very choosy of habitat, and it is pretty well limited to a few areas where, for some reason, it will thrive. But it is never plentiful at best and is usually thinly scattered. Tourists traveling Route 15 from Nogales to Hermosillo may see the *palo santo* by following these directions: When about 130 miles south of Nogales start looking for a high ridge of rocky terrain flanking a pass, on the righthand side of the road. The ridge can be seen for several miles, and there is a white cross on top of the cliff. The place is known as the *Divisidero de León* (Lion's Pass). A few scattered *palo santos* will be found on both sides of the road for perhaps a quarter of a mile before the pass is reached. The distance from Hermosillo is forty miles. From there on, fine specimens may be seen on both sides of the road, but never very many in any one area. About ten miles south of the *Divisidero* look for a shrine on the left side of the road. Nearly opposite it, on the right, is a fine specimen that may be examined without crawling through a fence. It is much photographed by tourists.

The *palo santo* is remarkable for its bark and blossoms. The bark is pale and smooth, a light gray with an almost iridescent quality as though the trunk had been covered with aluminum paint. Its blossoms are large and white, and some two inches across. They somewhat resemble a flattened morning glory bloom, hence the name used by English-speaking people. They flower at the ends of rather thick twigs. There may be a good-sized shower of blossoms on a tree, but the branches are never completely covered as in the case of the paloverde. During summer rains large dark green leaves appear rather sparingly on the branches. The tree is never heavily foliated, and the leaves do not remain long after the rains stop. During the season of heaviest tourist travel, from mid-November to March, the trees remain decorated with thin showers of blossoms without the interference of leaves. It is as though they are proud of their unique beauty and wish to show it to all who would behold. The *palo santo* is a medium-sized tree, reaching a height of about thirty-five feet on the average, though I have seen a few specimens near a wash a few miles outside Hermosillo that were considerably larger. The trunk sometimes attains a diameter of two feet or slightly more. A few *palo*

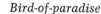

Bird-of-paradise

santos grow in small limited areas along the road from Hermosillo to Guaymas; then they occur spottily on down through Sonora, Sinaloa, Nyarit, and through the west coast area to Oaxaca. The *palo santo* is a beautiful and remarkable tree.

The tree tobacco is a plant that originally came from South America, but over many years it has spread so widely in the desert that it is commonly seen almost everywhere at elevations below 3,000 feet. It is now practically regarded as a native form. Of rapid growth, the plant makes an interesting little tree reaching a height of about twelve feet. 82

Catclaw, or "wait-a-minute" bush
(with blossoms)

The trunk and branches are slender and the form is usually rather un-symmetrical. Leaves are large and broad, lance-shaped, and have a slight bloom. The tree is evergreen except in severe frost periods, when the foliage withers and drops, but is soon replaced by another crop of leaves. The most desirable feature of the tree tobacco is its flowers. They are formed on the ends of twigs, and consist of trumpet-shaped blooms an inch to two inches long. New blossoms are greenish at first, maturing to yellow. It is an ambitious tree, blooming continuously throughout the year in areas having no frost. While the tree-tobacco flowers are pretty enough alone to justify planting around the home, probably its most important virtue is the attraction the blossoms have for humming-birds. The tuberose-like blooms manufacture quantities of nectar, and every hummingbird in the area will visit a tree from dawn to dusk. It is a veritable avian paradise.

Another alien species of tree has become so firmly established, and has such a widespread distribution, that it has come to be regarded as a native, even though its existence in this country covers only little over half a century. This is the tamarisk, known as the salt cedar. Because of its dense feathery foliage, it has been planted extensively for shade, and is valuable as a windbreak along the edges of fields. There are two species of tamarisk. The smaller, known as the smoke tree, reaches a height of about fifteen to twenty feet and spreads rapidly over bottom-lands, often becoming a pest. It requires moisture, a hot climate, and soil with some salt content. This species bears plumy flowers of a delicate smoky lavender in the spring. A stand of the smoke trees in bloom is a pleasing sight. The large tamarisk is similar in appearance, but when mature it makes an impressive tree with a great spread and a height of

Barberry, or "desert holly"

Creosote bush, or greasewood

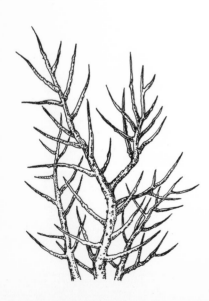

Crucifixion thorn

seventy-five feet or more. When planted for shade and ornamental purpose in towns and around homes, the big tamarisk requires severe pruning periodically. It may be cut back to what might seem a dangerous point, but it will soon send out new growth in profusion.

Still another exotic plant is spreading rapidly over areas of the desert near towns, ranches, and settled communities. The bird-of-paradise is a handsome shrub, sometimes growing to a height of ten feet, bearing showy flowers of red and yellow in masses on twig ends. It belongs to the pea family, and the seeds are produced in flat pods that twist open when ripe to expel their contents with some force. Leaves are compound. The seeds germinate readily, unlike those of the palo-verde, and plants soon appear quite far from the parent bush. An example of this may be seen at the Palo Alto Ranch on the Sasabe Road, fifteen miles south of Three Points. Shrubs in all stages of development line the highway for about a hundred yards, the result of natural sowing. The bird-of-paradise has long been established in Mexico, and is a favorite shrub in Sonora.

Closely related to the mesquite are the mimosas and acacias. They belong to the legumes, and produce pods. Several species of each are common throughout the desert, but a description of one will serve to give an idea of these attractive though often temper-trying shrubs. I have chosen the common catclaw, so called because of its sharp hooked thorns that liberally cover the branches and hook in toward the main stem. Why nature has so armed the catclaw, whether to defend the plant or as a means of scattering the ripened seeds, I have never been able to discover. No one will disagree with the general verdict that the catclaw is a plague on man and beast. Hikers and horsemen in particular have a special and justified hatred for the catclaw. They risk the danger of laceration every time they venture out. The shrub is also known as the "wait-a-minute-bush" because of its diabolical habit of literally seizing one who brushes against it and clinging like barnacles on a ship's hull. There is no use trying to bull through; the more you struggle, the deeper the thorns tear. The only remedy is to back up slowly and retreat, uttering the mildest ejaculations that seem to fit the case. If you discount the cussed nature of this shrub and look at it esthetically (this can be done by keeping out of its grasp), you will find that it has much to commend it. The leaves are compound, like those of the mesquite, though finer and more delicate. In the spring the catclaw bears many pale yellow blossoms that look a little like pussy willows. Flowers on other species of acacias and mimosas vary from this shape to little pom-poms; some are pink, others deep yellow, and several are sweet-scented.

The mesquite has often been called a wise tree, because of its habit 84

Burroweed

of not leafing until the danger of frost has passed in the spring, though even the mesquite sometimes gets fooled. But the acacias and mimosas are smarter still—or lazier. In the northern part of their range in the Sonoran desert they look like dead brush until late in May. Then, using only what water their long and intricate root systems can find, they slowly send out small leaves that take a long time to develop to maturity.

The hollygrape, sometimes called desert holly, belongs to the barberry family. It is a very attractive shrub from three to eight feet in height, and is often found in bottomlands and along washes. The foliage is dark glossy green and the serrated leaves are provided with sharp points. In the period from February to April, depending on locality, clusters of golden blossoms appear. They are very fragrant and their pleasant perfume fills the air, especially in the evening. Flowers develop into small purple berries in the early fall, and they are eagerly eaten by small mammals and birds. They make delicious jelly. A broken branch reveals wood as yellow as saffron. By steeping the wood, and particularly the roots, of the bush in water the Indians obtained a brilliant yellow dye.

If the orderly-minded reader objects to my placing a plant completely out of context with its family I must apologize. But I have never been able to think of the nightblooming cereus as anything but a shrub. In fact it closely resembles a dead stick standing on end under a greasewood. The queer plant that bears such a wonderful blossom, known as "queen of the night," is a cactus. It is never plentiful anywhere, and must be searched for. Rarer still is the happy event of timing the blooming period (it may be only one night in the year), so that the observer may see and enjoy the marvelous fragrance of this rare flower. The stems are long, fluted, and dark gray in color, and the blooming season occurs in June or July. Searching for the cereus and, having found it, waiting for the night it will bloom amount to an outdoor sport with many desert plant enthusiasts.

85

The commonest and most widely distributed shrub on the desert is the despised creosote bush. This is the "greasewood" of common parlance. There is a saying that creosote will grow where nothing else will, and certainly it is the characteristic vegetation of worn-out rangeland, with the possible exception of cholla.

The name comes from the strong odor of the resinous material given off by the plant. This is particularly noticeable after a rain. The Mexicans call the creosote bush *rama hedionda,* stinkweed. Those who have a kind word to say for the bush are few indeed, but nothing can be so bad as not to possess some small virtue. The creosote bush has foliage of a lovely bright olive-green color that it keeps throughout the year, and in the spring it bears pretty yellow blossoms.

The thin branches of the creosote bush are very brittle and sharp when broken. If you drive over even a small one, you will risk a punctured tire.

Many fascinating varieties of thornbushes accent the desert. The large spined crucifixion thorn is common and interesting. The blackthorn and a large and dense variety of shrub hackberry the Mexicans call *garambullo* are covered with glossy dark green leaves, and furnish cover for small birds and animals.

Two forms of shrublike weeds are found in profusion in areas barren of better vegetation. They are the burroweed and snakeweed. These, too, are symbols of run-down rangeland. Growing to a height of about two feet, they make a decorative pattern in sandy and rocky areas. According to ranchers, nature just about hit bottom in producing these pests, yet for me they have a reason for their existence. I find them very useful as accessories in painting desert foregrounds.

Petroglyphs, pecked into rock. This example is typical of many to be found throughout the desert. It is on a ranch in the Sasabe region. Note how a section of rock has split away from the main mass because of weathering.

SEVEN

GLEANINGS
FROM
THE PAST

The ancient people left treasures behind them

THE SHADOW of Baboquivari, the sacred mountain of the ancient people, moved slowly toward a sunny spot where an old man sat at the edge of the village above the river. As the shadow covered him, he arose stiffly and winced from rheumatic pain, but in his hand he held the object that had occupied him for many days. It was finished; he had pecked the last touches, and smoothed the ragged surfaces of this ceremonial stone vessel. In the morning he would present it to the shaman. The shaman was all-powerful, the maker of big medicine, and he had ordered the making of the bowl.

The old man paused for a moment to look toward cone-shaped Cerro Prieto, eternal sentinel of the sahuaro country, and southward toward a land that would someday be called Mexico. Then, as he shuffled slowly homeward, he gave his work a final critical inspection.

It was good. The stone was rough and dense, a warm creamy gray, lit by sparkling black rhyolite crystals. He had hunted far before picking up the rough piece that he knew was exactly right. The shaping of the bowl was merely tedious; any good artisan could have done it. But working out the intricate design called for something beyond a craftsman's skill; it was a task for an artist, and the old man was an artist.

The bowl was three inches across and two inches high. It was beautifully proportioned, but what lifted it above the commonplace was its wonderful design. With consummate skill he had carved, in three-eighths of an inch relief, a rattlesnake winding in regular curves around the outside. The snake was almost fifteen inches long. Its head started near the top of the bowl, and its tail ended almost at the bottom edge. Five notches at the end of the tail suggested rattles. He had wrought his masterpiece without the use of measurements, by eye and feeling alone. There were no rulers or calipers in the days of the great prehistoric irrigation experts, the Hohokam, who lived in the area for more than a thousand years before the coming of Europeans.

Twilight descended, and many small village fires poked glowing red holes into the curtain of dusk. The pungent fragrance of burning mesquite scented the air. The old man sat cross-legged before his fire and was given food—roasted jackrabbit and corn cakes made from meal ground in a stone metate. The hunters had been lucky; there were also some mule deer and peccary, a small piglike animal that roamed the desert then as now. He sat by the fire, and mused, satisfied with his work. A sickle moon hung low in the western sky, just over the sacred mountain, and the chill of the desert night crept down. Gradually, voices ceased and the village became quiet. The old man retired to his pit house, drew a rabbit-skin robe about him, and drifted off to sleep.

We found it pleasant at the site of the old village that October afternoon. The sun was still high enough to light Baboquivari, and my wife

Rare bowl of light-colored stone, with rhyolite crystals, carved with rattlesnake motif

88

Baboquivari, the sacred mountain of the ancient peoples
From a watercolor by the author

and I were sitting on a sandy spot, basking in the warmth. After some moments her voice roused me suddenly out of a dreamy mood.

"Well," she said, "are you going to sit there all day, or shall we go out and hunt some more? I'd like to find something myself."

"I still can't believe it," I replied, staring incredulously at the rattlesnake bowl in my hand. "Things like this just don't happen." For years I had wanted to find a bowl with a rattler carved around it. I had seen one or two illustrated in books on archaeology, but they are rare in the best collections. And now I had found one! "I just can't believe it," I said. "I'm afraid I'll wake up. Kick me."

She lunged out playfully, and the toe of her boot caught me squarely on my shin.

"Ouch!" I exclaimed. "I'm awake, all right. And I really do have the bowl, don't I? Let's go."

I had run into this treasure in a wholly unexpected manner. We had worked over the ground of this old village, which we had discovered several years before, without finding anything but a small arrow point and a turquoise inlay piece. We had almost concluded that it was worked out—at least until a gouging rain might uncover something else. Then my wife called me from a hundred yards away.

"Come over here," she said. "I just found a fine quartz crystal, and there's sure to be something else around when Ab gives me one of them." Ab is my wife's special spirit who accompanies her in her searches. When he is in a genial mood, he points out treasures, sometimes things partly concealed. But when the old boy has a mad on, as he frequently does, he lets her down scandalously.

I walked over, scanning the ground as I went. Three-fourths of the way across I suddenly stopped. There on the ground in front of me was a small ring of stone. I called Jo and she ran over. We stared a moment, afraid it would turn out to be a swindle of some sort. It looked too perfect. Then she started to poke at it with her metal-tipped gleaning stick. "Just a minute," I said, "you might scratch it." The soil was sandy and I ran a finger around the edge, loosening the earth. The bowl felt lumpy, and I remarked that it must be a crude thing, not carefully ground. But when it popped out and I brushed off the dirt, we nearly fell over. "Snake!" we both yelled at the same time, as though we had seen the real thing. But this was much more exciting. There was something weird about this find. It was as if old Ab himself had read my thoughts and guided me to the treasure.

The avocation to which my wife and I are devoted occupies much of our spare time. We call it "gleaning," since we search old village sites for whatever may be visible on the surface, or is just coming out. We do not dig or excavate. We are not "pot hunters," and are as opposed to the ruthless and indiscriminate looting of villages as are the archaeologists. We are strictly amateurs, and, so far as our collection is concerned, we wouldn't pay a nickel for the finest point—or sell anything we have found at any price. Furthermore, we know where everything we have came from, so our collection is not a hodgepodge of "Indian curios." We have catalogued every item, down to the tiniest bead, by marking it with a number that refers to a list of the villages from which the material came. In this way we feel that we are doing a good work by preserving not only the artifacts themselves but also by keeping a record of their source. It is obviously impossible for archaeologists to visit and excavate all sites, and each year more fine things are washed away than are ever recovered. Some artifacts have considerable monetary value— palettes, axes, drawknife scrapers, effigies, for example—and unfortunately there are many "professional" hunters who weasel their way through known sites and dig indiscriminately. The fact that this is against the law does not deter them. Items in the "take" are sold to curio shops, which in turn vend them, sometimes at outrageous prices. The buyers do not know where the artifacts came from, nor do they particu- 90 larly care. Much valuable information has been lost forever by this pernicious practice, and we hope it can be stopped.

As a youth I had assisted in excavating some mounds of the Hopewell Culture in Michigan, while working for a museum. Often when hunting or fishing I would pick up an arrowhead or ax in a plowed field. These things aroused my interest, but school, a world war, and many other factors interfered with this delightful occupation and I all but forgot about it.

When we first came to the border country of Arizona to spend winters, we were shown some arrowheads and other artifacts that had been found by local people. They showed us some gleaning grounds, and we became interested in looking for artifacts. It is not easy at first, but with practice the eye becomes accustomed to separating odd-shaped pieces of stone from the general rubble often present, and these often turn out to be points or scrapers. We gradually began to build up a collection.

Gleaning is a fascinating occupation. It is hard to describe the thrill of looking on the ground and, after a long search, at last seeing a perfect arrowhead, or better still a beautiful sky-blue turquoise pendant. The urge for artifact hunting grows on you like prospector's fever. You never know what will turn up next, or where you are going to find it. Sometimes the richest villages with the "hottest" evidence fall flat and yield nothing; and the dullest spots often give up treasures. Many of the village sites we hunt over are widely known and have been visited for many years. Some have been excavated scientifically by museums and other official groups, and then abandoned. But each rainstorm may bring out a few pieces, so such grounds are worth revisiting occasionally. In a village that had one time yielded over a hundred fine points and three shaft-smoothers, my wife turned up a magnificient light sand-colored stone gorget, milled with a design around the edge, and bored near each end with holes for suspension. It is about four inches long by two wide, elliptical in shape and beautifully made, with a smooth finish. We had visited this village for several years previously without finding anything, but decided to give it another try, "just for old times' sake." The ornament lay, unbroken, in a steep rocky gully that led to a bottomland. It would have rolled down in the next rain and been lost forever.

Other villages are more remote and have seldom been hunted. Among these, the best are the ones we discover ourselves, by the process of deduction. Finding a new village is almost as much fun as finding things in it—especially if you have surmised that there ought to be a village there, and then hit it right on the nose! Deducing where a village ought to be may sound silly, but actually it isn't at all. We have geological survey maps of a lot of the country, and by studying contours along

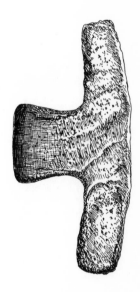

Slate drawknife scraper with polished blade

91

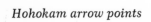

big washes, rivers, and tributary arroyos, we look for situations that are apt to have possibilities.

The Hohokam were largely agriculturists. Practically every village has metates—usually broken or worn out, though we have found a few fine whole ones—and the handstones known as manos, used for grinding corn. Metates are large rocks, sometimes well shaped, with hollows deepened by much grinding. There are usually shale hoes and potsherds, some of them decorated with interesting designs, and many chips of chalcedony, agate, obsidian, chert, and other materials that were struck off in the process of making arrowheads, knives, and scrapers. This "rubbish" is what we look for and is evidence of a village. The prime requisite in establishing a permanent site, not just a temporary camp, is a sizable piece of flat land, suitable for farming. Water was necessary then as now; but the fact that there are no living springs or streams at present does not necessarily rule out a site, for in Hohokam times the country was much wetter than it is now. A third factor is a good spot for the dwellings, usually one on an eminence commanding a view of the surrounding countryside, where the inhabitants could have warning of a surprise attack.

Sometimes we drive as far as we can go over poor ranch roads, then take out across the desert without benefit of any road at all, and hike four or five miles to the assumed village site. If we are in luck, we find the usual shards, grinding stones, and chips. If the village had a more elaborate culture, broken shell bracelets, a fragment of a stone ring, or perhaps ornaments of nacre may be found. And if we are very lucky, we may find an arrow shaft-smoother, a stone ax, or a bowl carved from granite or scoria. Arrowheads may be big utility points that were used for hunting or warfare, or they may be exquisite little ceremonial pieces, made of agate, opalite, obsidian or, rarely, clear rock crystal. Often we find beads and pendants of shell, turquoise, steatite, and green serpentine.

Sometimes we are given a tip by a rider on horseback, who has spotted a place that might have possibilities. One evening a cowboy friend, himself a gleaner, came over to visit. The conversation came around to our favorite subject, and he said: "Folks, I was ridin' range yesterday lookin' for some calves when I found a li'l'ol' piece of ground with pottery and chips. Didn't have time to look around much, but I did pick a nice hunting point. The evidence is scarce and I don't think there's much there, but you might like to give it a try." Acting on his advice, we took off the next day and found the spot. The evidence certainly was thin: a shard every fifty feet or so and only a few rough chips. It reminded me of a scraggly little village that a friend and I once visited. After a futile search of an hour, he said, "H-m-m, must have been very poor people lived here."

Hohokam arrow points

This time the prospects appeared to be no better. We came up with a broken point of red agate and a crude stone knife, nothing more, and were about to quit when I hopped over a little drain made by the rain. I thought I saw something sticking out of the side of a bank, as I jumped. Turning back I took a careful look, and the object proved to be a squared-off piece of stone, about an inch by an inch-and-a-half in size. It looked suspiciously as if an old Indian had been fiddling with it. I started scraping with my gleaning stick, and unearthed a curve of stone, then two more curves. Finally loosening the object, I flopped it out on the surface and emitted a most undignified but appropriate war whoop. It was a ceremonial dish 12½ inches long, 9 inches across at one end, and 4½ at the other. It was beautifully made, with projecting ears at both ends, and in perfect condition. One of the ears had been all that was visible, and that was what gave me the hint that there might be something there. No, we never sell short even the dimmest village.

On a later trip to this place, my wife saw an irregular, flat white granite stone, iron-stained and curved at the edges. It was not unlike dozens of rocks, but she flopped it over with her stick, just to be sure. I was nearby, and heard her squeal with delight. She had found a fine "free-form" stone dish, carved with loving care, ages ago. Of our collection of stone vessels and bowls, just one was found completely out on the surface; the rest showed only a hint of projecting stone. So our motto is: SUSPECT EVERYTHING.

Once my wife spotted a piece of rounded stone about two inches wide, and dug out a fine polished green diorite ax. In another village I saw a piece of carved stone no larger than a postage stamp, just like many other insignificant pieces, *except for the carving*. It turned out to be about the best shaft-smoother in our collection. The edges are milled with notches, and there is a ridged shoulder on one side. The maker had incised a big *X* on one face. His mark? We have another with this same *X* symbol. Part of the fun of this game is trying to guess what was in the minds of those ancient ones.

Pottery fascinates us greatly, and we have a considerable collection of decorated shards with interesting designs. Unless one excavates, the chances of finding a whole pot are rare, though we have had a little luck here and there. The first time we discovered our "Rattlesnake Bowl Village" we had had a fruitless day up to late afternoon. We had "rim-hopped" a lot of rough country, up and down steep arroyos, and were pretty tired. But a piece of benchland in the distance looked promising, and we decided to give it a try. My wife went to it directly and I made a scouting loop around. Coming to the head of a small drain, I saw the rim of a buried pot, then another and another. The edges were eroded, and I looked further, hoping to find a perfect one. Then I saw something

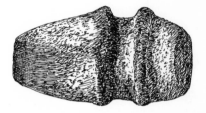

Granite ax

93

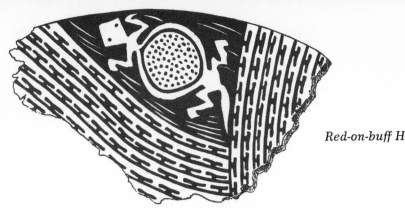

Red-on-buff Hohokam-type shard

sticking out of the side of the little gully—the blade of a small green granite ax. It was perfect, and as I lifted it out I called to my wife: "Come over, I've found some buried pots and an ax—" I glanced a few feet farther along and there lay another one, an old walloper with a deep groove and polished blade.

"For goodness' sake, *please* stop finding things," she pleaded, "and give me a chance." But this seemed to be my day. The drain contained a remarkable pot with several rows of raised lumps like peas below the rim. Plastered against the pot, where it had been carried by the force of a freshet, was a slate palette. My wife later found a magnificent T-end smoky obsidian arrow point and several others of fine quality. One of the plain pots was perfect. As usual it contained only cremated bones (this was the Hohokam burial custom). It was one of the best finds we had ever made, and we were very happy. But we couldn't know then that we had missed the best treasure of all.

A regular gully-gouger of a rainstorm came up before we could go back to the village again. When the roads dried out, we packed a lunch and were off. At the village we found several fine points, a couple of turquoise beads, and two shell pendants, one of which was carved with a puzzling design. But when we got to the burial area where we had found the former treasures, we got a shock. On the side of the drain we saw a wonderful decorated pot—or rather pots—badly broken and partly washed away. Apparently they had just worked out and a cow had stepped on them. We worked to salvage what we could, digging out the the main pot and picking up all the available shards for later reconstruction. We got a great deal of the main pot, but of the very ornate shallow cover pot only about a third remained. It had a beautiful linear design, and incorporated, besides, four strange reptile motifs that were probably

Casas Grandes polychrome-type shard

meant to be conventionalized horned toads. (See illustration.) We were glad to save this much, but regretted not having found it whole the first time.

Another pot fragment, found in a different village, has as a motif a stylized bird, upside down, in buff, black, and reddish color. This is Casas Grandes polychrome ware, and was undoubtedly traded from a far distant village, as much barter went on between tribes.

Spindle whorl　　　　*Green serpentine ear spool*　　　　*Arrow-shaft smoother*

When we first began, arrowheads were the chief object of our search. But we soon built up a good collection of them, and now a point has to be superb before we gloat over it. Beads, pendants, effigies, stone disks, and spindle whorls in stone and clay, shaft-smoothers—these are now the most wanted objects of our quests.

We once ran into an exceedingly elaborate culture in a village, and found many fine tubular beads of sea-green stone, besides several spindle whorl-like ornaments, which turned out to be ear spools, of the same material. When we were in New York on a trip, we took the beads and ornaments to Dr. Gordon F. Eckholm of the American Museum of Natural History, the eminent authority on Southwest and Meso-American archaeology, for an opinion. They looked like jade, and we hoped they were.

"Hm-m-m," said the doctor, "they look like jade, all right; mind if I scratch one?" He drew a needle across the stone, and a chalky white line appeared. "No," he said, "unfortunately not jade—too soft—but still pretty fine. They're probably high-grade serpentine, and hardness is the principal difference."

We keep on trying. The hunt is the thing. There's that white sandstone pestle we found; the carved red stone miniature shaft-smoother with suspension hole that looks Aztecan; a shell pelican and a lizard, unfortunately broken; a shell bird effigy that resembles an owl; several finely carved nacre ornaments; serpentine effigies of eagles and a crow. There are nose plugs, shell needle ornaments, chipped and ground effigy pieces—cruciform and "reel-shaped" objects. Among the larger ob-

jects in our collection we treasure several drawknife scrapers, made of shale, with beautifully ground and polished blades. They were probably used for fleshing hides. I should not neglect to mention two phallic pieces so embarrassingly realistic that modesty forbids our displaying them in the case where many of our artifacts are shown to visitors.

What next? That's what keeps us going, with growing eagerness. It's always the night before Christmas. In Never-Never Land, a turquoise monkey that my wife has been begging for may be waiting; or another fine shaft-smoother; or clay figurines and stone effigies. Who knows?

From the foregoing account of some of our adventures, it might be assumed by the casual visitor that the Arizona part of the Sonoran desert, where we do our gleaning, is strewn with treasures waiting to be picked up. This is not true, nor was it ever exactly the case. Gleaning entails a lot of what might be termed hard work, were it not so much fun. It also involves some knowledge concerning sites, and how to recognize old ones, or find new localities.

Every year gleaning becomes more difficult, and the results are increasingly meager. Some days, in fact several days in a row, may pass without our finding more than broken pieces; we return home without a single item of "case material"—a piece worth putting into the collection. But we keep on looking over old, worn-out villages, and once in a while we are rewarded with something really fabulous. Actually, what we are looking for is a chance to get away from things, take some exercise "on the hoof," and study wildlife as a sideline.

Another interesting angle to roaming the countryside in search of villages, and surface artifacts they might contain, is the ever-present possibility of discovering rocks, or cliffs in remote areas formerly unknown to us, having petroglyphs. We know the location of many such sites and have photographs of the strange figures found there; but since something different in the way of motifs may turn up we are always on the lookout.

A petroglyph is a design, pecked into rock, so that the lines are incised, leaving shallow hollows that expose the lighter colored stone underneath and show the work. It is sometimes confused with the pictograph. The latter is a painted design, usually done in earth colors, and the ones that are preserved are those that necessarily are protected from the weather—in caves or the faces of rock in deep, overhanging cliffs. In most of the desert area petroglyphs predominate. They may occur almost anywhere, but usually are found in the vicinity of ancient villages. Designs are varied, sometimes being spirals, concentric rings like targets, swirls, loops, and other abstract forms. In other cases, conventionalized animals and human figures appear.

96

Hohokam ornaments:
shell, slate, and serpentine

Though much study has gone into the subject, the exact meaning or interpretations of these cabalistic symbols has not yet been exactly determined. Nor is the identity of the people who made them accurately known. Often great areas of a rock wall are covered, as is the case at "Picture Rocks," a few miles north of Tucson in the foothills of the Tucson Mountains. Again, an isolated stone, no larger than a bushel basket, having pecked work, will be found in a remote place on the cattle range.

Several fine examples are to be seen at the Elkhorn Ranch, a few miles off the Sasabe Road. They comprise quite realistic representations of deer and antelope. One of the largest and finest is a huge rock on the Zepeda Ranch (San Carlos) in Sonora, about thirty-five miles south of Sasabe. A few typical designs are illustrated here. They were drawn from rocks in the northern part of the Sonoran desert, but petroglyphs occur throughout the entire area, and in Mexico as a whole.

There are two reasons for the present scarcity of artifacts. One of these is the increasing popularity of hunting for them, as a diversion, or even owning them by purchase from a dealer. The other, and perhaps principal, factor is the weather. For many years there have been cycles of drought, lasting for several periods of what should have been rainy seasons. The land dries up to powder, grass fails to grow, and the shallower-rooted vegetation browns off. Then a spell of violent rains strikes, gullying the parched earth and washing countless acres of topsoil off into washes and rivers, to be lost forever. With it go many fine artifacts.

Burials of the ancient people were made at a certain depth, and as successive rains of wet seasons washed away the earth and lowered the surface, pots and artifacts gradually came into sight. This is what we call the "grave level," and below that lies nothing. We were fortunate in arriving in the Southwest at a time when this process was, we think, at its height in most of the villages we searched; so we were able to make a very good collection. Not all burials were at the same level. They varied considerably, perhaps, in different villages. And the soil also differed in density and porosity, so that there are doubtless many buried treasures in the way of artifacts still to come out for many years.

We advise visitors to look on the ground when hiking over the desert. If potsherds are found, it probably means that there was a village, or at least a camp, there at one time. The chances are good that the site has already been looked over by many people, but no one can get everything. If you find arrowheads or other artifacts, please mark them and keep a record. In that way they will have meaning.

Those who wish to pursue the subject further will find some informative books on the Hohokam, and other early people, listed in the bibliography.

Cruciform ground pitchstone

Reel-shape: chipped obsidian

Pendant: red mudstone

Hohokam ornaments

EIGHT

THE DESERT IN BLOOM

When conditions are right,
a glorious spectacle

THE DESERT IN BLOOM! Among the many evocative expressions commonly heard, this one has come to be a byword. It summons forth visions of beauty, color, romance, and escape from the ordinary chores of a routine life to the dream world of a kindly nature who puts on special shows, now and then, for mortals, wearied by care, to refresh their souls. If this be a poetic thought, surely there can be no harm in it—even though scientifically it may not be strictly true. Only cynics will argue against it, and they are miserable people, anyhow.

There is not a month during the entire desert year when plants of some variety do not bloom. Even in the coldest months of December and January many winter species, such as the various asters, lend color to the countryside in the northern part of the Sonoran desert; and farther south in Mexico, below the frost belt, the numbers of species that bloom are practically unlimited.

While most desert plants—trees, shrubs, cacti—bear blossoms at some time, the big show is produced in the spring, roughly from early March to late May, depending on latitude and locality. The term "the desert in bloom" is generally used to denote this period, and the performers in this great spectacle are mostly the low flowering plants, many of them verbena, penstemon, poppies, primrose, and lupine. Given the right conditions, whole hillsides and stretches of desert floor may

99

Martynia, or devil's-claw. A very interesting, though economically useless, plant. The upper part shows leaves, fuzzy stems, flower, and pods. Below are the "devil's-claws" produced from the ripened pods.

be thickly patterned with carpets of brilliant blue, yellow, orange and red, sometimes gayly mixed in a crazy, haphazard design. Try to put it down on canvas and it would look like the devil; but nature does it without offending.

Many people have come to the desert with the hope of seeing this magnificent sight and have gone away without having their wish fulfilled. While a few plants will bloom every year in localities where the earth has stored water near the surface, really big displays come only when all the factors are right. These consist of temperature and water. When winter rains come early, in November and December, and then practically cease, there will be no big flower show in the spring. Late frosts may also kill off blooming plants, and in the northern part of the desert frosts severe enough to kill young mesquite leaves have occurred into early May. The condition is unusual, but it can happen.

During the winter of 1959-1960 several good rains filled the ground with water so that it held ample moisture through February. In mid-March we made a trip to Punto Peñasco near the upper end of the Gulf of California. From Sonoyta, on the border, to Punto Peñasco, a distance of some sixty miles, the display of flowers was simply incredible. Besides verbena, poppies, and the commoner forms, there were many plants of the fascinating ajo lily in full bloom. In the following spring, 1960-1961, we made the same trip, at the same time, and found only a few patches of blooming plants in widely separated areas. The difference was water; no important rains had fallen since December.

One might assume that if a spring passes without flowers there will be none the following year, even if conditions are propitious. This is not true, because the seeds of annual plants have the fortunate ability to lie dormant until the exact conditions for their germination and development occur. It may take two or more years, but the seeds will be right on the job when the time comes. Old-timers in the desert can predict pretty well what the flower possibilities will be by keeping track of the winter rains. They are seldom wrong, and it will pay anyone contemplating a trip to see the desert in bloom to get in touch with an observing old resident.

One of the handsomest and most interesting of desert plants yielding blossoms beautiful in both form and color is the penstemon. It varies from a few inches in height to about three feet, and blooms from April through late May. The penstemon usually grows in small colonies, or may be found as scattered plants at almost all but the highest elevations. It is common along many roads both in Arizona and Sonora, and there are usually fine colonies to be found flanking Route 15 on the way south to Hermosillo. It is generally at its best there in late April. Clusters of trumpet-shaped rose-colored flowers form along the top of the tall 100

Penstemon

stem, and several stems or stalks usually grow together. The Mexicans in northern Sonora and near the border call the plant *San José*.

Among the plants contributing to the spring flower display on the desert, the lupine holds a high place. The wild form may grow to a height of two feet, but generally plants are much shorter, averaging perhaps a little more than a foot. The lupine is popular in gardens, in the cultivated form. It varies somewhat in color, according to locality, but in general is a purplish blue. Some individual plants are lavender or even rather pinkish. The lupine belongs to the pea family, and the seeds are formed in small pods that break open on ripening and are scattered by weather and birds, thus spreading over large areas. It is not uncommon to see an acre or more thickly covered with this beautiful and desirable plant.

The verbena is another plant that often grows in large beds, and in association with plants having flowers of contrasting colors, forms interesting patterns of blue. It is a low, clumpy plant, about a foot or slightly more in height. The flowers are formed in clusters and are about half an inch across. They are a mixture of pinkish lilac and a little white. The effect at a distance is blue, and the flowers are usually thus classified. The verbena is widely distributed. While the principal blooming season is in the spring, this little plant seems to disregard protocol, and blooms whenever it feels like it. We have seen plants in full flower in the fall and even early winter, and again in February. It is a common roadside plant. The stems are described as being hairy. Actually, they are covered with myriads of little spicules that sting like fire in contact with the skin. It is a good idea to wear stout gloves when handling the verbena.

The covena, sometimes called desert hyacinth or wild onion, is not a spectacular plant because it does not mass in large beds. But it is a dainty and lovely little addition to the flora of the arid lands, and is much appreciated by flower lovers. It is of wide distribution in regions below 5,000 feet. Near settled communities, however, it is becoming scarcer yearly because of its unfortunate habit of producing an edible bulb. This is a little onion-like tuber that has a pleasant flavor. Children are particularly fond of the bulbs, and eagerly dig them up and eat them as nibbles, thereby destroying the plants. In our hikes in early spring, usually in late February, we look for small dark green, very narrow leaves crawling out of the ground like worms and lying flat on the sandy earth. They look like wide blades of grass. A month later the blade-like leaves have assumed an upright position and the plant has sent up a central stem that bears a small cluster of lovely light- to deep-blue bell-like flowers. There are from seven to eight blooms on a stalk, and the plant reaches a height of about a foot.

Covena

One of the earliest plants to bloom in the desert is the dainty and modestly pretty fairyduster. It is a perennial sprawling shrub growing close to the ground, and it is seldom over two feet in height. The branches are woody, dark brown, and the leaves are delicately fernlike. Blossoms are formed in tufts, like plumes, two inches or less wide, and are white and light red, giving them the appearance of a ruby. The fairyduster is sometimes called false mesquite. It produces small beans and is much eaten by cattle. It grows along washes and arroyos as well as on level ground, and is valuable as an erosion-control agent. A stand of fairyduster in bloom affords a charming sight, especially when it covers the ground under ocotillos, which bloom at the same time in early spring.

Among the purplish-blue flowers asters have an important place in the decoration of the desert. They are of many varieties, and while commonly thought of as fall-blooming plants, some species flower in the spring and throughout the summer. They grow in sandy and sometimes rocky soil along roads and in wastelands. The small lavender aster with a bright yellow center has the ability to resist cold to a remarkable degree. When we lived in Sasabe, numbers of this species bloomed in the late fall and persisted throughout most of the winter, in spite of temperatures that often went into the low twenties.

The chief performer in the spring desert show is undoubtedly the poppy. To see these brilliant yellow-orange flowers massed so closely together as to form a veritable carpet of gold (the description most commonly heard) is to experience one of life's brighter moments. Often areas of desert floor embracing countless acres will be so covered with poppies as to dazzle the eye. And when, as often happens, the solid pattern is broken with patches of verbena, lupine, and other flowering plants, one can really say, "I have seen the desert in bloom!"

The true wild desert poppy is of the genus *Eschscholtzia*, closely related to the common California poppy which is often planted in gardens in almost all parts of the country. The plants have delicate, deeply cut-in leaves, somewhat like a geranium leaf, and yellow to orange blossoms. The flowers have four petals, and average perhaps two inches in width. Poppies grow from three inches to a foot in height, depending on soil condition and moisture. The plants have many stems, forming a compact mass of blooms. Though the huge displays of blooming poppies (and other plants) occur only in years having late winter rains, the plant is an eager bloomer and will take advantage of any spot that affords even a little moisture. It may not bloom to its maximum size, but bloom it will. I have often seen poppies, in dry periods, with blossoms no larger in diameter than a dime, growing from stems barely two inches long.

The desert poppy is very widely distributed throughout southern

Fairy duster

Arizona and Mexico, and it blooms, according to latitude and elevation, from February through May. It does not restrict itself to flatlands, but delights in climbing the slopes of foothills and even the sides of the lower mountains.

Though this is one of the few true poppies growing in the desert, another very beautiful and abundant plant that resembles it is the caltrop, popularly named Arizona poppy. It is, strangely enough, related to the creosote bush. The leaves are compound, somewhat like those of the mesquite and acacias. The flowers have five petals instead of four, an important difference in distinguishing the two forms. They vary in hue from bright yellow to almost orange. The growth habit is sprawling, and the plants do not grow in masses, but singly. In the Sonoran desert confusion is eliminated without close examination of the plant by the growing season. The caltrop is a summer bloomer, appearing generally in mid-July and lasting throughout August and September.

Plants growing close together form large masses of handsome color that cover great areas. Arizona poppies may be seen commonly in wet seasons along almost any road, and in open lands not used for pasturage. They are restricted to elevations below 5,000 feet. At a time when the spring display of flowers has passed, the caltrop is a welcome and colorful addition to the countryside.

When driving through the desert at almost any season of the year the motorist is apt to see tall prickly plants bearing large, handsome white flowers with yellow centers. This is the thistle poppy, one of the commonest perennial plants in the desert. While the prickly stems and deeply notched, spine-covered leaves are very similar to those of the thistle, the plant is a true poppy. It grows to a height of about thirty inches and is seen in single clumps or in colonies of several dozens, forming scattered groups. The fruit is a spiny burr; in fact everything about this rather formidable item of desert flora is prickly but the blossom. Though the thistle poppy is a handsome addition to the countryside, its usefulness ends there. Among ranchers and agriculturists it is considered a pesky weed. Cattle will not eat it, and it creeps into corn and cotton fields and stays there with the persistency of a gadfly. Once established, eradication becomes a real problem. A plant near the foundation of a house we lived in kept coming up from roots in spite of hoeing and even of burning the surrounding dry grass. Its inherent toughness enables it to grow and thrive under all weather conditions.

Arizona poppy, or caltrop

Thistle poppy

It ignores cold, drought, and other adverse factors. Even grasshoppers shun it. This compelling urge to overrun the land causes the plant to bloom in the coldest midwinter weather, at times, although the normal blooming season is in the spring.

Sometime in late February or early March carpets of pretty yellow flowers suddenly make their appearance. They are evening primroses, delicate and decorative little plants that grow close to the ground and bear blossoms from an inch to an inch and a half in diameter. There are four petals, and the color may be either yellow or white. The blossoms open late in the afternoon, but fade soon after sunrise on the following day. Each plant produces many buds, one or more of which are ready to bloom every day, replacing the exhausted blossoms. The primrose thus has a flowering season that extends over a period of several weeks. While there are several species of primroses, some of them attaining a height of five feet, the commonest are the low ground-hugging cover plants. At times they contribute greatly to the grand spring flower show.

In seasons when the desert pulls out all the stops and builds the floral spectacle up to a grand crescendo, the mariposa lily plays an important role. Then it may be found in large beds, adding its brilliant orange hue to the contrasting blues, yellows, and purples of neighboring flowering plants. This does not, of course, always happen, but in any season a few mariposas may be seen. It may grow to two feet, in warmer parts of the desert, but farther north the plant usually attains a height of less than a foot. Stems usually twist and curl somewhat. The name "mariposa" means "butterfly" in Spanish, and individual flowers remind one of these gaily colored insects. The three petals are creamy yellow to peach color on the outside and brilliant orange to vermilion inside, with purple streaks.

A rare member of the lily family is one of the handsomest of all desert plants, though unfortunately it is severely restricted in distribution. The ajo lily is found only in a small area of southwestern Arizona and northern Sonora. It does not grow at altitudes greater than 2,000 feet. Mention has previously been made of the fickleness of this wonderful plant. Copious rains at exactly the right season, late winter, are needed to make it appear. One may find a few specimens in any year, but it may take a lot of looking. "Ajo" means "garlic" in Spanish, and the bulbs of the plant are edible and have a garlic-like flavor. The plant is a perennial, growing to about two feet, with a slender stem and narrow leaves. The blossom consists of several, generally three or four, lovely white lilies in a clump, each flower having six petals and being two to three inches wide. They are extremely fragrant, and a bed of ajo lilies will fill the air with delightful perfume. The town of Ajo in southwestern Arizona was named for this plant, also a range of mountains and a valley in the vicinity. The best place to see the ajo lily is in this area, and from there south from Lukeville into Sonora. The right time extends for about a month after mid-March, and it is a sight well worth the effort. Let's hope you have luck!

Mariposa lily

Ajo lily

Locoweed

THE DESERT IN BLOOM

Visitors to the desert in late winter and early spring will find quantities of graceful little plants with compound blossoms, purplish blue, sometimes mixed with white, almost anywhere. The leaves are fernlike, medium green, and slightly curled. It is an innocent-looking little plant that uses beauty to cloak its real nature, for this is the dangerous locoweed. "Loco" in Spanish means "crazy"; it is a word so commonly used that it has long been adopted into the English language. Cattle and horses eating this plant literally become crazy, and often die. There are many species of locoweed throughout the Southwest, and seventy or more are recorded from Arizona alone. They vary somewhat in size and shape, and not all species are poisonous; these are dangerous only when eaten, and the plant may be picked and added to bouquets safely.

A plant that dips its brush in brightest yellow to paint its flowers is the much-appreciated brittlebush. It blooms from late fall throughout most of the winter, at a time when the majority of plants are resting. The brittlebush is of the genus *Encelia,* a member of the vast and far-flung sunflower family. Here it might be noted that if you wish to get involved in the intricacies of trying to classify desert plants—and since the subject is so fascinating this is almost inevitable—the sunflower family is a perfectly splendid place to begin. While there are many small closely related species, some annuals, others perennials, the true brittlebush (*Encelia farinosa*) is perhaps the most spectacular. It grows in thick clumps, is a perennial, and reaches a height of from two to three feet. Masses of small tapering leaves cover the woody stems. They are gray-green and present a silvery appearance that affords a contrast to the deeper green of most other plants. The blossoms appear on long stems at the top of the bushes, forming a crown of golden color very pleasing to the eye. The brittlebush grows at lower elevations, from 3,000 feet down, and thrives best at perhaps half that height. It likes sandy soil and apparently gets along with very little moisture. It is abundant in such locations throughout southern Arizona and much of northern Sonora. In wasteland areas where grasses and forage plants do not grow well, great masses of brittlebush light up the landscape, during the height of the blooming season, with a golden glow.

Sometimes in a hike over the desert, or along almost any road, you will come upon a curious horny pod, four or five inches long, tapered at both ends and terminating in a tonguelike affair and two long brownish-black wickedly sharp curved hooks. This is the devil's-claw, one of the most interesting of the arid-land plants. If you are in the desert in summer, from May on, you will see gourdlike leaves on vines growing in clumps in many localities. In a short time a few delicately beautiful flowers, somewhat resembling little orchids, will appear. They will be hidden by the dense foliage, and must be looked for. In color they are reddish purple or sometimes white, with orange and yellow streaks. These flowers mature and produce pods that look like little pointed summer squashes in shape. They are velvety in texture, sticky to the touch, and light green in color. The pods grow from a stalk and droop downward. There may be as many as eight or ten on a stalk. In the early fall when the pods ripen the outer skin cracks and peels off, revealing a number of black seeds tucked into the inner shell with its two claws. These spread apart, drop to the earth, and are ready to hook themselves into the feet of animals or human pedestrians and be carried off.

The devil's-claw is of the genus *Martynia*, technically, and besides being unique and interesting the dried claws have several uses. The Papago Indians strip the shiny blackish bark from the claws and use it to weave into their fine baskets, to create dark-color patterns. A whimsical use of the claws is their employment in the making of grotesque little animals and birds. The curved claws may represent the horns of hoofed creatures, or the tusks of elephants. By the addition of twig legs, bits of driftwood, and other natural materials some weird and laughable creations result.

Throughout the late spring and summer months a handsome large plant sprawls over the earth in a vinelike growth. It is the datura, or giant jimsonweed. It grows very commonly over a large range, at elevations of from 1,000 to 6,500 feet. In lower Sonora the plant starts blooming much earlier than in the north, and is often seen by late-winter visitors. The jimson is poisonous in all its parts, but only if eaten. Blossoms are large, three inches across, and very spectacular. In color they are predominately white with a lavender tint. They open in the late afternoon and close when the sun strikes them in the morning. An individual plant may reach a height of two feet or more, and sometimes spreads over a large area of ground. The fruit is roughly spherical and dries into a hard shell, thickly coated with sharp spines. Leaves are large, gray-green, and spearhead shaped, with slight indentations along the edges.

A beautiful little plant bearing violet blossoms that are produced on a curling stem is of the genus *Phacelia,* sometimes called wild heliotrope.

Encelia, or brittlebush

Spiny fruit

Datura, or giant jimson

It grows in large colonies and is another contributor, in certain areas, to the spring flower show. The edges of the leaves have rounded serrations, similar to some species of oak, and the stems are generously covered with prickles, reminding one of the verbena. It is wise to use gloves when handling the plant. The ordinary blooming season of the phacelia is February to June, so it may be enjoyed by late winter and spring visitors.

In the hot months of summer, when tourists come to the desert less frequently, there are many beautiful and often spectacular species of plants in bloom. Those who contemplate a summer trip, or who are thinking of settling in the desert, will want to familiarize themselves with two very interesting and lovely species.

One of these is the trailing four-o'clock or three-flower. It is a plant with slender stems that trail over the ground to a length of thirty inches or more, covering a considerable area. The vinelike stems are rather sticky, with small prickles, and they send out shorter branches that bear both leaves and blossoms. Leaves are elongated, slightly pointed, and shallowly indented along the edges. The blossoms are a wonderful rosy pink to violet color, about an inch in diameter, and divided into three flowers; these in turn are cut by two notches so that they give the appearance of being subdivided into three more petals. The flowers open in the evening and stay in bloom until the sun heats up the earth in the morning. This very attractive plant prefers sandy soil, and is common on benchlands and along washes.

Another summer blooming plant with showy flowers is the wild potato or purple nightshade. It grows to a height of about two feet and bears a good number of blossoms, pale bluish-purple in color with yellow centers, and an inch or so in diameter. Leaves are long, lanceolate, and slightly indented, or wavy, along the edges. The fruit that develops in the fall is a small berry. The unripened fruits and the leaves contain an alkaloid that is poisonous.

Among the most spectacular and beautiful flowering plants of the desert are the cassias or desert sennas. They are of several species, varying somewhat as to flowers and seedpods. One commonly seen along roads is the slim-pod senna. It is one of the finest and showiest plants on the whole list. The large flower heads, made up of many small blossoms, 108 are deep yellow and bronze and resemble a little the cultivated stock in growth habit. Leaves of this species are compound and dark glossy green. The ripened pods, as the name suggests, are very narrow and long, and contain innumerable small seeds. This is one of the most desirable of plants for the home garden, and is frequently cultivated.

The study of plants is a fascinating occupation when regarded as an avocation. It can also be a baffling and mind-muddling task if one takes it too seriously. A field guide, of which there are several good ones on the market, is a necessity; but works that are too technical and go into great detail about the number of anthers, stamens, sepals, and petals, complicated with Latin names and scientific terms, can definitely mix up the reader and dampen the fun.

Trailing four-o'clock, or three-flower

Reference has been made to the confusion in common names by calling a thing something in one section and another thing somewhere else, or by two different names in the same place. But it is not so staggering as to have to start out cold with, say, a blue flowering plant that has rather prickly leaves, rounded—or are they *exactly* rounded?—a branching stem; or is it vinelike?—and so on. You see the plant and try to fix its characteristics, then start looking under "blue flowers." You find one with the right flowers, but the leaves are wrong. The next blue-flowered plant goes along fine almost to the end; then you find that the stem is thorny and it should be smooth. The trouble is that there are just too damn many plants with blue flowers; or yellow or orange or red. Your head begins to spin. Don't give up. In the first place avoid botanical textbooks. They are fine for their purpose, but not for the ordinary person without special training who has had the pleasure of discovering a fine plant and merely wants to know what to call it. The simple well-illustrated field guide will provide most of the answers by the shortest and most painless route. And asking questions of local people who have spent much time in the desert will usually fill in the blanks.

Remember that most flowering plants in the Southwest have a Spanish name, besides from one to three common English names.

In camp at Kino Bay. Venus casts a path of silvery light across the calm waters of the Gulf. Tiburón Island is in the distance

NINE

LIFE IN THE OPEN

The star-studded sky is your ceiling

TO ABORIGINAL MAN camping was a way of life—there was no other; to us, who have climbed so high on the ladder of evolution and are literally saturated with the products of civilized man's ingenuity (some of which we might be better off without), it is still a way of life—but in a far different sense. We look upon camping as a sport. Actually, it goes a little deeper than that. Those of us who are so fortunate as not to have had the love of nature "civilized" out of us, who still retain a sense of wonder and reverence for the works of the Creator, feel a compulsion to make periodic trips into the open, to live there a few days, even weeks or for several months. This desire for solitude is a direct heritage, handed down to us from the dim past, and we can count it a blessing. It is the real reason we go camping.

Now, as everyone who has spent some time in the open, without benefit of motels and hot showers, knows, the word "camping" is a very loose term. It can mean comparative luxury or it can descend, at times, to the depths of abject misery. Everything depends on several factors; the type of rig used, the spots chosen for the camp, the knowledge the camper has of life in the open, and his ability to meet circumstances and to take care of himself. I am no advocate of the rugged life. It makes precious little sense to go out and torture oneself, when it is possible to live outdoors, without elaborate equipment, in a sensible manner.

One has only to look at a catalog nowadays to see how far we have come, in a score of years, in the way of rigs and camping equipment in general. Trailers have developed to a point where they now have show-ers, refrigerators, butane gas, *and* electricity. Some huge overcab coaches, mounted on trucks, are similarly equipped. Built-in beds are luxurious. There is panel-ray heat for chilly nights, a cooler on the top for hot weather. Does one want a dish of hashed brown potatoes for breakfast? Start the electricity, plug in the electric frying pan. Much simpler than cooking over a mesquite fire or old-fashioned gasoline camp stove.

Equipment like this can be purchased for as little as $4,000, though one may have to go to $7,000 or more, depending on how much one can't do without. Now I have no gripe about this sort of thing. If it pleases people who have the means and they want to do it that way, that's strictly their business. But I question their accuracy in the use of the word "camping." To me, camping is a much simpler and more fun-damental thing. The whole object is to get away from the accustomed luxuries and conveniences of life, not to take them along. This does not mean that one has to sleep in a pup tent on the bare ground and cook in a tomato can. There is a nice point of balance between luxury and dis-comfort, and it can be reached economically and sensibly through a little forethought.

Experienced campers who have rigs of various types, and have   112 trekked much through the more temperate parts of the land, do not need advice concerning equipment or general camping technique. But the camper, veteran or beginner, should know that camping in the desert region involves a number of factors that differ from living in the open in other types of country.

Practicable and modestly priced camping rigs include tents that can be erected quickly and easily. The umbrella type is a favorite. A tent can be folded into a comparatively small package, and is the best possible solution to the problem of shelter when the camper must travel with the minimum of equipment. It takes little room in the trunk of even a small car. But, in a land where there are scorpions and other crawly things, it must have a sewed-in ground cloth and screened windows for protection against flying insects. Most of the desert areas are blessedly free of mosquitoes, but there are still gnats and miserable little flies known as *jejenes* (hay-heń-ace) in Spanish. They are the equivalent of the no-see-ums of the North, and fully as bad.

A rig used by an increasingly large number of people, and the one preferred by us, is a station wagon with seats that fold down to make a sleeping platform. We use air mattresses and sleeping bags, if the weather is cold; otherwise sheets and a thin blanket. For trips of a few days we find this to be an ideal arrangement. Stove, iceboxes, folding chairs and table and other things are put out on the ground; the bed is made, and you are in business. For longer trips a small tent in addition is a great convenience. One with an extension flap will protect the camper in case of rain or wind, and still permit him to cook and be out of the weather.

With such an arrangement you are up off the ground and out of reach of prowling things. The same holds true, of course, in the case of a tent with sewed-in ground cloth. If the tent interior is thoroughly sprayed with insecticide before retiring, it is safe enough to sleep on the ground on an air mattress, but folding cots are a little better and don't take up much room in the car.

Every camper knows the necessity of taking along plenty of bug bombs and fly dope, no matter where he stays. Insects of some sort are everywhere. Once, in the heart of the Maine wilderness, in the Rangely district, we were plagued with, of all things, common houseflies. But the precaution is doubly necessary in the desert because of the incidence of scorpions and creatures not found in a colder climate. There are special

sprays known as scorpicides which, if used regularly, will control all insects, spiders, and other crawlies, besides scorpions, and remove this worry from the camper's mind.

Iceboxes are, of course, a necessity. They should be large enough to hold a fifty-pound cake of crystal ice. We carry two; one filled to capacity with just ice, the other holding twenty-five pounds, which

leaves room for food that must be kept refrigerated. Under normal conditions, in winter camping, ice will last for close to five days. Most of our camping is done in Sonora, so we must carry water for drinking and cooking. Five-gallon army-type water cans are ideal for this. We always take along a galvanized pail or two to catch the water that is drained from the melted ice, and this we use for washing.

The method employed in camp cooking is a subject that is argued wherever there are campers. Purists contend that nothing but a wood fire and grate should ever be used. Some will concede the use of charcoal, but only where wood is scarce or of poor quality. We always carry a grate, but use the open wood fire mostly for broiling steaks. Bending low over an improvised fireplace on the ground doesn't exactly contribute to the comfort of an aging back, and is an occupation better left to younger folks. There is no greater comfort in camp than a sturdy and reliable two-burner gasoline camp stove. Set up on a folding aluminum table, at handy working height, it leaves the cook free to work in comfort.

In some localities a stove of some kind for cooking is a necessity, owing to the scarcity of good wood. This is particularly true of places along the Gulf of California, where in traditional camping areas people have cleaned out practically all the good firewood. There is a vast difference in the burning quality of the various woods, as all outdoor people know. In the Southwest, mesquite is rated right up at the top. It is very hard and burns slowly, with streaks of bluish flame here and there. It   114 makes wonderful embers for broiling that last for hours. It also has a pleasant fragrance when burning. In mountainous areas oak is the favorite firewood and has much the same virtues as mesquite. Although juniper, which grows at high altitudes also, is a softer wood, it burns steadily and the smoke is extremely fragrant. Ironwood, or *palofierro*, is excellent provided you can find dead branches; but don't try to chop large dried chunks. As mentioned in a previous chapter, this is almost the hardest and toughest wood found anywhere in the temperate zone.

Of all the trees growing in the desert, paloverde affords about the worst firewood. It burns poorly and gives off volumes of acrid smoke that fills the air with a most unpleasant odor. Stench would be a better word, for the stuff actually stinks. Years ago when our friends the Strangs came to Arizona they visited a camp of Yaqui Indians. Mrs. Strang said the place stank, and she thought the Yaquis must be a filthy lot. Some time later Mrs. Strang made a fire, using dead branches of a paloverde tree. Then she knew.

Besides the ever-necessary axe, another indispensable item is the shovel, preferably a long-handled one. In addition to its ordinary uses around camp—digging a pit for a cooking fire and burying rubbish (which every good camper does)—it may prove a friend in need. When traveling dirt roads off the main highway, where many of the most interesting spots are located, there is always a chance of getting stuck in a sand pocket or hollow filled with loose silt. These areas are innocent-looking enough, but they can give you trouble if you drop into one. This is particularly true in hot weather. Heated sand has a tendency to cramp tires and make traveling difficult. With a shovel to remove loose sand, one can get out of most any situation, though it may take a little time and some effort.

Another use for the shovel lies in leveling off slight humps on the ground where the tent is pitched; and of course, if there is danger of rain, in digging a trench around the tent to carry off surface water. When sleeping in a station wagon it is important to see that the vehicle is as level as possible. Nothing is more annoying than to sleep on a sidewise tilt, with the head higher than the feet, or vice versa. Some of the choicest camping spots, with respect to view and other conveniences, seem to have the perverse habit of being on slopes. One of these on high

land overlooking a charming cove at Kino Bay was located on a sloping hill that would normally give the car a steep slant. We overcame this by digging the earth on the upper side sufficiently to drop the wheels below the slope, thus leveling the car.

Aside from a mechanical breakdown, which shouldn't happen if the car is in good condition and thoroughly checked before starting out, one of the worst things that can happen is to run out of gas or oil, far from the nearest supply. Here again camping in the desert differs from most parts of the country. Distances are great, and a factor not taken into consideration by some motorists is that driving rough back-country roads—some of them, while passable, are little more than trails—eats up gas and oil at an appalling rate. Carry extra supplies. Often some stretches must be traveled at a rate of ten miles an hour or less, and it entails the constant shifting of gears. If a car averages eighteen miles to the gallon on a paved road, this rate may be cut by a third to, in some extreme cases, a half, depending on how rough the terrain is. From this the wisdom of carrying an extra supply of gasoline, in a can specially made for the purpose, is obvious. This advice will not be needed by the majority of campers, who will stick pretty close to traveled routes having campsites with supplies of almost everything needed within handy reach. But there will come a time when some remote place will offer an irresistible lure. The desert has a habit of bewitching people. That mountain range that looks so tempting may appear to be twenty miles away, but actually it may be closer to sixty, with some pretty tough wheeling in between. The motorist who says, "Oh, we have enough gas, let's go," may be in for a peck of trouble. The desert demands foresightedness in many things. If the rules are followed it can be as kind to travelers as any other land.

Where to camp is a problem in any part of the country where modern nomads trek along the gasoline trail. Many spots that appear to be ideal, on the surface, are unsuitable for a variety of reasons. Sites like this will be found along all main highways. A few yards off the road is a clump of mesquite trees—level ground—no fence—no sign reading KEEP OUT. Wonderful! Why not camp? Well, because it is probably the most dangerous spot one could choose. The newspapers contain many items each year that give readers the cold chills. Campers are robbed, their property and cars stolen; they are beaten, even murdered. In spite of regular police patrols this desperate condition not only exists but is increasing at an alarming rate. Emphatically, it is not safe to camp along any highway in an unsupervised and unguarded camp site.

In Arizona, finding such sites is a simple problem. There are many state and national parks and monuments, conveniently spaced, and equipped with running water, toilets, fireplaces, and other conveniences. 116

Campers are usually permitted a stay of two weeks, and they may leave their tents and equipment during the day with the knowledge that things will be safe. At night they may sleep peacefully, because all these campsites are efficiently guarded.

But suppose the visitor wishes to get into remoter country, away from organized campsites. It can be done by a very simple procedure. The great majority of land in southern Arizona is devoted to stock raising. Ranch spreads are vast, often covering many sections (square miles). In almost every case the major part of a ranch holding consists of land leased from the state or federal government. The balance is owned outright and is known as deeded, or patent, land. Leases to ranchers cover only grazing rights for cattle and do not prohibit access to the public for hunting, fishing, camping, and recreational purposes, as well as prospecting for minerals. While it is a liberal law, it carries certain responsibilities on the part of both rancher and the public. It does not mean that one can go anywhere indiscriminately and set up camp. The rancher has a big investment in expensive stock, and unfortunately cattle thieves still roam the range as in the old days. He wants to know who is on the land and what their purpose is. The West in general is noted for its hospitality, and southern Arizona is no exception. The camper who has his eye on a nice spot has only to go to the ranch house, introduce himself, and visit a while. A short chat will almost invariably result in granting permission to camp. When the owner or manager of the ranch knows that the campers are good people, not goons, he will do much to help them and to make their stay a pleasant one. He will acquaint his cowboys and range riders with the fact of their presence, and while the campers may never see them, except at a distance, they will be as safely protected as though they were in a park campsite.

Down below the border, in Sonora, public camping sites are not numerous, but the owners of spreads ranging in size from a small jacal to a huge hacienda are invariably courteous and extremely hospitable. Often they will present you with tortillas, fruits, and other little gifts. They will refuse money, but little *regalos* of candy or cookies are welcomed by the children. A slight knowledge of Spanish is helpful, but lack of it is not necessarily a barrier. The Mexicans are very intuitive, and travelers who are friendly and courteous find themselves welcomed with a minimum of words.

TEN

GAME-BIRD GUNNING

It's different, and it can be exciting

Gambel quail
From a watercolor by the author. Reproduced by courtesy of the
owner, Mr. P. Huber Hanes, Jr.

"HOW'S THE BIRD-SHOOTING out your way?" is a question I am frequently asked by sportsmen friends who live in the East.

It is something that can't be answered in a few words, and I generally reply that it is good, but different; how different can be understood only by one who, like myself, was brought up on gunning in the brushy coverts, fields, marshes, and reedy shores of lakes in the East and Midwest, and then exposed to desert shooting.

From the time I was a lad in my teens, in Michigan, to the age of more than fifty, days off in autumn were devoted to the pursuit of the ruffed grouse, woodcock, pheasant, bobwhite quail, jacksnipe, and wildfowl. My book of memories is filled with adventures in pursuit of these grand game birds through many golden autumn days in the Midwest, before World War I, and, after discharge from the Navy in 1919, again in New York and New England. Birch and alder thickets where the long-billed woodcock climbed skyward on whistling wings; the roar of a crafty old grouse beating on fast pinions in headlong flight to the safety of dense cover; the nerve-shaking clatter of a flushing covey of bobwhites, fanning across a field of goldenrod and joe-pye weed; the staunch old setter, locked in a classic point; flaming maples and birches, bittersweet vines clad with gay berries—these are the pictures that come back vividly over the path of the departed years. To sportsmen in the North, South, East, or Midwest this is the mirror that reflects the image of field sport; it is the essence of traditional upland gunning.

Now take a gunner who has known nothing different (myself, for example), drop him off in the desert with a shotgun and shells, and just enough explanation of the game laws so he won't get in trouble, and it isn't difficult to see that he'll be a pretty confused fellow until he gets the hang of it.

In the desert, instead of a warm gunning coat (and sometimes a sweater on a cold morning) most of the time he will be hunting in shirtsleeves. If he has a tender shoulder and hard-kicking gun he had better wear a light skeleton vest, with shoulder pad. In place of alder and second-growth hardwood thickets, he will do his brush gunning in groves of mesquite, paloverde, or ironwood. He may be clawed and scratched by *garambullo* and wait-a-minute-bush, but this will be one of the few things to remind him of his home covers—for is there anything more torturing than bulling through a jungle of catbrier or wild blackberry brush?

He may miss the hardhack-covered open fields, punctuated with patches of goldenrod and povertyweed, but they will be replaced by vast areas of burroweed and brittlebush where game birds hide. If he is devoted to the pursuit of the ruffed grouse, in its native wooded cover, he

119

will be less than pleased, for the desert offers no substitute for this unique game bird.

But if the spirit of adventure and the joy of discovery are in him he will find many things that will surprise and even delight him. Should he yearn for the color of autumn foliage, he may often find enough along washes and dry riverbeds to satisfy his esthetic sense, and convey at least a little of the flavor of the traditional gunning to which he is accustomed. There will be brilliant cadmium-yellow leaves on the alamos (cottonwoods), pink-bronze foliage of the ash, in places even wild grape and sumac. But the biggest surprise to the first-time desert gunner will be the object of his quest—the game birds themselves. Having to forego old friends he will make new acquaintances, some of which may surprise him in more ways than one.

Much of American sporting literature is devoted to gunning for bobwhite quail. In all parts of the Deep South and West, through much of Texas, in the Midwest and north to southern New York and even parts of southern New England, the bobwhite is the favorite game bird of upland gunners. There he is hunted with fine gun dogs, pointers and setters, who find the coveys, point, and hold them for the first shot—the thrilling covey flush. Then singles are followed and pointed by the dog whose sensitive nose locates them even in thick brush. This is sport of a high order, followed by countless sportsmen who cherish upland gunning in the grand tradition. When the term "quail" is mentioned it means, to the vast majority of sportsmen, only one thing—bobwhite.

Quail shooting in this sense is a refined, almost sophisticated occupation, entailing certain codes of ethics (one must never follow singles of a flushed covey too long and shoot it down too low), well-trained and expensive gun dogs are needed, and, in the South, good saddle horses are imperative because of distances covered.

Now in contrast to all this, desert quail shooting presents a picture so directly the opposite in all its aspects as to be positively shocking to most of the devotees of orthodox quail shooting. To begin with, quail of the arid lands are nonconformists. They are gay, rowdy little fellows with a mind of their own. Their most exasperating habit is running;

Gambel quail

Gambel in flight

they will run all day long and think nothing of it, flushing only when cornered and there is no other way out than taking to wing. This is Strike Number One against them, from the standpoint of the gunner who expects to have his birds lie before his pointing dog and afford a good honest wing shot when they flush. Desert quail, except perhaps under very exceptional circumstances, simply will not lie to a dog. They will run—and run—*and* run. So the use of a pointing dog is out, and to most upland gunners that removes a great deal of the fun. There is a compromise that is employed by some desert quail hunters who like the companionship of a dog. A good retriever, Labrador, springer, or cocker perhaps, who will stay strictly at heel until given the command to fetch, is a valuable asset. He will find birds that have fallen into a thorny mess of brush, and best of all, retrieve ducks that have been shot over a *represa* or *tanque*.

The quail of the Sonoran desert commonly hunted are Gambel, scaled (blue or cottontop), and Mearns. In the southern part of the desert, near the Sinaloa line, there is also the elegant quail, but it is never plentiful enough to rate along with the other species as a game bird.

The commonest of the desert quail is the Gambel (named after the noted naturalist). It ranges from the northern limits and extends east and west to the southern border of our desert, in most of the region of moderate to low elevation. It is strictly a desert dweller and never goes very high into mountainous country. This is rated by most bird devotees as the handsomest of the quail. The bird is leggier than the bobwhite, and the tail is considerably longer. It averages slightly heavier in weight. Color of the neck, cape, and back of the cockbird is a handsome slaty gray with a bluish tint. The breast is cream, with a black band somewhat in the shape of a horseshoe. The crown is chestnut, and face and throat are black with separating white lines. Side coverts are deep mahogany, broken by a pattern of white stripes. The hen is slightly duller in general cast, with the hint of a brownish wash over the slate-

Scaled quail (blue quail or "cottontop")
From a watercolor by the author. Reproduced by
courtesy of the owner, Mr. P. Huber Hanes, Jr.

Mearns quail (harlequin or fool quail)
From a watercolor by the author, reproduced by courtesy
of the owner, Mr. P. Huber Hanes, Jr.

gray plumage. She has no dark breast marking and her head is not distinctively marked. The distinguishing feature of the Gambel is the curved black plume that projects from the crown of the head, in front, and bobs up and down in front of the bill. The plume of the hen is slightly smaller than that of the cock. An interesting fact sometimes not observed is that the plume is capable of being moved by muscular action of the bird's scalp. While it is generally carried in the form of a forward loop when the quail is running, or at ease, it is usually straightened out and extended well over the back when the bird is feeding, drinking, or sometimes just when it is alert or on guard.

The scaled quail is more restricted in range, occurring chiefly in the eastern part of the Sonoran desert, over to the Baboquivari Mountains, and somewhat down into northern Sonora. It is the important quail of western Texas and New Mexico, and this area of the desert might be said to be a western extension of its range. In recent years it has become more plentiful. In appearance, it differs greatly from the Gambel. The general color cast is bluish-gray, but the body is covered with an intricate pattern of blackish curved lines that give the effect of scales. It is somewhat shorter and chunkier than the Gambel, but slightly larger in overall dimensions than the bobwhite. The unique bobbing plume of the Gambel is replaced, in this species, by a tuft of whitish feathers that can be raised as a crest, and from this it derives the popular name of "cottontop." In parts of the range a variation in color in the form of a dark reddish brown patch on the underpart of the bird occurs. This is a subspecies, the chestnut-bellied scaled quail.

The third form of quail is a comical character popularly known as the "fool" quail or harlequin. He resembles a circus clown and is badly mixed up in color and design, but handsome in spite of it. This is the Mearns quail, again named for the naturalist who first discovered the species. This little character is dumpy and chunky, with a surprisingly large body for its limited overall dimensions. In striking contrast to the long-tailed Gambel, the Mearns has a tiny tail less than an inch long! The back of the male is a soft cinnamon brown, with darker brown and tan patterned markings. The belly is a rich mahogany with black edging at the lower part, and the sides are grayish-black, liberally sprinkled with white dots. The most striking part of this odd bird's assembly is the head. It is almost grotesquely large, with a tan-brown crest that extends from the bill to the back of the head and droops down like a shawl around the short and chunky neck. The side of the head is patterned with black lines and patches that give him a comical look. His feet are disproportionately large—and very capable for use in running over the rocky terrain he inhabits. The Mearns quail is found only in the foot-hills, in open country near oak and manzanita brush, at an elevation of

123

White-winged dove

about 4,000 to 5,000 feet. The bird is nowhere plentiful, and though there is usually a short open season in Arizona it is not much hunted, nor is it considered top game.

Unlike the bobwhite, which travels in small coveys, desert quail are gregarious and often band up in huge gangs. It is not unusual to run across as many as thirty to sixty or more in one aggregation. The Gambel is a noisy and raucous bird, gabbling and cackling most of the time. When it sounds off with a scatter call it is almost as vehement as a domestic rooster, and the sound can be heard for half a mile or more. This trait, foolish on the part of the bird, is an invaluable aid to the hunter (who, goodness knows, needs all the help he can get) in locating coveys.

If what has been written sounds like a condemnation of desert quail hunting, let me hasten to say that nothing of the sort was intended. Some of the finest days I have spent on the desert have been devoted to the pursuit of this galloping little waif. What I wanted to emphasize is the difference between ordinary, or regulation, upland gunning, and desert sport.

It is entirely possible to hunt quail alone, but two or three gunners in a party, acting as a unit, will be much more successful. Our system —and when dealing with this smart little bird a system is needed, especially since the gunner does not have the valuable assistance of a pointing dog—is to work along in a line through likely country, keeping eyes and ears alert. When a covey is located ahead, the two end men advance to cover the flanks, and we all move in at a steady pace. If the ground cover is fairly thick, we can probably get close enough for a shot. The last act consists of rushing in at a signal and "busting" the covey to get them in the air. One or more of us usually get a chance for a single or double.

Following singles, after the covey has scattered, is a far different thing from hunting up single bobwhites. You mark a bird down, a hun-

124

dred or two yards off, by a burroweed or little mesquite where it has pitched in. Now, if it were a bobwhite, which is courteous and gentlemanly, you might reasonably expect to find it somewhere near there. But not the Gambel. No, sir! It didn't like the sound of the gun. It flew only because it had to, and its fast little legs started pounding the ground the instant it lit. It doesn't trust to protective coloration or any fine theory that might be written about it. If the gunner expects to have even a ghost of a chance to flush a single that has pitched in, he must take off the instant the quail hits the ground and run as though the devil were after him. If he is lucky he *may* get a shot, but chances are he will be puffing so hard that he won't be able to hold the gun right. From this it will be readily seen that desert quail shooting is an athletic occupation, best suited to vigorous souls in good physical shape who are devoted to the strenuous life.

Now, there is a milder form of the sport, and one that is better suited to more phlegmatic and older people. This involves cruising around on back roads slowly and looking for birds. When a covey is located—quail pay little attention to a car—it is often possible to slip out of the off-side door and get a shot or two.

This brings us to the question of ethics. The purist will assert that it is never permissible, under any circumstances, to shoot a bird running on the ground; it must first be flushed and in the air for a wing shot. A very pretty theory, but has the purist ever hunted desert quail? Probably not, or he would be a purist no longer. I think of my good friend Ernest Miller who was one of the finest wing shots I ever knew, and also a thoroughly ethical sportsman in every respect.

"Damn the cussed things," Ernie used to say; "when they start running instead of flushing the way a decent game bird should, why, sluice 'em on the ground with the right barrel and then you'll have a chance for a wing shot with the left."

Desert quail are delicious as food when properly cooked, as good as bobwhite, I think, but they must be treated right in the kitchen. My wife browns them quickly in a pan with a little butter, then lets them

Mourning dove

simmer slowly with a cover on the pan until they are tender and cooked through. We have found that roasting, unless carefully controlled, has a tendency to dry out the flesh.

Another upland bird that is vastly popular with gunners in the desert, and is extremely plentiful, is the dove. The term is used collectively, for there are several species of doves. Two of them furnish sport to the gunner—the mourning dove and the whitewing. The mourning dove is one of the commonest birds of North America, being found from coast to coast, up into Canada, and far south in Mexico. The desert form is a subspecies, known as the western mourning dove, but the difference between it and the eastern form is so slight as not to be noticeable.

The white-winged dove is a handsome bird, slightly larger than the mourning dove. It has more of a blue-gray cast to the plumage, and the tail is slightly semicircular, when the bird is in flight, like that of a domestic pigeon. A white band, or speculum, on each wing distinguishes this bird from the mourning dove, in flight, aside from the shape of the tail, which in the mourning dove is long and pointed and edged on each side with small white patterned feathers.

While mourning doves are never very plentiful in most sections of the North, and in the middle and eastern sections of the United States, they abound in the South and simply teem in the West, and in the desert during the spring and fall migrations. There is also a large resident population. The apparent scarcity of this bird in northern regions, owing to its habits, sometimes leads well-meaning but uninformed people to agitate for its protection and to have it removed from the game-bird list. That this would be nothing short of a calamity, any southern or southwestern agriculturist will attest. Doves descend on wheat and rice fields, and many other crops to their liking, in clouds of many thousands and make short work of the farmers' labors. For this reason alone, dove

Cinnamon teal

seasons in the West are long and bag limits generous. In Arizona there are usually two seasons, one in September and the other later in the autumn. Since laws often change from year to year it is necessary to check when obtaining a license to shoot.

Anyone who has shot doves will affirm that here is the trickiest form of wing shooting, with the possible exception of jacksnipe. The dove has a twisting erratic flight that makes it a most difficult target. Just as the gunner pulls ahead of a swiftly flying bird, presto! it isn't there. He corrects his swing, and the perverse creature has changed its course again. Finally he pulls in desperation and sends the shot charge three feet off the target. Dove shooting can be a thrilling game or a cause of black despair; it also enriches the ammunition makers.

When doves are coming in over a *represa* or pond in the evening, they fly fairly steadily and the sport is then similar to pass shooting for ducks. Any average shot can kill doves under those circumstances, and that is how most of the desert dove shooting is done.

Whitewing shooting lasts only a few days after the season opens in September, as this species migrates very early; but there are always mourning doves throughout both seasons.

Duck shooting in the Arizona part of the Sonoran desert is very limited, as might be expected, because of the scarcity of lakes, marshes, and other typical wildfowl areas. Most of it is done on *represas* and small tanks. To be very successful, two or more gunners are needed to cover a small body of water. Since the banks of these artificial ponds are high, the gunners can deploy and take positions opposite each other, meanwhile keeping out of sight of the birds that may be on the water. A sneak-peek will tell whether they are there or not. If ducks are in, the gunners rise at a signal and yell. The flushed birds must go somewhere, and someone will probably get a shot or two; then it's all over for that spot and you'll have to drive to another water hole, hoping that someone hasn't beaten you to it. Though I have shot some fine ducks over *represas*, it has never appealed to me greatly as a sport to get excited about.

The duck list in the desert would correspond pretty closely to that of most other parts of the country, since wildfowl are migratory, with a couple of exceptions and additions. The wood duck and the black duck are the exceptions; they do not occur in the desert. And the additions are the handsome little cinnamon teal (in addition to blue-wing and green-wing) and the black-bellied tree duck.

Wildfowlers know, of course, that ducks and geese are protected by federal law in the United States, and the number and species that may be taken in any one day are strictly limited. A Federal duck stamp is also required, in addition to the state hunting license.

127

If duck shooting, as the wildfowl *aficionado* knows it, is a rather poverty-stricken sport in most of the Arizona region of the Sonoran desert, the exact opposite is true of parts of Sonora. Great areas of this important Mexican state are given over to agriculture, and among the principal crops are wheat, corn, rye, barley, and rice. Any and all of these items, at harvest time, which usually corresponds to migration season for wildfowl, are to a duck what lobster Newburg is to a gourmet. The result is easy to see. Hordes of wildfowl overrun the grain fields like flies on a picnic pie. They stuff and cram until they can scarcely fly. Shotguns are expensive in Mexico, and ammunition is high. Even if there were many gunners they could not make a dent in the duck population. This would seem to be a perfect setup for the visiting sportsman, and it is—but there is always a fly in the ointment. This is it: While the sportsman may take his pet gun across the Mexican border for hunting purposes, the necessary procedure is so complicated that it would stagger all but the most enthusiastic devotee. It is also exceedingly expensive. There is no point to going into it here. Those interested may obtain full information by applying to any Mexican consulate. Most of them will be discouraged by the prospects. All of the above is in addition to the fee that must be paid for the privilege of shooting—simply stated, a hunting license. But there is a way out, and most sportsmen who wish to shoot in Mexico take it. In all the good areas where ducks, doves, and other feathered game are found there are "sporting clubs" whose business is to rent guns and ammunition. For a nominal fee, the visitor can "join" and be issued a gun and ammunition. In addition, he must buy a hunting license, the fee for which, for a short period, is not exorbitant.

For information on laws and complete procedure (which may change from year to year) the interested tourist should write to:

Prof. José Dávila Cárdenas
Sección de la Conservación de la Fauna Selvática
Dirección General Forestal y de Caza
Aquiles Serdan 28, Mexico, D.F.

If you have digested all the above and still want to go to Duck Heaven (having lived a good life, of course), all you have to do is get your pen and some paper and sit down and write.

According to current information that I obtained from a customs officer at the Port of Nogales, the legal limit of ducks for Mexico may be imported to the United States, provided they are plucked and cleaned and the carrier has in his possession a valid Mexican hunting license. Since laws change frequently, this point had better be checked on both sides of the border.

One of the most typical of arid-land birds, the roadrunner, or chaparral cock, is a veritable symbol of the desert. He never takes to the air unless forced to, and then only for a short escape flight. Though clumsy in looks, his reactions are incredibly fast.

BIRDS—BIRDS—BIRDS!

A land of never-ending surprises.
No bird watcher has seen all
until he has visited the desert

SINCE BIRDS of some form are found everywhere, they are a part of our daily lives. The reactions of people to birdlife vary greatly, as they do to everything else. Some are genuinely fond of birds and enjoy them, but evince no desire to learn about them. Others profess no interest whatever and frankly say so, but I have never yet seen anyone who didn't get a chuckle out of a robin tugging at a big worm on a dewy lawn, or a tiny wren struggling to place a twig in a nest. The third class consists of the genuine enthusiasts, persons who not only love birds but who are also eager to learn all they can about species, habits, range, and the many other fascinating facets of their lives. There are the "bird watchers," about whom we hear much these days and shall hear more. In recent years their growth has rivaled that of mushrooms. Observing birds and making notes is one of the finest and worthiest of avocations. All the equipment needed is a notebook, field glasses, and an observant and eager mind.

Bird enthusiasts who have filled many notebooks with records of the feathered inhabitants and migrants of various parts of the country, but have never visited the desert, are in for a real treat when they first come to this totally different, arid land. Here, adaptation plays an important role in the lives of birds, as it does with plants and mammals. Many species of resident birds are able to get along with practically no water for long periods of time, deriving what moisture they need from succulent insects and green vegetation. Certain types of birds common to nonarid parts of the country are represented in the desert by most interesting and sometimes strange forms, many of which seem to have no relationship to the familiar forms.

The study of ornithology, even in a popular and sketchy way, is, as every enthusiast knows, a huge and never-ending occupation. In a

Cactus wren

work of this kind it is impossible to do more than touch on some of the strange and often exotic forms of birdlife to be found in the desert, with the thought of giving the visiting bird *aficionado* enough of a taste to whet his appetite. A list of most of the birds common to the various life zones of the Sonoran desert will be found at the end of this chapter. There will be some old friends, in slightly different form, but also many new acquaintances to be made.

One of these is a chattering, talkative, positively raucous bird, pert and inquisitive, often hopping up on window ledges and peering into the house. In size it might be described as slightly larger than a bluebird. The color is basically brown with a whitish chest that is liberally covered with spots. There is a white stripe over the eye and there are white spots along the outer tail feathers. To most newcomers the identity of this bird is a puzzle. When told that it is a wren they are incredulous, as I was at first. Wrens are supposed to be tiny mites of things, but this one disregarded the rules, and grew up. He is the cactus wren, one of the most ubiquitous and at the same time comical characters of desert birdland. The nest is constructed of twigs and is usually placed in the thickest and meanest mess of spines to be found in a cholla. There it is safe from most marauders, and that is probably the reason why the cactus wren is so successful in increasing his tribe.

Everyone knows the cuckoos, yellow-billed and black-billed. They are among the commonest birds of much of the country. People who have never been west but who have read a great deal are familiar, through word and picture, with the roadrunner, or chaparral cock. This ludicrous, long-tailed, frowsy-headed bird (often more than twenty inches in total length) would surely seem to belong to a group far removed from the cuckoos; yet, to the surprise of most people, it is a cuckoo. Its song is a series of soft coos, not unlike the note of a dove, diminuendo in pitch, and having a soothing and gentle effect on the listener. It is deceptive of the bird's true character; one might be led to believe that here is a mild and sweet-natured creature. Quite the contrary, the roadrunner is a belligerent, cocky individual, and a holy terror to many forms of wildlife. While it feeds largely on lizards— imagine how fast it must be able to move in order to catch one—it will tackle almost anything, including fairly large snakes. It has been said to kill and eat small rattlers. Were it not for its unfortunate habit of fancying nestling birds it would be given a 100 percent clean bill of health; but bird lovers who have watched a nest of young develop, only to be cleaned out at one swoop by a roadrunner, have no love for the creature. This is a restless, roving, and somewhat noisy bird, making a metallic, rolling sort of clacking sound by vibrating its mandibles rapidly. It paces the desert ceaselessly, and will not take to wing unless absolutely forced to do so. It generally shows little fear of man and will often allow a close approach. The plumage is a metallic green above, showing bluish tints in certain lights, and "scaled" with cream-colored triangular markings. Its tail is solid green, with a bronzy cast, and edged with cream. The breast is tan to almost white, with dark brown penciled streaks. Its crest is large and exceedingly unkempt, as though the bird were in need of a haircut. The roadrunner is everywhere a subject of heated controversy; to some he is pure devil and should be eliminated without mercy, while others overlook all his faults, and staunchly defend him. But even his maligners agree that the desert would not be the same without the familiar figure of this long, rangy bird trotting across almost any road one drives.

The cardinal, with which most people are familiar, occurs freely in most parts of the desert, and needs no description. There are several color variations in the species, but the male is predominantly brilliant scarlet, with a small black patch under the bill. The female is more somber (the bird family affords one of the few instances in which the men get a break in the wearing of gay and bright apparel), being principally of an olive-brownish cast, with a little red. The subspecies known as the Arizona cardinal inhabits the entire Sonoran desert, and is said to be the most intense in color of the cardinals.

A close relative of the cardinal that is found only in a limited range of the Southwest is a handsome bird called the pyrrhuloxia. It, too, is crested with a jaunty topknot. The predominant color is gray and red—rose-colored or ruby on the breast and crest, with a medium-gray back. The female resembles somewhat the lady cardinal, but the difference is easily noted. In the pyrrhuloxia the color is gray, not olive, and

Pyrrhuloxia

Phainopepla

the breast is yellowish. There is a bit of red on the wings and crest. The bill is large and almost parrot-like, and an important difference is the color; yellow in the pyrrhuloxia, dark reddish in the cardinal. This bird is one of the best singers in the desert, and during nesting time and well into the summer his loud crisp whistle can be heard at a considerable distance. He has a variety of calls, and at least one of them sounds almost exactly like a human whistle. A young lady visiting a guest ranch once told me that the first time she heard this whistled call of the pyrrhuloxia she thought it was some fellow trying to get fresh!

A bird that is unique in that none other resembles it, and one that never fails to intrigue bird watchers, is the phainopepla. It is trim and dapper with a markedly upstanding and ample crest, and is about the size of an oriole. Dressed in glossy black plumage it has an elegance that borders on dignity. This illusion is somewhat dispelled by the white wing patches, when one looks at the bird in profile, and especially when it is in flight. It then becomes a misplaced study in black-and-white in an otherwise colorful world. The female is dark gray, and lacks the white wing patches. Unlike the cardinal and pyrrhuloxia, the song of the phainopepla is rather weak and vacillating, an uncertain warble with no

133

particular theme or apparent enthusiasm. While nowhere very common in comparison with many other species, several of these birds may usually be seen along roads in the course of a day's drive through the country.

Admirers of the romantic mockingbird will have plenty of opportunity to meet their famous songster in the desert. From early spring throughout the nesting season the air is filled with the melodious notes

Curve-billed thrasher

of this versatile little musician. Like most of the thrasher family, to which the mockingbird belongs, this bird possesses a truly remarkable repertoire of themes and variations. Sometimes its mood is loud and raucous, at others soft, dulcet, and evocative.

A very common bird found only in the Southwest is the curve-billed, or Palmer's, thrasher. It is about the size of a robin, but with a long tail and markedly hooked bill, curving downward. In color the back is brownish gray and the belly is tinged with lighter brown. The eye is light orange with a staring black pupil which gives the bird a wild look. It is entirely justified, for this thrasher is an exceedingly active character, moving across the ground with flashing speed and stopping just as suddenly. It is aggressive, and will often make passes at other birds at a feeding station or watering place. Like the pyrrhuloxia, the Palmer thrasher has a sharp crisp whistle which is very penetrating, something like *wheet, wheet!* If unaccustomed to the sound, one would be almost sure that it was a man calling a dog. The song of this bird   134 is similar to that of the mockingbird, but perhaps not so varied or versatile.

Attempting to identify sparrows accurately, as every bird student knows, is practically equivalent to looking for a green bead in a lawn— at least for the amateur. In the desert alone, distinguishing two of the white-crowned sparrows—Gambel's and Nuttall's—is not an easy or always successful task. But one little member of this vast family is so distinctive that it will never be mistaken, once it is learned. This is the desert sparrow, smaller than average for this group of birds. It is gray on the back and whitish underneath. It has pretty white face stripes and an angular jet-black throat patch that sets it off from all other sparrows. If sparrows in general give you trouble, start in by learning this one. You can't miss!

Several members of the goatsucker family occur in the desert. Nighthawks, flying across an evening sky and making a booming sound as they dive, are a familiar sight to most people. The species known as the Texas nighthawk is the common bird of the desert region. It is slightly smaller and browner than other nighthawks, and the white bar on the wing, noticeable in flight, is near to the tip of the wing.

A very interesting member of this family is Nuttall's poorwill. It is nocturnal and is never seen during the day except when flushed from its hiding place in a clump of brush or pile of rocks. Then it flutters away like a great bat, uncertain of its flight. It is often encountered along back roads at night, where it likes to crouch on the warm gravel, and will flush in the glare of the headlights, affording a rather startling sight. This peculiar habit is the basis for the Spanish name, *tapa camino* (road cover), which the Mexicans give it. The call note is distinctive and very melodious when heard across a stretch of lonely and silent desert land. It is quite similar to the call of the familiar whippoorwill, with the omission of the first note. A friend once said to me. "There's a funny bird out here that I can't figure out. It must be a whippoorwill— sounds just like it—but it has never really learned to call. Leaves off the 'whip.' " The poorwill has a strange practice of partial hibernation during cold spells. It may hide for several days without coming out to feed. Once

Desert sparrow

while we were looking over an old Indian ground we came upon a poor-will hidden in a rock pile, with just its tail sticking out. It was so protectively colored that it matched the rock and was difficult to see. When touched it seemed dead, and made no attempt to fly off and escape.

Many birds belonging to the flycatcher family inhabit the desert, or are migrant through it, stopping for periods during the spring and fall flights. Among them are the wood pewee, phoebe, Mexican crested and buff-breasted flycatchers. Members of this group are so numerous that the inexperienced—and sometimes even the veteran—bird observer may have difficulty in distinguishing the species. But there is one, the male of which at least, can never be mistaken.

The vermilion flycatcher is unique. This handsome little bird is very active, as are all the flycatchers, and is an aerial feeder, going through all sorts of comical antics, twisting and turning, to catch an insect on the wing. The male is a brilliant vermilion of a flaming hue except for the back and head, which are a warm black. It is slightly crested. When seen against a clump of green cactus, or the foliage of a desert tree, the effect is truly startling. The female is dark brown on the upper parts with a white breast and belly, and there is a slight pinkish cast to the under-tail coverts. This little flycatcher is one of my very favorite birds, and I always watch for the first one to appear in the spring. This is usually about the first week in March, in the vicinity of the Mexican border at an elevation of around 3,600 feet. Some individuals winter in southern Arizona, but this is a rather rare occurrence. Most of the birds drift down farther into Mexico. We found them plentiful all through Nyarit and Jalisco during January.

One spring a neighbor said, "Oh, I saw a little baby cardinal this morning."

"Baby cardinal?" I replied, "Are you *sure*?" It was in the first week of March, and I had just noted the first vermilion flycatcher that day.

"Very sure," she replied, "it was in a mesquite tree right outside my window, and I had a good look at it. It was bright red and black—just like a cardinal, only small. Mrs. ——— saw it too, and she said it was a baby cardinal."

I asked her if she knew when cardinals nested, how long it took a brood to mature, and whether she had ever taken a good look at young birds and checked as to size and color as compared with the parents. She didn't have any clear answers to that, and when I showed her a color illustration of the vermilion flycatcher in a bird book she looked puzzled but, I'm afraid, not entirely convinced.

Several handsome and large jays inhabit the foothill and mountain areas of the desert, and one must go there to see them, as they rarely

Lark sparrow

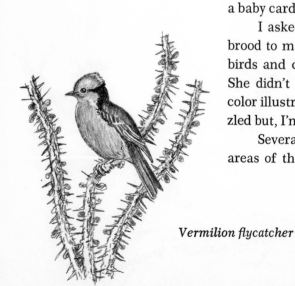

Vermilion flycatcher

136

Arizona jay

leave the high country. The most spectacular of these is Steller's jay, a bird a foot or more in length, dark blue with black markings and a definite crest. The Arizona jay and the Piñon jay are both smaller and somewhat duller in color, and lack the crest.

Visitors to the desert for the first time will see many large black birds, often in great flocks, slowly flapping, sometimes soaring across the sky. They will be identified immediately as crows, and unless one is seen close enough to be compared to a known-sized object the mistake is understandable. Actually, they are ravens, birds very much larger than the common crow. Another distinguishing mark is the call. The crow caws, loudly and raucously, but the raven croaks—a sort of hoarse *cr-r-uck,* usually repeated several times, and not so loud in pitch or with the carrying power of the crow's caw.

The soaring flight of the turkey vulture—commonly called buzzard —is familiar to almost everyone. This is the common vulture of the desert, and is numerous everywhere. It performs a valuable service in cleaning up dead creatures, a veritable Department of Sanitation. Great flocks may often be seen wheeling over the land, searching with incredibly penetrating eyesight for even the smallest morsel. A vulture can see a crust of bread, abandoned by a picnicker, from an unbelievable height in the air. Once I was sitting in a patio in Hermosillo with a Mexican friend, sipping a tequila sour. Overhead a large flock of vultures soared with scarcely a wing flap. With the dry humor typical of his race, he said, "Dat's d' Mexican Air Force." The turkey vulture is a big bird with a wingspread of about six feet. Its head is red and naked, and

137 the primary and secondary feathers of the wings are light tan. They

Gila woodpecker

can be plainly seen when the bird is soaring aloft, and this feature distinguishes it from another similar bird.

This is the black vulture, smaller by perhaps a foot in wingspread, and black in color, including head, with the exception of a white patch on the underside of the wings. The tail is shorter than that of the turkey vulture, and the flight habit is different. Instead of almost continuously soaring, the black vulture flaps a good deal, then soars for a short distance and uses its wings to pump forward. An interesting fact about this species is that in very recent years it has gradually been extending its range, from Mexico, and penetrating northward. Black vultures are a rather common sight now in southern Arizona, whereas they were rare as few as a dozen years ago.

Our largest raptorial bird (aside from the rare condor), is, of course, the eagle. But the bird of the desert is not the one used as our national emblem—the bald eagle. Here it is replaced by the other one of the two species, the golden eagle. It is noticeably larger than the turkey vulture in flight, sometimes spreading as much as 7½ feet. The head is massive and the body large and powerful. Observed from below, when the great bird is in flight, the appearance is solid black; but when it flares and tacks so that the top of the tail can be seen it will show white, with a black edging band.

The golden eagle is a mountain bird and may sometimes be seen soaring over a range or lower foothills. On rare occasions it may be encountered close by in higher country. One morning we started out on the road early, and near a cattle guard we were treated to the rare sight of three eagles on the ground. We were able to coast to within fifty yards or so before they spread their massive wings and slowly pumped air to rise majestically into the upper reaches of safety. An examination of the ground showed that they had been feeding on a couple of dead jackrabbits that had been killed by a car. Here was a further proof of the fact, often noted, that, though the eagle is a most efficient hunter, he is not above accepting a bit of fresh meat that is handed to him, without his having to go to the trouble of butchering it.

Hawks and falcons abound in the desert. Some species are rare and seldom seen—the prairie falcon and extremely scarce aplomado falcon. Others, Swainson's hawk, a red-tail, and the ferruginous rough-leg, are quite common. The gray hawk called "Mexican goshawk," zone-tailed, and Mexican black hawks are found only in the lower parts of the desert, in Sonora, and are well worth studying. One hawk that will be seen commonly after one gets into Sonora is a striking bird known as Audubon's caracara. It is large and has long legs. On the undersurface is a pattern of alternating light and dark. The throat is a warm white, and the belly and breast are black. The tail is white, rimmed with a brownish-black shade. The bill of the caracara is massive and powerful. This is a most interesting bird. Though very common in Mexico, it is seldom seen in Arizona, and there only in the area along the Mexican border.

The woodpecker family is represented by a great number of species, both in the mountains and low regions. One of them that will often be seen and is unique to the desert is the Gila woodpecker. It is a medium-sized bird with a black-and-white-striped back. The head is a dull brown with a bright red patch on top. White areas on the wings may be seen when the bird is in flight. The female is similar in coloration, but lacks the red pate spot. Gila woodpeckers are very busy birds, and spend much time exploring the cracks and crannies of tree bark in an endless search for insects and larvae.

If space permitted, an entire chapter might be devoted to the owls alone, since so many species inhabit the desert. Two of these highly specialized forms of birdlife are particularly notable. The pygmy owl is a little rust-brown mite of a thing (compared with his huge cousin Bubo, the great horned owl), and his habits differ in that he is often diurnal. This bird can be recognized readily because of the habit of carrying its tail at a jaunty angle from the body, instead of straight down. It has a smaller head, in proportion to the body, and a longer tail than most owls. Since the pygmy is a daytime hunter, it is dreaded and despised by small birds of all kinds. Its voice is expressed in a series of melodious notes that seem to roll—*too-too-too-too-too*, ending with *took-took-took*. It can be memorized and imitated readily by one with a good ear. When a reasonable facsimile has been mastered, the performer can then hide himself in thick brush and start calling. In a short time the air and branches of nearby bushes and trees will rapidly fill with a scolding, screaming chorus of outraged small birds.

The smallest of all owls is a tiny little bird near the size of a sparrow.
139 The elf owl lives in areas of sahuaro and makes its nest and home in

hollows of the giant cactus. It may sometimes be seen perched in such an opening during the day, and it presents an odd appearance. This owl is reddish-brown in color, and has white eyebrows.

While the eastern part of the United States and most of the nation, in fact, is host to only one hummingbird—the lovely little rubythroat—the desert is rich with a wealth of these magnificent little flying jewels. About ten species occur throughout the range of the Sonoran desert, either as residents or migrants. Though they vary greatly in color, and in some cases in size, they can be identified rather easily, with the help of a good color plate, because of their habit of feeding on the nectar of flowers by hovering in the air. By approaching cautiously one can walk almost up to a feeding bird without alarming it.

Several species of birds that occur rarely, really as accidentals that drift north from Mexico, are seen only by bird enthusiasts who are willing to go into their habitat and search them out. The easiest of these to find would probably be the rose-throated becard, a handsome small bird looking something like a flycatcher, but with thick head and large bill. The male is gray with a black pate and cheeks and beautiful rose throat. It is unique in that it builds a tremendous long, hanging nest. In Arizona becards sometimes nest in a grove of trees along a small living stream on the Patagonia Road, about sixteen miles east of Nogales. They may be found more commonly in Mexico in mountainous areas, especially along washes and streams.

A chunky green bird having a heavy black bill and red forehead is occasionally found as far north as the Baboquivari Mountains, in southern Arizona. This is the thick-billed parrot, a common bird of the mountainous regions of Sonora.

Another rarity for Arizona, also inhabiting mountains, is the coppery-tailed trogon, a relative of the great quetzal, or resplendent trogon, that played so important a part in the lives of the Mayas and Aztecs. This bird is about eleven inches long with head and back dark glossy green and belly and underparts bright rose. A band of white extends around the shoulders in front of the birds, separating the green of

Elf owl

Screech owl

Saw-whet owl

the head from the pink breast. A good many records of this trogon have been made in Madera Canyon, in the Santa Rita Mountains, a short distance south of Tucson. It occurs much more frequently in the mountains of Sonora. This is another species that presents a challenge to the bird watcher who is looking for out-of-the-ordinary items. It is well worth finding and recording.

The western subspecies of the well-known sandhill crane is the little brown crane, a term that has always seemed a misnomer, because there is very little difference in size between the two birds. This long-legged bird is nowhere plentiful, and obtaining a record is not an easy matter. Great blue herons in flight have sometimes been mistaken for cranes, but there is no valid reason for confusion. The heron always flies with its head tucked back on its shoulders, showing a decidedly crooked neck, while the crane stretches its neck out to full length. In color, too, the difference is very noticeable. The crane is grayer in color and has a bald red head.

On two occasions my wife and I had weird experiences with these rare and interesting birds. In hiking through some thick mesquite growth one fall, during the migration season, we saw the motion of some large creature ahead of us, traveling quite rapidly. I ran as fast as the brush would permit, but failed to catch up with the galloping thing in front of me. After a chase of a few hundred yards, in which the

Here is a desert rarity well worth looking for. The rose-
throated becard builds a tremendous nest, usually in a
tall sycamore or cottonwood tree. Look for him in canyons in the mountains of Sonora and in a couple of
localities in Arizona mentioned in the text.

creature gained on me rapidly, I got a clear sighting of it as it crossed an opening in the trees. It was a little brown crane. With head bent low, all that was visible was the rump of the bird, with its droopy back feathers strongly resembling the bustle of the skirt of an old-fashioned era. Two days later the performance was repeated, this time with two birds in the act. We both saw them distinctly, and they ran as before, easily outdistancing us. I watched the sky after the birds were lost to sight, but, so far as I could learn, they did not take to wing. Why, I have often wondered.

Coppery-tailed trogon

The following list of land birds (water birds are treated separately in another chapter), though not complete, is offered with the thought that it may be of assistance to the more advanced bird watchers. It is divided roughly into zones, though many of these may overlap, and is intended as a popular rather than a scientific approach to bird study.

Birds of Mountain Ranges in the Sonoran Desert
("Island" habitats) from upper oaks to fir forest

Band-tailed pigeon
Golden eagle
Whippoorwill (Stephen's, a darker bird than eastern)
Whiskered screech owl (the "syncopated" owl)
Mountain pygmy owl
Flammulated screech owl (rare)
Spotted owl
Thick-billed parrot (rare visitor to mountains)
White-eared hummingbird (rare in Arizona)
Rufous hummingbird (on migration)
Calliope hummingbird
Rivoli's hummingbird
Blue-throated hummingbird
Broad-tailed hummingbird
Red-shafted flicker
Acorn woodpecker
Lewis woodpecker
Olivaceous flycatcher
Buff-breasted flycatcher
Coues' flycatcher
Steller's jay
Piñon jay
Beechey jay (Sonora)
Scrub jay

Arizona jay
Clark's nutcracker
Mexican chickadee
Plain titmouse
Bridled titmouse
Bushtit
Brown-throated house wren (Chiracahuas and Huachucas)
Robin
Western bluebird
Mountain bluebird
Townsend's solitaire (winters)
Solitary vireo
Calaveras warbler
Olive warbler
Audubon's warbler
Black-throated gray warbler
Grace's warbler
Red-faced warbler
Painted redstart
Western tanager
Hepatic tanager
Pine siskin
Red crossbill
Oregon junco (winters)
Pink-sided junco (winters)
Gray-headed junco (winters)
Red-backed Arizona junco

Birds of Desert and Lower Grass, Yucca, Cañon Oak Foothills

White-winged dove
Mourning dove
Inca dove
Ground dove
Roadrunner

Ferruginous rough-legged hawk
Aplomado falcon (rarest raptor in the United States)
Mexican black hawk
Gray hawk ("Mexican goshawk")

144

Prairie falcon
Mearns quail
Gambel quail
Gila woodpecker
Cactus woodpecker ("ladderback")
Arizona woodpecker (in oak zone)
Western gnatcatcher
American pipit
Sprague's pipit
Phainopepla
Hutton's vireo (oak zone)
Bell's vireo
Gray vireo
Orange-crowned warbler
Virginia warbler
Lucy warbler
MacGillivray's warbler
Western meadowlark
Yellow-headed blackbird (winters)
Hooded oriole
Scott's oriole
Bullock's oriole
Brewer's blackbird
Boat-tailed grackle
Red-eyed cowbird
Cardinal
Pyrrhuloxia
Black-headed grosbeak
Varied bunting
House finch
Green-backed goldfinch
Green-tailed towhee (winters)
Spotted towhee (oak zone)
Brown towhee
Abert's towhee
Rose-throated becard (see text)
Scaled or blue quail ("cottontop")
Nuttall's poorwill
Trilling or "Texas" nighthawk
Vaux swift
Little green kingfisher (sometimes seen on a stream near Patagonia. See text on becard.)

Broad-billed hummingbird
Lucifer hummingbird (accidental)
Black-chinned hummingbird
Costa's hummingbird
Coppery-tailed trogon (see text)
Gilded or Mearns flicker
Rough-winged swallow
Raven
White-necked raven
Verdin
Bewick's wren
Rock wren
Cactus wren
Canyon wren
Mockingbird
Bendire's thrasher
Curve-billed thrasher (Palmer)
Leconte's thrasher
Crissal thrasher
Sage thrasher (winters)
Lark bunting (winters)
Vesper sparrow
Lark sparrow (breeds and winters)
Rufous-winged sparrow
Rufous-crowned sparrow
Botteri's sparrow (very rare)
Cassin's sparrow
Desert sparrow
Clay-colored sparrow
Brewer's sparrow (winters)
Black-chinned sparrow
Gambel sparrow (a white-crown)
White-crowned sparrow
Desert song sparrow (rare breeder on the desert)
McCown's longspur (winters)
Chestnut-collared longspur (winters)
Turkey vulture
Tropical kingbird—brown tail
Cassin's kingbird—black tail
Western kingbird—black tail, white edging

Sulphur-bellied flycatcher (sycamore groves in mountain canyons)
Mexican crested flycatcher
Ash-throated flycatcher
Black phoebe (along streams)
Western (Say's) phoebe
Vermilion flycatcher
Beardless flycatcher
Horned lark
Black vulture
Zone-tailed hawk

Burrowing owl
Elf owl
Screech owl (call is different from that of eastern screech owl)
Cactus pygmy owl
Masked bobwhite quail (extinct in U.S., but still occurs in a few grassland areas of northern Sonora)
Elegant quail (southern Sonora)
Audubon's caracara

Tropical Birds That Reach Navajoa, Sometimes Guaymas

Western fish crow (winters occasionally at Navajoa)
Mexican crow
Red-billed pigeon

White-fronted dove
Groove-billed ani (species of cuckoo)
Scarlet-headed oriole

The Alamos Faunal District lies about twenty-five miles east of Navajoa and is the first area in Mexico in which the visitor, coming from the north, could expect to see typically tropical birds. This is the Short Tree Thorn Forest Region, which adjoins the Sonoran desert southeast of Navajoa. Here is a partial list of birds that may be seen there:

Urubitinga, or great black hawk
Laughing falcon
Bat falcon
Chachalaca
Green macaw
Blue-rumped parrotlet
White-fronted parrot
Squamulated owl
Ridgeway's poorwill
Nutting's flycatcher
Red-billed pigeon
Squirrel cuckoo

Sinaloa wren
Happy wren
Rufous-backed robin
Brown-backed solitaire
White-lored gnatcatcher
Golden vireo
Yellow-green vireo
Fan-tailed warbler
Rufous-capped warbler
Musical euphonia
Rusty-crowned ground sparrow
Beechey jay

The American egret is a large, stately bird with pure white plumage. It affords a fine sight when seen against a background of mangroves, where it is frequently found. It may also be seen at times along the shores of freshwater lakes and ponds in the northern part of the desert.

TWELVE

AQUATIC BIRDS

For the best show, go down to the sea

ON ALMOST any of the small bodies of water in the Arizona part of the desert, wildfowl, herons, shore birds, and other species may occasionally be seen, especially during migration time. But the bird enthusiast interested in aquatic forms will waste no time in going to Sonora, from the upper end of the Gulf of California along the coast, to the Sinaloa line (marking the Sonoran desert's end, and of course to the south).

Watching water birds is one of the most rewarding of occupations, and about as profitable a way of loafing as could be devised, in keeping with the true spirit of a vacation. A comfortable folding chair, preferably placed on an overlook above the beach, glasses, notebook, and pencil constitute the equipment. The show goes on in front, and it's all free.

Mornings and evenings are the periods of largest concentration, as a rule, but when schools of sardines and other small bait fish are running, the air will be filled with great masses of birds, yelling and screaming in the manner of a bunch of school kids at recess. They dive with great skill, creating splashes of white spray, and come up with small fish, rarely missing. Terns and gulls are graceful, but anyone who has seen a pelican dive knows what a ludicrous sight he presents. He folds his wings several feet above the water and, seemingly without taking particular aim, simply falls in with a great splash. Should he come up with a fish too large to swallow at once he will be plagued by terns and gulls that follow him and attempt to snatch the quarry.

Meanwhile another show is going on in the water. Great schools of mackerel, corvina, and other species are chopping at the bait fish and breaking the surface, churning the water into white froth. This, of course, is the time for the angler to be in action. But it also presents a problem. The mass of milling birds is so dense that it is easily possible to hook one when casting. I saw this happen once with a pelican. The big fellow was hooked lightly through the skin of the neck and was pretty mad about it, but when released unharmed he resumed his fishing as though nothing had happened.

The brown pelican is the common bird of this family in the Gulf region and along the Pacific coast. Brown pelicans measure about six and a half feet in wingspread, being smaller than the white pelican. They fly in long lines, a few feet above the water, alternately flapping and coasting. An interesting thing about this is that they all flap and coast in unison—a sort of "follow-the-leader" game. Flocks often number from fifty to one hundred birds, and when trading over the water they resemble a long freight train.

Cormorants, which are much smaller birds and predominantly black, fly in long lines, sometimes in wedges like geese; there are several species inhabiting the Pacific Coast region.

The list of wildfowl—ducks and geese—will correspond to that of

Brown pelican

other parts of North America, with the exception of the black duck, and the inclusion of the cinnamon teal and black-bellied tree duck.

Ducks commonly seen along the coast will, of course, be the divers, as is true everywhere. Among them are: goldeneye, bufflehead, merganser, canvasback, redhead and broadbill (scaup). The dabblers—pintail, teal, mallard, shoveller, widgeon, and others—largely confine their range to the inland area, especially the rice and wheat fields where pickings are good and life is easy.

Grebes and loons are common, and may be seen diving and working the waters near shore at almost all times. The two species of the former are the Pacific loon and the red-throated loon.

One of the most fascinating of the Gulf birds is the frigate, or man-o'war, bird. Anatomically, it is almost a freak. Its wings are disproportionately long to the bulk of the body, some seven-and-a half feet, very narrow and angular. The body color is black, and the male has a patch of orange on the throat. The female has a white breast. The head is set close to the body, and the tail is long and forked, like that of a swallow. This is apparent when the birds are wheeling and banking for a turn. In soaring flight the feathers are apt to be drawn together, presenting the appearance of an unforked tail. A flock of a dozen or more frigate birds, soaring against a deep blue sky, affords a sight that, to the bird lover, is alone well worth a trip to the Gulf region.

A bird never very plentiful, but well worth the effort of searching for, is the roseate spoonbill. You may have to spend some time and perhaps cover considerable ground; or in the right locality you just might have the luck to see one in flight. This beautiful pink-plumaged bird is well known through illustrations, even to people who have not seen it in life. It occurs in Florida and other semitropical regions. Along the Gulf Coast it frequents bayous and muddy estuaries, starting in the mangrove belt, which reaches about to Kino Bay, and becomes more plentiful farther south.

In the same type of terrain one may occasionally see a whitefaced glossy ibis, a bird of medium size, with a long down-curved bill. It is dark brown in color, and in contour somewhat resembles a large curlew.

Rails are familiar to observers interested in marsh birds, and the large California clapper rail and smaller Virginia rail are partial to salt marshes, while the well-known sora rail is found in fresh-water marshes farther inland.

The purple gallinule also occurs. It differs from the eastern form in coloration, having dark purple underparts and a light blue patch on the bill. Its legs are bright yellow.

The coot, or "mud hen," is much in evidence all over the desert

Glossy ibis

wherever water is to be found, and is distinguished at first sight from a duck by the pointed ivory-colored bill.

A very large group of birds, although of different families, is roughly classed under the category of waders or "shorebirds." Many of these, being widely distributed over the country in general, are familiar to most bird watchers. Among them will be the killdeer with its plaintive call, greater and lesser yellowlegs, spotted sandpiper, knot, and marbled godwit.

Many of these birds comb the beaches, following a receding wave and hastily picking up tidbits washed in, then quickly turning and trotting back to avoid a wetting. They are among the most graceful and interesting forms of birdlife, and their presence on the shore contributes a certain atmosphere that fits perfectly into the marine picture. Groups of from a pair to several dozens may usually be seen on any beach not crowded with people, but large concentrations are frequently found on mud flats, in estuaries and shallow coves at low tide. At such a place, near the railroad bridge south of Empalme, we saw a congregation of thousands of waders, representing many species, and varying in size from a peanut of a sandpiper to a great long-legged stilt. This was during the fall migration.

The curlews, of two species, are among the most fascinating of shorebirds. They are distinguished from other members of the family by their down-curving bills and are sometimes popularly called "sicklebills." The bills of most shorebirds are straight, except those of the godwit and avocet, whose bills curve slightly upward. The larger of the curlews, which is not infrequently seen, is an impressive bird, as much as twenty inches or more in length and standing high on long legs. The bill alone is six or seven inches in length. These birds are so large that, when seen flying in the wedge formation often employed by wildfowl, they may be mistaken for ducks at first sight. The long-billed curlew is the name given to the larger species; the other one is the Hudsonian curlew, a somewhat smaller bird, having the same mottled and patterned plumage, but darker brown in color, and with a shorter bill.

The marbled godwit resembles the curlews rather closely in color, but is distinguished from them at once by the upturned bill. This is a rather common bird of the beaches, and is usually seen singly, plying its trade of snooping among the rocks for tidbits.

A very handsome wader that is common is the western willet. It too is a large shorebird, gray and white in body color and having a very distinctive wing pattern of black and white, not obvious when the bird is on the ground, but unmistakable in flight. Another large shorebird is the black-necked stilt, white underneath, with a black back. There are no markings on the wings, and the legs are very long and red. While

Willet

151

these two species are similar in size, the markings distinguish them at once.

One of the largest and most strikingly beautiful of all the waders is the avocet. It is about the size of the marbled godwit and, similarly, has an upturned bill. Body color is black and white, with a distinctive pattern on the back and on the wings when in flight. The bird is at its best in the breeding season, when the plumage of the neck and head turns a lovely shell-pink color. One year in April we camped at Puerto Libertad for a week's fishing, and a group of a dozen avocets stayed on the beach for several days. They came close to us as we cast from the shore, and were very tame and unafraid. Their pink, black, and white plumage seen against the reddish-brown rock, yellow sand, and aquamarine green of the shallow water created an unforgettable picture.

The black turnstone is a small, predominantly blackish bird, with a white breast. It likes rocky areas along the coast rather than sandy stretches, and is always busy, prying into crevices and crannies of the rocks, searching for food. Its relative, the ruddy turnstone, has orange legs and, in breeding plumage, an exotic pattern of black and white, giving it a harlequin look.

The wandering tattler is a medium-sized shore bird that frequents the same areas preferred by the turnstones—rocky places along the coast. All shore birds are sociable and get along well together. (This is a virtue not always found in doves, particularly the mourning doves, which are supposedly the symbol of peace but which frequently chase and snap at one another, and drive away birds of other species on a feeding ground.) The tattler is gray above, with a white line over the eyes. In breeding season the white underparts become barred with black bands, giving the appearance of another species.

Avocet

If you see a long-billed bird of medium size, very closely resembling the Wilson's snipe (jacksnipe), feeding along the flats or beaches, it will be a dowitcher. The jacksnipe is most frequently seen by gunners, in fresh or brackish marshes, and then only when flushed. It flies a zigzag course and utters a harsh, rasping note that sounds like *scaipe!* It has a mottled back and striped black-and-white breast, with brownish-orange tail, banded with black and white. The dowitcher, on the other hand, is always distinguished by a white rump. While it may sometimes be found in marshy freshwater areas, feeding with the Wilson's snipe, the latter never uses the sea beaches.

Terns, which are among the most graceful of seabirds, are found in great abundance all over the Gulf area. While they resemble gulls, they are more slender and have forked tails, like those of swallows, and, in most species, black caps. Some have red or orange bills, and whitish bodies, with grayish wings. Among the species ordinarily seen along most of the coastal area are the royal, elegant, Caspian, and black terns. Since members of the various species resemble each other closely, identification becomes a difficult matter, except for the advanced student of birds.

Terns are among the most active of aquatic birds, and small groups of them will be seen diving and questing for food, even when other species are resting. When feeding, a tern descends in an arrowlike motion, cleaves the water cleanly, and seldom misses. The performance is similar to that of a kingfisher.

Gull

Gulls are of such occurrence in all marine areas, and on many large inland bodies of water, that their general appearance needs no description. Identifying species, however, is a different matter. The observer who is interested should obtain a good bird guide and study closely the distinguishing markings. Of the several species found in the coastal area of the Gulf, ones commonly seen are the glaucous, California, ring-billed, laughing, and Heermann's gulls.

In general, gulls are heavier and larger than terns, have thicker bills, slightly hooked at the ends, and their tails are square, or a little rounded in almost all species. While the coloration might seem similar in most gulls, there is considerable variation among the different species. Body color of mature birds is usually white, or slightly off-white. Young birds are brownish to buff. Wings are gray, from a light to fairly dark value, and most species have wings with white edgings. The primary feathers on some gulls are dark—from gray to black. Several species have black heads. Legs, too, vary greatly. They range in color from flesh-colored to yellow, reddish brown, dark red, to black. Some species have greenish or yellowish-green legs. From the foregoing rough description it can be seen that the observer who wishes to keep accurate records has his work cut out for him.

Gulls are among the boldest of birds, and soon lose their fear of man when they know they won't be harmed. They become confirmed mendicants, and will circle around a camp, uttering a chorus of notes that sometimes sounds almost human. They are expert at catching pieces of bread or other tidbits that are tossed into the air by softhearted

154

people, and they seem to be able to locate a camp of "suckers" with un-erring accuracy, no matter how far back from the sea it is placed.

The great osprey, or fishhawk, is so common everywhere that all outdoor people know it. A good many of these interesting birds fish along the coast, and it is a thrilling sight to see one plunge to the water with great speed and seize a corvina or mackerel from a school that is feed-ing on the surface. The osprey is a powerful bird; it can carry an in-credibly large fish in its talons and fly aloft with apparently no effort. It grasps its prey with its feet, not its bill, when fishing.

If you have a stroke of luck, when in a mountainous area of the coast, you may see a rare wildlife drama. The golden eagle is a notori-ous pirate, a bird that prefers to rob, rather than to do his own fishing, whenever there is an opportunity. From a high crag he scans the sea, spots an osprey making a catch, then takes off in swift pursuit. Unbur-dened by a heavy fish, he soon catches up, and makes a pass at the un-fortunate fisherman, who drops his still-squirming burden, and flees. The brigand then circles slowly to the ground and enjoys a feast on his ill-gotten gain. Crime is not confined to the human race!

No notes on water birds would be complete without the inclusion of a most fascinating group of birds, the herons. Perhaps the commonest of these, in all parts of the country, is the great blue heron, mistakenly called "crane" by the uninformed. It is not only an impressive bird, stand-ing almost four feet high, but a most decorative one, with blue-gray coat of plumage, black crest, whitish crown, and long neck plumes. When standing in a statuesque pose in shallow water it has great dignity, and adds a fine touch to the landscape.

A magnificent bird, smaller than the great blue heron, is the Amer-ican egret. It averages about forty inches, and its plumage throughout is purest white. The legs and feet are black, and the bill is yellow.

The snowy egret is smaller, about twenty-four inches, and its bill is black, as are its legs; but, differing from the American egret, its feet are yellow. Egrets are nowhere plentiful, and the sight of this spotless bird, encountered standing against a mass of mangroves in an estuary, affords a fresh thrill every time it occurs.

Another water bird, the reddish egret, occurs sparingly in this region, and is seldom seen. The Louisiana heron may occasionally be

Stilt

observed, and also the black-crowned night heron, which is known to most bird watchers. Anthony's green heron is a little fellow (for herons), and when he raises his crest he looks like a very tough and fierce character.

Considering all the varied and often exotic facets of nature afforded by Sonora's wondrous Gulf Coastal region, water birds rank right up at the top. They are vibrant, living creatures, always putting on a show that may be enjoyed without the necessity of buying a ticket.

THIRTEEN

FURRY AND HAIRY CREATURES

In addition to many well-known mammals
that make the desert their home,
some truly exotic forms

UNLIKE BIRDS, mammals have the annoying habit of keeping out of sight most of the time. One of the desirable things about bird-watching is that the enthusiast can take binoculars, notebook and pencil, a lunch and water, and go out for a day in the field, practically assured that he will return rich with results. Birds are everywhere, and are willing to oblige by showing themselves, performing what to us are sometimes amusing antics, and often providing delightful concerts of avian music. But do mammals cooperate? Not on your life!

It is true that one often sees such small animals as ground squirrels, rabbits, and gophers; or occasionally coyotes and foxes or deer, in the course of a drive or hike over the desert, but these encounters may be laid to pure chance. One summer evening, as we were sitting on the porch of our home in the foothills above Tubac, a bobcat came strolling leisurely across the yard. Now, if I were asked by a visitor to take him out and show him a bobcat I could truthfully reply that it would be about as easy, on the spur of the moment, as it would be to produce the genie from Aladdin's lamp. Unfortunately I don't have the lamp, nor does anyone else. The mammal watcher, a member of a race about which one hears little as compared to the bird watcher, has a tough and weedy field to cultivate.

Not that the desert does not abound in mammalian life; to the contrary the region is exceedingly rich with a long list of mammals common to many regions, besides a number of exotic creatures that occasionally cross the border into southern Arizona, and are much more common below it in Mexico.

Difficulties that beset the mammal observer are many, but they largely fall into two classes. One of these is the unfortunate habit possessed by a large proportion of animals of being nocturnal. And from long association with man, all but the smallest of diurnal creatures have learned of his wicked ways, and take good care to avoid him. A whiff of man scent, at a long distance away, will send a deer or antelope off kicking gravel in an instant.

Of the two great North American cats—mountain lion and jaguar —the former, which inhabits areas of most of the states west of the Rockies and in Mexico, is found throughout much of the suitable range in the Sonoran desert. While it lives principally in the mountains, it makes forays into the grasslands cattle-range areas, and kills many calves. Very rarely one may be seen skulking early in the morning or at dusk, but we see the large, unmistakable pugmarks in sand or soft soil frequently, giving ample evidence that a prowler has been abroad. The mountain lion (cougar, puma, or panther) is, on the whole, a furtive creature, and not dangerous to man unless cornered. The Mexicans call him *el león,* and say he is *un cobarde,* a coward. But with *el tigre,* the tiger, which is the great spotted jaguar, the case is entirely different, and no Mexican *tigrero* takes him lightly. He is highly unpredictable and dangerous.

It may come as a surprise to some to learn that the jaguar, whose normal range is Mexico, Central, and South America, makes an occasional foray into southern Arizona. About ten years ago a couple of hunters had killed a mule deer and were cleaning it out, when they heard a crackling noise in the brush. Looking up, they saw an amazing, almost incredible sight. Stalking with belly close to the ground, a jaguar crept slowly toward them. It was only a few yards off when one of the men stopped it with a well-placed shot. This incident affords a perfect example of the brazenness and nerve of this great spotted cat. It had smelled blood, and, following the scent, had found the source. It seems incredible that the cat could not see the men working, yet it kept coming. Whether the performance of this cat was normal for the species, or otherwise, can best be left to professional hunters who have had a great deal of experience with the beasts; but I think it pretty safe to say that no mountain lion would do such a thing. This jaguar was a big one, and fully adult. The lucky hunters collected a bounty from the State of Arizona and an additional one from the Cattlemen's Association. The in-   158

The peccary, or javelina, is a piglike animal common to much of the desert. It is fond of the roots of the opuntia, or prickly pear, and often digs up large areas of the plants. It is hunted for sport and food.

cident took place in the Cerro Colorado Mountains, a small range that
may be seen lying fairly close to the road between Arivaca and Kinsley's
Ranch, in Pima County.

A newspaper item, dated July 28, 1961, noted the kill of a jaguar
on the Empire Ranch, near Sonoita, Arizona. It had killed many calves
and had been hunted for two months before being driven into a cave by
dogs, and shot. This big cat weighed 160 pounds—quite a formidable

customer! In all, records show that about fifteen jaguars have been killed in the region near the Mexican border in the last several years.

Hunters interested in this type of sport will find guides, with packs of good dogs, in several of the mountainous areas of Sonora who will take out parties. While the quarry is the mountain lion, an occasional jaguar is encountered.

Deer, which are plentiful in all parts of the country, even straying into villages and towns and often making a nuisance of themselves on the highways, are found in good numbers in the desert. They are of two species: the large mule deer, or blacktail, and the very small Arizona and Sonoran whitetail. The desert mule deer does not average much larger than a big eastern whitetail, in weight and body size, but an old buck may have an impressive set of antlers.

Once, when I was driving my brother-in-law over a stretch of desert road, a big mule deer with a huge rack of antlers crossed a hundred yards in front of us. "Stop the car," he exclaimed, "there goes an elk!" I had quite a job explaining that it wasn't an elk, but a mule deer, or blacktail. He lives in Westchester County, New York, where deer are plentiful, and he was sure he knew what one looked like—until this wondrous creature showed up.

The desert whitetail is a very small animal, in comparison not only to the mule deer but to the eastern whitetail as well. A large example will perhaps weigh 125 pounds, but most of the whitetails shot during the hunting season will average under 100 pounds. The antlers of the two species differ in that single tines come off the main beam of the whitetail, whereas in the case of the mule deer the tines, or prongs, are branched. The color on the top of the mule deer's tail is largely black, with white edging and underparts.

A good many species of animals found in most parts of the country have desert cousins, which may differ a little; or in some cases, greatly. The desert cottontail rabbit, for instance, is smaller than several of the eastern forms, but he has noticeably longer ears. This little fellow abounds almost everywhere, and often lives in the patio and garden areas of homes in large cities.

The jackrabbit is another symbol of the West, and while it is common to a vast area of the country, it is very abundant in the desert. The family is represented by two species—the antelope, or Allen's jack, and the blacktail jack. The former is a highly specialized creature, with enormously long ears that are translucent. When seen against the sunlight in certain situations, the erect ears glow with a brilliant coral pink hue, and resemble some strange, exotic blossom. The hind legs of the antelope jack are very long and angular, and when it sits up the resemblance to a kangaroo is striking. When alarmed, the jack leaves the 160 scene with a speed that soon leaves any dog but a greyhound or whippet far behind. Its powerful hind legs seem to contain steel springs, and it covers several yards with a single leap. Often it will make an observation bound into the air to eye its pursuer, jumping almost straight up to a considerable height. We were once treated to the sight of two antelope jacks engaged in a scrap of some kind. They danced on their hind legs and boxed one another like pugilists in a ring. After several minutes of this performance, one of them landed a haymaker on the other one's chin and sent him spinning. He got up, shook himself, gave his opponent a dirty look, and slunk off into the brush. Decision: a technical knockout.

The blacktail jack is heavy, but not so long-geared as the antelope; nor does he possess such enormous ears, although they are certainly ample. In color he is more of a uniform gray, tinged with a buffy overwash, while the antelope jack has a white belly, rump, and foreparts up to the neck, with only a slight patch of brindly color on the back. I have seen several antelope jacks with so little color that at first sight they seemed almost to be albinos. Rabbits are one of the exceptions to the statement that animals are not often seen on the desert. In most sections they are so commonly met with that one soon wishes something different would show up.

When it does it could easily be a coyote. Aside from small fry like ground squirrels, this doglike animal is probably the most frequently seen, next to rabbits. Don Coyote is a carefree vagabond, wandering over great areas of the desert, making his living principally on small mammals—mice, gophers, voles—and rabbits, which he catches readily with the aid of his pack in a well-planned relay race. He keeps no regular hours, is both diurnal and nocturnal, often hunting by day and serenading the desert night with wild, maniacal ululations. The weird chorus of a pack of coyotes, expressing their innermost feelings, never fails to thrill the desert lover. Don Coyote is an integral part of the desert picture, like the sahuaro and the roadrunner, and though there are inter-

Badger

ests that would like to see him eliminated, I feel that even they would miss his picturesque figure, trotting across the mesa; and even more, his nostalgic, soulful outpourings on a moonlit night.

The coyote resembles, probably more than anything else, at a distance at least, a small German shepherd dog; but unlike most dogs, it carries its bushy tail tucked between its legs when trotting or walking.

A tawny yellowish animal, much smaller than the coyote, may sometimes be seen padding across an open area; or perhaps crouched in a site where there are gopher or ground-squirrel burrows, awaiting a chance to pounce on an incautious individual who gets too far from its hole. This is the desert fox, one of the swiftest of the arid-land creatures. He lives largely on small mammals, and is of great benefit, from an economic standpoint. Differing from the other members of his family, he has the ability to climb trees, and may sometimes be seen sunning himself in the crotch of a paloverde, or taking a nap in a twisted old mesquite.

The raccoon, a somewhat comical and highly intelligent character, chose most of North America as a home, ages ago; and in making the choice he did not overlook the desert. Being a highly adaptable animal, he is choosy about the particular region he lives in. He must have cover and water, the latter not only for drinking purposes but also as a necessary compliance with his ancient, built-in habit of first washing the food he eats. While coons often wander some distance in the course of

Pack rats (wood rats) are mischievous little rodents—from the human standpoint. They are the gadgeteers of the animal world, and fancy all sorts of bright objects—often valuables such as jewelry—to embellish their elaborate nests.

a night (they are nocturnal), they live, for the most part, in the canyons of foothills and mountains where there are living springs and *tinajas* of water trapped in rocky depressions. The raccoon is a notorious thief, and, being omnivorous, is not averse to robbing a henhouse of eggs. Every farmer who has a patch of corn knows what happens when a family of coons makes a raid. They seem to have a talent for selecting the finest and ripest ears.

One might not expect to find porcupines in the desert, but they are here. Since this "walking cactus" feeds on the foliage of trees, he is to be found in the high country, mostly at elevations of 6,000 feet or more. The western porky is somewhat larger than his eastern and northern cousins, and the color is yellowish, mixed with gray. Almost everyone now knows that the story of the porcupine having the ability to throw his quills, with deadly accuracy, is a myth; but the quills are very loosely attached, and a switch of the animal's tail can play the devil with the man or dog who gets too close.

The powerful "perfume" of the skunk is a scent known almost everywhere. Where there is land there will be skunks, as well as the nauseous stench emitted by their scent glands when they are disturbed by something, which is frequently. Several species of these black-and-white animals occur (in what most people consider too great numbers) in all parts of the desert.

The common striped skunk is here, and a little fellow known as the spotted skunk. It is really a handsome animal with an interesting pattern of black and white markings. It has a white spot on the forehead and one under each ear. A large member of the family is most interesting because of its anatomical variation. This is the hog-nosed skunk, which has a long, naked snout. It is found only in the southwestern part of the United States, but is plentiful all through Mexico.

Skunks do a great amount of good, as they are largely insectivorous, but they do have a weakness for eggs and will sometimes raid chicken coops, and the nests of birds that rear their young on the ground, like the desert quail. Before an extensive study of the causes of rabies was carried on, years ago, the trouble was largely laid at the skunk's door—among wild creatures. Cowboys called them "hydrofoby skunks." We now know that many mammals—coyotes, squirrels, woodchucks, and, most recently discovered, bats, are carriers of this dread malady. But fortunately, through research, immunization is now available by a series of inoculations.

The badger, a flattish yellow and gray animal with harlequin markings of white and black on its head has an extensive range from the Great Lakes region, through the Midwest and West, down into a considerable part of Mexico. This puts him in the Sonoran desert, a region he seems to like well, judging from his numbers. He has extremely powerful front legs, with long claws—an animal forerunner of the bulldozer—and, as an old desert resident once said, "He's the diggin'est animal they is." The amount of earth a badger can move in a few moments is simply astonishing. Once on a hike in a sandy area I caught a badger off guard, away from his hole. It was open country, and the animal was about a hundred yards off. Seeing me, he sized up the situation and then began to dig, throwing a cloud of dirt like a dog burying a bone. Though I hurried, he had practically disappeared; only the tip of his tail showed some six inches down in the hole. Horseback riders have very little use for the badger. His extensive excavations are always a source of danger, especially when concealed by grass. Horses, stepping into badger holes, sometimes break a leg.

Kangaroo rat

Many interesting small mammals inhabit the desert, as would be expected, and among these the one perhaps most discussed is the pack rat, or more properly, wood rat. Its habit of stealing all sorts of small bright-colored objects and carrying them off to its nest is well known. There have been cases in which valuable items, such as jewelry

164

Ring-tailed cat

and even watches, have eventually turned up in the maze of sticks, leaves, and rubbish out of which this little animal constructs its nest. The pack rat seems to have a badly mixed-up personality, and is utterly lacking in plain horse sense. A stunning example of this is evident in some of the impossible situations in which it chooses to build its nest. One day upon returning from a drive, my wife sniffed the air when I stopped, and said, "I smell something burning, like weed-fire smoke." I lifted the hood, and a cloud of acrid smoke arose from the manifold pipe and the metal surrounding it. There, in a great mass, was a collection of mesquite beans and twigs that had been scorching during the drive, and might have caused real trouble had it not been discovered in time. The car was housed in a shed with only the end open, and the rats had decided that it would be just the dandiest place to build a nest. I cleaned out the mess, and next day again opened the hood. During the night they had piled several quarts of bean pods, plus some twigs, *on top of the battery.* I tried trapping the rascals, but they were too smart. Our neighbor had the same trouble. It went on for some time— the little rodents were not to be discouraged—until some kind soul told me to leave the hood of the car up at night. That did it. I was never troubled again.

Kangaroo rats are among the most interesting and handsome of all the small desert animals. There are several species, having an extensive range through much of the Southwest. The desert kangaroo rat is a good example. It is pale tan and white, with the extremely long tail, terminating in a tuft of hair, typical of the family. The hind legs are long and powerfully muscled, enabling the animal to make long gliding leaps. The tail acts as a rudder to stabilize its position, and the action is more like flying than the motion ordinarily connected with a terrestrial creature. Kangaroo rats are harmless little things—they don't have designs on man's possessions, or upset his household—and they keep to themselves. The desert kangaroo rat lives in sand and is often found in dune country. It is nocturnal, and delights in performing a weird little dance on moonlight nights. It is like something out of fairyland.

One of the oddest of desert mammals is the ring-tailed cat. It bears a superficial resemblance to the raccoon, in that it has a fluffy tail of gray, encircled with rings or bands of darker gray or black. But there the likeness ends, for the ring-tailed cat (which is not really a cat) is more slender and much smaller. It has big ears and a little wizened face, with pointed nose and large innocent-looking eyes, encircled by wide bands of buff. Though common in Mexico, its range extends only a little way north of the border. Being nocturnal, this is one of the animals rarely seen, although it is quite plentiful throughout the desert area.

Another exotic animal, whose original home was the tropics, has been extending its range until it has now reached the border and has crossed it into southern Arizona. This is the coatimundi—usually just called coati. It has a brindled hairy coat, long tapering snout with black-and-white patterned face, and stands high on its legs. The tail, which is practically as long as the animal, is tapering, and is ringed faintly with bands of dark brown. The coati carries its tail high in the air, and its ambling gait reminds one somewhat of certain kinds of monkeys. These animals travel in packs and feed mostly on grubs and insect larvae, which they root out of the ground. But they are also fond of the roots of certain plants and tubers. This, of course, includes potatoes and yams, and a band of coatis has been known to do great damage to a crop in the course of one night.

The jaguarundi cat is a true cat, belonging to the genus *Felis*. It is a most handsome animal, about twice the size of a house cat, and weighs fifteen pounds or more. There are two color phases, gray and red, without other color markings. The tail is almost as long as the body. This is a southern animal, found in Mexico, though nowhere is it apparently very abundant. It strays occasionally into the United States, barely crossing the border. I have always wanted to see a jaguarundi in the wild state (the chances are about as good as winning on a ticket in the Irish Sweepstakes), and maybe I did; I say, just *maybe*. Late one afternoon we were driving along a dirt road in the mountain country overlooking Lochiel, a lonely little village on the Mexican border. 166

The land on each side was heavily forested with trees thick with foliage. As we rounded a bend an animal sprang from the brush on one side of the road and, quick as a flash, crossed over and disappeared. It was gray, rangy, and had a long tail. Its head was distinctly catlike; that was my impression from the quick glimpse I had, but this creature was longer and bigger than any tabby or tom I had ever seen. And if it were a domestic cat, it was certainly out of context, for the nearest house was miles away. From the briefness of the encounter I can't claim it as a record; but at least I'm getting closer.

This strange creature is a coati-mundi, or chula. It originally came from South America, worked up through Mexico, and is now found in the lower parts of the Southwest. The range has been extended noticeably in recent years.

One other desert animal deserves a note. It is the peccary, commonly called javelina. This piglike animal (it is not a true pig) travels in bands, sometimes numbering up to twenty or thirty members. It is warm gray in color, with a coat so rough that it reminds one of a porcupine, at a distance. It may reach a yard in length and weigh up to forty or fifty pounds. The boars have vicious curved and very sharp tusks, capable of ripping a man or dog badly. This has occasionally happened, though javelinas mind their own business when not molested. They are herbivorous, and spend most of their feeding time grubbing in the ground, digging out the roots of prickly pear, a food of which they are particularly fond. The javelina is a favorite quarry with hunters in the desert, and there is an annual open season. It has musk glands along the back near the rump, and these must be removed immediately after the animal is killed, or the flesh will be strong and unpalatable when cooked. While I do not hunt javelina, I have eaten the flesh on several occasions. Once or twice I rather enjoyed it, but felt that venison and some other wild meats were better.

When, a few years ago, we were invited to a meal at a guest ranch, in which we learned that javelina would be the entree, we found an excuse for not going. One of our sons attended, tried a few bites, and was not impressed. He had killed a few "pigs" in the past, dressed them properly, and when cooked the meat was palatable. But this was different. None of the guests could get up any enthusiasm, and there were no bids for seconds. The cook, who did the barbecuing, saw how the thing was going, and finally said, "Anyone want any more of this damned stuff before I throw it out?"

To my way of thinking, he had described it perfectly!

Misión de San Pedro y San Pablo, Tubutama, Sonora

FOURTEEN

THE MISSION TRAIL

*Padre Eusebio Francisco Kino's gift
to the desert—Christianity, culture, cattle*

IN EVERY ERA of history certain individuals have appeared, often from obscure and unsuspected sources, to make outstanding contributions to cultural and material progress. The mysterious gift called genius chooses its children at random; it may lay its benevolent hand upon the brow of king or peasant, and it is mindful of neither time nor place. In the latter part of the seventeenth century it favored a part of Spanish-America, the land now known as the Sonoran desert—more specifically the region termed the Pimería Alta—in the person of Father Kino. For Kino was an undoubted genius, a man of such stature in many fields that his labors and influence brought culture and a better way of life to the several tribes of Indians living in this vast area, in the short space of a quarter of a century.

Padre Eusebio Francisco Kino was born in Segno, Italy, in 1645, near the Bavarian border, and was principally educated in Germany. There he studied for the priesthood, and was ordained in the Jesuit Order. His burning zeal engendered in him an intense desire to become a missionary, and he petitioned his superiors to be sent to the Orient. It is our good fortune that he was assigned, instead, originally to Baja California, and later to the Pimería Alta. After a period of work with the natives in Baja California, a study of native tongues and the new life that lay ahead of him—which called for knowledge of pioneering, map making, colonizing, and many other phases of work in a raw and partially unknown land—he was ready to take up his duties. The year was 1687.

Father Kino was one of those rare individuals whose resources seemed boundless and unending. He was utterly devoted to the work of God, deeply devout, modest and self-effacing—a true ascetic in his personal life, but with an all-embracing love for humanity, to the extent where no sacrifice or hardship was too great in the achievement of his object. This was the conversion of the Indians, whom he called his "dear children." But in his great wisdom he realized that spiritual values cannot be separated from material things. He knew that people with ample food and good living conditions would be far more willing to listen to the Gospel than would those whose lot was less fortunate. So, from the beginning his great concern was the material welfare of his charges, in addition to their conversion.

With seemingly inexhaustible energy he labored ceaselessly, driving himself, as well as the natives, in building houses and developing communities, breeding horses and cattle, introducing better farming methods, with superior varieties of wheat and other crops. His bed consisted of a rough mattress of two sheepskins, placed on the floor, and his pillow was a pack saddle; for covering he used one or two thin blankets. He seldom allowed himself more than four or five hours' sleep.

The example set by Father Kino was so impressive that the Indians 170

Misión de San Antonio de Oquitoa, Sonora

needed no persuasion in doing his bidding. He possessed a rare and magnetic personality that seemed to radiate from his being and influenced everyone, inspiring them to better things. He was absolutely fearless, and on a number of occasions evoked the respect and admiration of the fierce Apaches, enemies of his people, the Pimas, in their raids on the new colonies.

He was a tireless explorer, traveling over great areas of unknown territory, meeting new tribes and seeking locations for his string of missions, which he had hoped to build clear to the Pacific. His feats of riding incredible distances over an unfamiliar land, filled with the hazards of heat, lack of water, and the possibility of meeting an unfriendly people are still marveled at by all who know the country. Often he would go in the company of only one companion and be off for weeks at a time, living off the land and using the seemingly inborn instinct he possessed for finding water, feed for the horses, and the other necessities of existence in a harsh land. His feat of riding on horseback from Dolores, his headquarters mission in Sonora, to Mexico City—a distance of some fifteen hundred miles in seven weeks—is still discussed with admiration by seasoned horsemen. He was fifty years old at the time!

Father Kino was literally a collection of talents, gathered together in one energy-packed individual. He was an architect, designing all the missions in varying styles; an astronomer; agriculturist; cartographer (his maps of a then unknown country are still accurate today); explorer; historian of his times; and humanitarian. One of his greatest achievements was the introduction of ranching, on a scale of efficiency that spread throughout the entire region, and became the forerunner of the industry in this part of the Southwest.

He was an organizer and planner with great vision, a leader who would start enterprises—communities, missions, ranches, and farms—turn them over to competent men whom he had trained, and then move on to a new field. Soon he had numerous groups of natives busy

Misión de San Diego de Pitiquito, Sonora

in constructive work, in widely separated areas. Never content to rest on a few completed projects, he constantly pushed on farther, baptizing, preaching, and saying mass, in formerly unvisited areas; then organizing the people, instructing them in work methods, and getting them started in building. Often he would work with his own hands, laying adobes and placing beams in buildings under construction.

For a long period his daily life became a round of journeys on horseback, with short pauses at his mission communities to superintend operations and continue his religious instruction. But the explorer's spirit in him never ceased to urge him onward. He made a trip to the northern limits of the territory and discovered the Casa Grande ruins, then swung westward to the mouth of the Colorado River. There he met with some Indians who brought him, among other gifts, some blue shells, in exchange for presents he had given them.

These shells, trifling though they were intrinsically, were of immense importance to Kino. If other factors fitted in, they would be the key to the solution of a problem that had long occupied him. It had been stated and believed that Baja California was an island, not a peninsular extension of the continent. For a while the padre believed this himself, but was never thoroughly convinced. When he was assigned to work in Baja California, he, in company with others, made a trip across the land to the Pacific side. There he found the same type of blue shell that the Indians of the lower Colorado River region had given him. He knew that the shells did not occur in the Gulf, and deduced that they must come from the Pacific. Questioning the Indians, he learned that this was true, that there was a direct land route to the sea from their country, and that the shells had been carried across it—north of the termination of the Gulf.

The discovery was of immense importance to Kino, for he visualized a means of communication by land from his own missions to posts in Baja California. And he dreamed of a western extension of the chain he had built, making a connecting circuit. But time was running out, and he never saw the accomplishment of his dream; it was a task to be left to others.

During the period of nearly a quarter of a century that Father Kino had unselfishly devoted to colonization, and to Christianizing his widely separated flocks, he had the satisfaction of having accomplished at least part of what he set out to do. He had carved his name indelibly on the hearts of his people, and had forged a new frontier, making one of the finest chapters of history of the desert. But the path had not been always smooth. There were Apache raids in which missions and communities were destroyed, and an unfortunate uprising among his own people, begun by malcontents. He overcame these obstacles through his great strength of character, and stayed to see them through, when some of his own associates fled to save themselves.

As age and his manifold duties pressed upon him, he became weary in body, but not in spirit. He refused to give up to the very end. On a spring day in 1711 he had ridden over the mountains to Magdalena to inspect the new chapel built in honor of St. Francis. In the morning he was to celebrate a solemn mass of dedication. Donning his gold vestments, he went to the altar and began to read from the missal. His voice grew weak, and he sagged into a fainting spell. He was carried to his room by Father Campos, a fellow priest. It was reported that he refused to be put to bed. He indicated with his hand the sheepskin mattress and pack-saddle pillow that he had used throughout his long career, lying on the floor, and there he was placed. He died as he had lived, spurning the comforts that might have been his, had he so chosen. He was sixty-six years old.

The life of Father Kino has inspired several writers and historians who, from old documents in the archives in Mexico City and Spain, have given us an inspiring record of the accomplishments of this great missionary and colonist. A complete account of the famous Padre and his times will be found in the carefully documented and sensitively written work by Professor Herbert E. Bolton, entitled *Rim of Christendom*.

In keeping with the advance of progress everywhere, the passage of two and a half centuries from Father Kino's day has brought great changes to the land known as the Pimería Alta. A vast cattle industry, begun by the missionary-rancher, has grown and spread over every available area of rangeland. Agriculture has paced ranching, and in some regions has outstripped it, both in Arizona and in Sonora. In some places this may be a mixed blessing, for the growing of cotton and other crops places a heavy demand on water, and the drilling of deep wells to reach underground water has lowered the water table. In Kino's day such streams as the Santa Cruz, San Pedro, and Gila rivers ran full courses during the entire year; now they are full only in times of freshet. A short way from modern roads the land is still wild and primitive, and a horseman, following the padre's trails, might still encounter some of the hardships with which he met. Most of his missions have disintegrated from neglect, having been exposed to the ravages of the elements, aided and abetted by the ever-present vandals and relic hunters. They might all have suffered the same fate, had it not been for the followers of Father Kino.

These were the Franciscans—Order of Friars Minor—with whom, for some reason not clear, the King of Spain saw fit to replace the Jesuits who had laid the groundwork of colonization in New Spain. They took 174 up the work where Kino had left off, after a considerable interval had elapsed from the time of his death, slowly developed some of the missions and almost entirely rebuilt others. The edifices now extant are not as originally built. They have been altered, added to, and embellished; but they stand on the sites selected by Father Kino, and many of them contain a good deal of the original materials used in construction, plus towers, facades, and other details. Further restoration has necessarily been carried on since the time of the Franciscans, so that now many of the buildings differ in detail, though not in original exterior structure and design.

Visitors who wish to follow the Kino Trail through Pima Land may do so comfortably, on paved or well-maintained graded roads, but they will see only a part of the original chain of missions and *visitas*. The original edifice, Dolores, which was Father Kino's headquarters, has long disappeared. The site is some distance east of Magdalena, in a valley bordering the Santa Teresa Mountains. Remedios was situated north of Dolores. It, too, is gone. Cocospera, the next mission above, still shows traces of its former existence by the sad picture of a ruin. Other missions have sunk into the earth from which they were made to rise, showing little or no evidence.

Starting from Tucson, one may go south and visit the best-preserved and most impressive edifice first. This is San Xavier del Bac, one of the three Arizona missions established. Of the other two, Guevavi and Tumacacori, only the latter remains. Tumacacori, now a National Monument, is thirty miles south of San Xavier del Bac on the Nogales Highway. A tour of both missions is a fascinating day's trip.

If time is no object, an interesting trip takes in a larger area of country, and will give the visitor an opportunity to see the Organpipe National Monument, formerly mentioned. It is located a few miles north of Lukeville, the port of entry to Mexico. The Sonoran town opposite is Sonoyta, and from it the main road south and east goes through several interesting little towns—Tajitos is the principal one—to Caborca.

This is a lonely and very beautiful stretch of country crossing the heart of the Sonoran desert, and accommodations are not yet plentiful, as the road has been but recently completed. There is a good modern motel at Caborca, and it is well to plan on staying there. You will have time to see the mission in the afternoon, and can make an early start next morning to complete the loop.

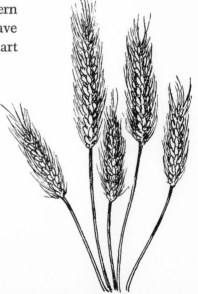

The Misión de la Concepción de Nuestra Señora is situated at the south end of town, on a dirt road, and is one of the finest of the remaining churches. It was built on the bank of the Río Concepción, the western part of the Río Magdalena (the names of rivers in Mexico are frequently changed as they pass through different sections). This is a broad watercourse, now dry during most of the year, but carrying an immense volume of wild churning waters in the rainy season. For a long period the church had been neglected, and erosion from flood waters had carried away part of the structure, including a convent that has not been replaced.

We first visited the mission in 1950, and work had begun on building a large stone dike to prevent further damage, and on restoration of the edifice. We climbed the narrow winding stairs of adobe bricks to the bell tower, where a fine view of the town and surrounding country may be seen. To our horror, we found the walls of the tower covered with initials, names, and other defacements, pecked into the mortar by the obnoxious goons who, unfortunately, infest every land. Some of the lettering was in Spanish, the rest in English, so the fault was not entirely due to the Mexicans. This occurred during the period of neglect, when free access could be had by anyone.

Work is now about completed, and a caretaker has charge of the premises. The altar and interior of the church have been restored in keeping with the original design, and services are held regularly.

The next stop east on the Kino Trail will be at Pitiquito, a small town lying a little way off the main highway. The church there is the Misión San Diego de Pitiquito. It is noteworthy for its very different construction, being built in a rather blocky form, with interesting domes. The main entrance is an arch, ornamented at the top. A series of broad steps, forming a semicircle, leads to it. The inside of the mission is very attractive, and has been well restored.

The small town of Altar is reached about twenty miles east of Pitiquito. It lies on the main highway, and in flavor and atmosphere it is indeed a bit of old Mexico. The church there is situated in the square, just off the paved road. Palm trees, shrubs, and lawns surrounding the building afford a contrast to most of the other missions, which are mainly situated on desert land, with only a few mesquites or *nopales* as accessories. This church was constructed in its present form long after Kino's death. Altar was a *visita* in the original group of missions, and the site was chosen by the padre, who visited his flock there on his rounds.

From Altar a dirt road leads to Oquitoa, and follows an irrigation flowage, which originates up in the Altar Valley from a large reservoir. The distance is about ten miles, and in the village the Misión San An-   176 tonio overlooks the valley. This is one of the most interesting of all the missions both in construction and surroundings. The churchyard is a large cemetery, filled with many ornate tombs and smaller decorated graves. This mission differs so radically in this respect that it is often commented on and is much photographed.

The building itself is different in design from the others, having a shell-like decoration over the arched doorway, with two columns rising

Misión de Concepción de Nuestra Señora de Caborca, Sonora

on each side to a horizontal ledge. Above this, a large semicircular section sweeps across the facade to the base of the bell tower, which contains two arched openings, each supporting a bell. This mission has been

Misión de San José de Tumacacori, Arizona

in use for many years, and has been repaired a great deal. Originally the structure was made entirely of adobe, and the long sweeping arch extending along the sides to the bell tower, together with the adobe texture of the front, gave the building a pleasing appearance that has been somewhat spoiled by the later application of stucco. The original texture may be seen on the sides.

Tubutama lies farther up the Altar Valley, along the irrigation ditch, and is the site of one of the most beautiful and ornate of the missions in Sonora. This is Misión San Pedro y San Pablo. The facade of the main structure is heavily ornamented with designs of shells, scrolls, and other motifs. It has been much worked on and restored, and probably has departed a long way from its original appearance when it was 178 completed by the Franciscans. The interior is beautifully done, with flowing arches, murals, and a simple altar.

The route is now retraced to Altar and the paved road, which leads east to Santa Ana, through a pleasant valley, bordered on each side by ranges of mountains. The distance is about forty-eight miles. The town of Magdalena lies eight miles north, on Highway 15, and its church is the Misión San Ignacio de Caborica. The present church is attractive, but it is not the original Kino structure, which has long been out of existence. It was situated several miles from the present church.

From Magdalena to the Port of Nogales is a distance of about sixty miles, and nineteen miles farther north, on the Tucson Highway, one of the most noted of all the missions is found. This is Misión San José de Tumacacori. While Father Kino did not build this church, he spent a great deal of time in the area and had a small temporary chapel nearby. The structure was erected by the Franciscans, in the latter part of the 1700's, and was slowly built over a period of years. It later became the scene of many bloody battles with the Apaches, who made periodic raids on the Pima occupying the region. It was then, of course, Spanish territory.

Tumacacori has had a checkered history. It passed through the hands of several families, and was looted, neglected, and left to the ravages of the elements. In 1908 President Theodore Roosevelt declared it a National Monument, after the property had been purchased by the government. While this act gave it protection, restoration of the edifice was not undertaken until about 1945. Only necessary repairs were made, and the structure stands now much as it was.

The museum on the grounds is an outstanding accomplishment in the graphic presentation of an era in history. It is a tribute to Kino and the other pioneer missionaries who, under the most difficult conditions, colonized this primitive land.

The several dioramas set in the walls are so realistic that they seem to be alive. Details are accurate and faithful, even to the expressions on the faces of the figures. One of them portrays Kino on his horse, accompanied by an Indian and his horse, overlooking the country from a knoll near a water hole, where cattle are drinking. Another depicts a bloody battle between the Apaches and the besieged garrison inside a mission building. The most impressive diorama is one showing the interior of the mission, restored as nearly accurately as could be determined from descriptions and the remaining vestiges of painted decorations and architectural construction.

The scene depicts a high mass in progress. The congregation, consisting mostly of the native Indians, kneels on the stone-flagged floor; there are no benches. At the rear are some Spaniards—*dons* and *damas*—dressed in their Sunday finery. The figurines are so skillfully made that the observer loses himself and is absorbed into the atmosphere of an age long gone, but that seems to be of the present. The illusion is completed by pressing a buttton on the wall. Soft music issues from the scene—the solemn strains of the liturgy, sung by a male *a cappella* choir: *"Agnus Dei, qui tolis peccata mundi—"*

The last mission of the chain is San Xavier del Bac, a few miles south of Tucson, on Mission Road. This is the largest and finest of them all, having received much attention in recent years. It lies in the Papago Indian Reservation, and the congregation is made up almost entirely of these people. The edifice looms up as a white form in the surrounding tawny desert, and is a landmark for miles around. Architecturally, it is a most pleasing structure, with towers, dome, and ornamental cornices. An unusual feature is the massive carved door, constructed of wide planks of mesquite wood. The altar is tall and broad, and is decorated with an intricate pattern of designs covered with gold leaf.

San Xavier is one of the tourist attractions of the Tucson area, and visitors are conducted through the church and grounds by priests who act as guides, and explain the history and background of the mission.

The mission era furnishes one of the finest chapters in the account of a fabulous land—the Pimería Alta, now better known as the Sonoran desert. Visitors who are not able to make the whole trip through Kino Land should at least see San Xavier and Tumacacori. They will evoke strange, and perhaps wistful, pictures of a period that lives now only in memory, and may someday be buried in the tumultuous events of our uncertain times.

FIFTEEN

DESERT SHORE COUNTRY

The fabulous Mar de Cortes is a land of beauty, mystery, and romance

THE WESTERN PART of the desert, in Sonora, encompasses a great area bordering the Gulf of California, which extends from the point where it receives the waters of the Colorado River, a few miles below the United States border, to its union with the open Pacific Ocean. This lies at a location slightly below the Tropic of Cancer, where the tropical zone begins, roughly with Mazatlán in Sinaloa on one shore, and Cabo de San Lucas in Baja California on the other.

The Sonoran desert might be said to stretch along about two-thirds of the eastern coast of the Gulf, with an extension to a great deal of the low-lying areas of Baja California. Owing to the rugged terrain of this vast strip of land, and lack of communication by improved roads, only a very small part of this fascinating country is presently available to tourists traveling by automobile.

Few regions in the many parts of the country through which we have journeyed, over a considerable number of years, have a stronger appeal than the area of the desert that lies along the Gulf in Sonora. To us it is truly *"La Tierra Encantada"*—The Enchanted Land. The fabulous Mar de Cortes is steeped in romance, both past and present. There the Conquistadores, in their explorations northward seeking the fabled Seven Cities of Cíbola, used the often-treacherous waters to sail the boats they had laboriously constructed; and, encountering the fierce *chubascos* that come up without warning, some of them came to grief. The Gulf is noted for its fickle moods. In fair weather it can smile, but when the fury of the tempest strikes it is one of the most dangerous areas of sea in this hemisphere. A place name suggests this ominous aspect. Between Tiburón Island and the mainland lies a narrow stretch of water where vessels from the earliest times even to the present meet with disaster. It is known as *el Estrecho de Infierno*, the Strait of Hell, and is popularly called the Graveyard of Ships.

Those who love the sea will find much to intrigue them—shrimp boats that put out from most of the coastal villages and towns; deep-sea fishing unsurpassed almost anywhere; a great variety of water birds; curving stretches of pure brilliant sand beaches, washed by waters that change from ultramarine blue in the distance, through purple to emerald and aquamarine, in the shoals, before breaking in a great surge of booming white surf. Grotesque masses of lava rock, the product of ancient volcanos, line the shores in places, or jut out of the ocean bottom to reach hundreds of feet into the sky. Seen as silhouettes in one of the matchless sunsets for which this region is noted, these angular scoria formations assume all sorts of weird shapes, some of which it is easy to imagine could be nothing more than petrified ghosts of the past.

In many parts of the coastal area great dunes line the shore and present wonderful windblown designs and patterns, accented by strange flowering succulent plants. The vegetation in the entire region is the delight of the plant lover.

Offshore, porpoises may frequently be seen, leaping in aerial maneuvers, their torpedo-like bodies cleaving the water in graceful arcs. And if you are lucky you may see a bewhiskered seal rise from the surface and eye you skeptically. The best part of this wonderful region is that here the visitor can be something more than a spectator. He can fish, from the shore or in a boat, for a great variety of finny quarry, dig clams, botanize, explore the fascinating low mountains back a little way from the coast, or search the beaches for beautiful, and sometimes rare, seashells. And if he is prepared to camp, as he must be to reach some of the more interesting places, the economy of the trip will be a pleasant surprise.

Starting at the upper end of the Gulf, one of the most readily available sites for visitors is Punto Peñasco, known more commonly by its English name of Rocky Point. It may be reached in an easy day's drive from Tucson, less than three hundred miles, all on pavement. As has been previously mentioned, the road goes through the Organpipe National Monument, and a visit to this unique area is well worth while.

The town of Rocky Point is an interesting little fishing village, and the harbor accommodates many shrimp and fishing vessels. On one of our visits in the spring of 1961 a small schooner, being made entirely by hand, was under construction. It had beautiful lines, and was much photographed by visitors. The village is situated on a hill overlooking the water, and is a quaint place, with interesting shops. About a half a mile before entering the town, a road on the right leads to a modern clean and well-kept motel with about sixteen units in the form of concrete buildings having two units to each structure. They are set high, well above the water, and afford a good view of the bay. Visitors who do not wish to camp can avail themselves of these facilities and be very comfortable.

Unfortunately, the shore at this site is very shallow and, being at the upper end of the Gulf, the bottom is muddy rather than sandy. The best fishing opportunities are located at Cholla Bay, about six miles from town on a sandy but passable road. This is another little fishing village where boats with guides may be rented for fishing of various kinds, according to season. An annual tournament is held at Cholla Bay, and the place has become quite popular. The shore fishing is not the best offered, because the bottom in most areas is very rough, with great masses of sharp volcanic rock, and the angler constantly loses rigs by getting hung up.

Another locality popular with fishermen who take their own boats is Puerto Lobos, the next good available spot south along the coast. "Available" is here used relatively, because Lobos has never been easy to reach because of the terrain. Though roads are occasionally worked on, they are difficult to maintain, and the trip is apt to be very rough and trying. This is another rocky area, and there are few good shore-fishing spots, but the more venturesome fisherman who takes a boat with him is often rewarded with superb sport.

Dropping down farther south along the coast, the next important point from the fisherman's view is Puerto Libertad. I write with affection of this lovely place, indented with little bays and sweeping stretches of curving shoreline. Rocky reefs jut out from the beach in several places, affording excellent points from which to cast a lure into the blue water. Here, too, one must be prepared to camp.

My wife and I first visited Libertad in the fall of 1949, in company with some American friends of Mexican ancestry, and a Mexican national and his wife who lived in Pitiquito. In those days the trip was rather rugged, much of it being over roads that were little more than desert trails. Without a competent guide it was easy to get lost on a *leñero's* (woodcutter's) side road and have to backtrack again to the main route.

We were living in Sasabe, on the border, and it was necessary to travel first to Altar and thence to Pitiquito, where a road that led to Libertad was picked up. In those days the road to Altar was badly neglected, and led, in a roundabout way, through several small communities—Los Molinos, Varselia, Paredones—over a badly gullied and often very sandy terrain. It was slow and painful going.

We had been to Altar, but knew nothing of the route beyond. In planning this trip, my wife asked Carlos what the total distance was.

"About a honderd an' eighty-five miles," he replied, after a moment of thought.

"And how much of it is bad?" she inquired.

"A honderd an' eighty-five miles," he answered with a broad grin. It was pretty nearly true, but things have changed vastly since then. The Mexican Government has taken an interest in promoting Libertad, along with many other attractive areas, as vacation spots for visitors. Work is being done on the road at regular intervals, in the way of grading and filling in bad rocky stretches. Since our first trip to Libertad, a hard road has been completed from Santa Ana, on Route 15, through Altar and Pitiquito to Caborca, the next town west. From there a new road has been established that cuts down much of the distance to the shore. If one is used to driving dirt roads and doesn't expect too much, it is no longer difficult to reach Libertad, and in much shorter time than was formerly required.

The community there is small as yet, but doubtless will grow. As this is written there are no motels, but they are being planned and probably will be built shortly. A series of communicating roads leads along the shores in either direction from the few buildings (one of them a clubhouse, privately owned) to a great number of secluded and desirable camping spots where one can be close to the water and have privacy.

From several standpoints the place that has appealed to us more than any other in the areas of the Gulf country where we have camped is Bahía Kino, Kino Bay. It is divided into two sections, Old Kino and, six miles north on a rough road made of coarse gravel fill, placed over 184 the otherwise impassable loose sand, New Kino. Old Kino is a typical little Mexican fishing community, with small adobe houses, many boats, and nets hung up to dry, making a picturesque setting. A couple of *cantinas* furnish beer, or stouter potables, to the thirsty, and a *tienda* has a few canned staples and some very nice straw hats made of native fiber, which can be purchased cheaply.

New Kino is much smaller, and the road to it follows a long curving strip of one of the most beautiful beaches I have seen anywhere. A short way out in the bay a pyramidal rock rises out of the sea to a considerable height. It has only a scant sloping shore before climbing upward. Much of the top and sides of this otherwise red lava rock are covered liberally with a white material that at first glance seems to be a patina of limestone. But a closer inspection through glasses shows it to be the guano deposited by countless generations of seabirds who roost there. This is Alcatraz Island, an unnotorious rock whose inhabitants are innocent of wrongdoing and crime. *Alcatraz*, in Spanish, in case the definition has escaped you, means "pelican." The word in more common use is closer to English—*pelícano*.

New Kino consists of a few cottages, at the end of the road, and a combination *tienda* and restaurant, run by a very nice family who have slowly built up the place. They have recently put in a long sloping pad of stone and concrete for the launching of boats brought by visitors. Several years ago they erected a series of half a dozen *cabañas*, made of black corrugated building paper, and braced against the wind by guy wires. Four of them are located on an eminence above a small cove, from which the view across the water, particularly at sunset, is lovely. Tiburón Island lies some fifteen miles offshore, and many seabirds trade back and forth. The shacks (which is really what they are) can be rented for a small fee. They have dirt floors and swinging wooden shutters that can be closed at night. Their big advantage, we have found, is a place of shelter from the winds that blow most of the time, and a handy place to set up housekeeping with folding table and camp stove. But they are not without certain perils. On one trip when we were unloading the duffel, a member of the party was about to place a box of provisions on the ground floor when he sprang back with alacrity. There in the spot he had chosen was a coiled diamondback rattler!

Sailfish

Having disposed of him in a permanent manner, we got busy with the insecticide and routed out several scorpions. One gets used to these things, but they should never be taken for granted. My wife and I always use the station wagon for sleeping and the cabins for housekeeping. But a number of our friends have slept in them, using cots, without incident. The water at New Kino is not trustworthy, coming from shallow wells, and it is necessary to bring along a supply that will last for the length of the trip.

The road to Kino Bay was improved and paved only a few years ago, allowing easy access to this fine resort area. With the completion of the gravel-road extension to New Kino, a development was started known as a *fraccionamiento* (subdivision). Lots were laid out, sidewalks installed, and water lines put down, to be serviced later by a large storage reservoir located on a hill nearby. A few cottages were built, but the development stalled for several years. It is now being resumed, and soon the place will be heavily populated with summer vacationers, mostly people from Hermosillo.

Temperatures are high all along the Gulf Coast in the summer, in spite of sea breezes, so it is not the best time to visit this area. Early November to about December (after which winter rains may be expected) and again in March and April are ideal periods, as few people frequent the place during the week. But weekends present a different picture, with crowded beaches, and are best avoided. The press of increasing population makes this inevitable in every country, and choice spots that still remain are hard to reach.

One of these is Tastiota (Estero Tastiota on the map), which lies south of Kino Bay. A hard road through agricultural country takes off to the south from the main Kino road, and leads to a large ranch, some twenty miles away. So far, so good, but then the ordeal begins. Tastiota is still twelve miles farther, and to reach it one must travel over one of the worst routes we have ever encountered. The "road" consists, for the most part, of pure silt, sometimes almost hub deep, which boils up in great clouds under the wheels, obscuring vision and all but choking you to death. The pace is a torturous seven or eight miles an hour, and you may easily get lost on one of the maze of trails that branch off in all directions.

Tastiota is a tiny fishing settlement, with a large lagoon connected to the Gulf by a strait several hundred yards wide. On incoming tides the fishing there is sometimes excellent; or it can be as flat as stale beer. Of the two trips we made to Tastiota, one was extremely successful from the angling standpoint, the other a complete washout. This is to be expected in fishing almost everywhere, but it seems to be particularly applicable to the Gulf. I have mentioned Tastiota in passing, but 186 without in any way recommending it. I would not care to incur the wrath of some reader who went there on my advice and had cause to regret it.

About ten miles north of Guaymas a road on the right leads to a resort area known as San Carlos. It has a good beach and is rapidly being developed, with motels and other tourist facilities.

The most popular of all resorts along the coast is Guaymas. It is world famous for its deep-sea fishing, particularly big game fish. There, annual tournaments attract anglers from many parts of the country who compete in what are known as "saltwater rodeos" for important prizes. Tourists who are interested in sea fishing can find dependable sport at any time of year. A fleet of good fishing boats is maintained, and they are captained by men who have grown up on the Gulf and know the best fishing grounds, besides the whims of the tides and weather. Guaymas affords all types of accommodations for visitors. It can be

Pompano

"plush" for those who want luxury in a fine modern hotel, or modest, in keeping with a simpler life. There are fine and reasonably priced motels, modern in every respect, and well maintained.

Saltwater fishing can mean several things, depending on what particularly interests the angler. If he wants big-game fish, marlin and sailfish, he can find sport throughout most of the Gulf area; but he will have to visit these waters during the summer and go out on a charter boat with a crew who know the game. In the cooler months there are many other species of fish—yellowtail, cabrilla, flounder, mackerel, to mention only a few—which can be taken by boat fishing. Heavy tackle, which is cumbersome, need not be carried, as it can be rented.

To a great host of fishermen, casting from the shore, in the surf or from a rocky point, offers something not found in boat fishing, and this is my preference. One can stroll from place to place, trying different

187

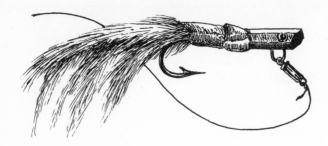

Feather jig, or pluma

spots and placing the casts to cover various areas of water that might harbor a fish in taking mood. The shore fisherman can be deliberate, taking time out between casts to watch the show being put on most of the time by the numerous seabirds, or stooping here and there to pick up a pretty shell along the beach.

The lure of the sea offers a powerful attraction to most anglers. Here is vastness and mystery. What lies beneath the surface directly in front of the fisherman? What strange marine creature may strike his next cast? The trout angler knows exactly what he is going to catch—trout. But he who casts his lure into the briny waters may hook almost anything; and he frequently does. These off-the-track experiences are what make the game so intriguing.

One evening at Kino as the sun was setting I decided to try a few casts before supper. It had been a dead day, with only a few small fish taking. Fifteen minutes of casting resulted in no strikes, and I was about to give up, when my wife called me to eat. "Just one more cast," I said.

Everyone who has ever wielded a rod knows the magic that may lie in that last try. I shot the wabbler out some forty yards, and slowly retrieved it with long sweeping pulls. It came within sight in the shallow water about twenty feet away, and suddenly a dark shadowy form swirled and struck it viciously. The rod arched and line stripped off the reel at a terrific rate—twenty, thirty, forty, fifty yards before I could stop the mad run. A sand shark, I thought, but as I had not brought a landing net I yelled to my oldest son for assistance. It took about five minutes to get the fish in close enough for a good look; much to our delight, we saw that it was a big corvina. It weighed fourteen pounds. When fishing in the sea one never knows what will happen next!

The Gulf offers a great variety of species, some of them among the most desirable food and game fishes to be found anywhere. Perhaps most abundant at all seasons of the year is a member of the weakfish family locally called corvina. This is a school fish that travels in large numbers and strikes artificial lures readily. A larger fish, growing sometimes to a hundred pounds in weight, is the totuava. It is a winter fish, usually appearing first in November. It often strikes a spoon or feather jig, and fish caught from the shore average about four or five pounds. My friend Art Almquist took one on a spoon, on one of our trips in November, and though we had no scale we estimated it to weigh 188 about fifteen pounds. On this same trip we took pompano, a small snook, and red snapper (*pargo,* in Spanish).

One of the finest of saltwater fishes, from the standpoint both of sport and food, is the *sierra,* or Spanish mackerel. It takes artificial lures readily and is a hellcat for fighting. A hooked mackerel will often whip its tail around a leader and sever it, or snap it by contact with its sharp fins, so a long bronze wire leader should be used on the rig. Mackerel are among the most delicious of food fish if cooked immediately after being caught; but storage of even a few hours on ice causes the oil to turn rancid and impart a strong and unpleasant taste.

Flounders are caught in the Gulf and may be taken with a spoon or wabblers in sandy situations. There is a trick to it that is worth knowing. Cast out and allow the lure to sink nearly to the bottom, then retrieve very slowly with little jerks. You can take flounders almost anytime by this method when school fish are not striking. The *baya* is a chunky, heavy-bodied fish that resembles a black bass slightly in conformation. It has an olive-colored background with irregular dark brown blotches. While it rates no claim to beauty or valor in a fight, its flesh is delicious.

Many other species of food and game fishes too numerous to recount here are taken; *pinta* and cabrilla are two of the most desirable. Among the oddities are small barracuda and triggerfish. The latter live among the rocks and may be taken with bait. Some people eat parts of them—they are mostly thick skin and bones—but when more delectable fish are not available I prefer hamburger.

Fishing from the shore may be done with various rigs—regular surf-casting outfits and bait-casting tackle are preferred by some, but almost everyone now uses spinning tackle. With a good rod, reel, and monofilament line, the best of sport is obtained. The tackle need not be heavy. I use a six-ounce rod, seven and a half feet long, and a small spinning reel that holds 250 yards of line, not over nine pounds test. It is amazing what can be done with this seemingly delicate tackle. If it is handled properly incredibly large fish may be brought to net.

Many types of lures are used. I have taken fish with bass plugs, both underwater and wabbling, in natural scale or red-and-white color. Probably the most effective all-around lures are metal wabblers, red and

Spanish mackerel, or sierra

Torote, *or elephant tree*

white, silver or copper, and feather jigs. (The Mexicans call them *plumas*.) They consist of a large hook with lead on the shank and long hackle feathers from a rooster, trailing out at the bend of the hook. Blue-and-white combinations are very effective, and sometimes red jigs work well. Mexican laborers, who seldom own tackle, fish with a *pluma* and coil of chalk line. They are expert at swinging the lure in a circle around their heads and letting it go at the right moment. As it zips out over the water the line, which is coiled on the beach, unwinds in loops and straightens out. They make casts of forty yards or more, then retrieve the lure in short jerks. It is a surprisingly efficient method, and a good performer can easily match a rod fisherman in results.

The coastal area of the desert is rich in a variety of strange plant forms, many of which are exotic and very interesting. It would require a considerable knowledge of botany to identify even the families to which some of these plants belong, let alone the exact species. Unfortunately,

190

popular guides, which are concerned with more northern forms, are of little help. But several oddities are easily identified and should be looked for by the visitor.

One of these is the *torote*, a strange, grotesque small tree that occurs in several locations along the coast. The trunk is thick in the lower parts, but loses diameter rapidly above. Twisted branches grow out at odd angles; they are thick and stubby. The popular name of this weird plant is "elephant tree" because of its shape and the color of its bark, which in old specimens is a grayish tint. The tree is generally small, but sometimes reaches a height of twelve to fifteen feet. Fruits are leathery and triangular, each bearing one seed. The leaves and sap are aromatic, having a pleasant fragrance. The sap is oily, and the inner bark, which is red, is sometimes used to make a dye or to tan skins of animals. On one occasion when firewood was scarce we used some dead branches of the *torote* to bolster up the evening campfire, but soon wished we hadn't. The smoke was so acrid that it drove us away. Specimens of the *torote* may be seen at Libertad, and there are many fine examples at Kino Bay.

In both of these localities, and in many other coastal areas, a giant cactus occurs. It resembles the sahuaro so strongly that it would pass unnoticed unless the difference was pointed out. This is the *sahueso*, or *cardón*. It grows from the earth in a single stout trunk, and

Sahueso, or cardón

old specimens bear many massive branches. In bulk and height it may be said to equal the sahuaro, but the principal difference lies in the texture of the branching limbs. In the sahuaro, these are regular and round throughout their length, but those of the *sahueso* are encircled by indented strictures at intervals, which roughly divide the branch into bulbous segments. This interesting cactus is found mostly near the coast, and does not grow far inland in its rather limited range. Going into Kino from Hermosillo, one first sees these giants about ten miles before the coast is reached.

In that area, and also in many others along the coast, the change in some—not all—of the pitahaya, or organpipe, cactus, already noted in the chapter on cactus, is very evident. The variation lies in the growth habit. The typical pitahaya sends it branches directly out of the ground in clusters, but in this variant, branches grow from a single thick trunk a yard or more in height.

Another interesting plant, not restricted to the Gulf region, but found growing at slight elevations back from the coast in the upper part of the area, is the *jojoba,* or goat nut. The leaves are leathery and gray-green, lanceolate and evergreen. It is a shrub from two to five feet in height. The fruit is a nut something like an acorn, edible, but not palatable because of a bitter taste due to a tannin content. The interesting thing about the *jojoba* is that the nuts contain an aromatic oil, which resembles a liquid wax and is used in the manufacture of pomades for the hair.

From Kino Bay south, mangroves begin to appear, marking a warmer belt. They grow in profusion along estuaries and brackish pools, and their twisted and matted branches, covered with decorative foliage, form refuges for many birds. The beautiful rose-colored *Murex* is found in this area, and many of the natives have the shells for sale. A large conch having a lovely pink and yellow interior shell also occurs in this mangrove region.

From the standpoint of unusual aspects of natural history, alone, the region of the Gulf of California in Sonora has more than enough to occupy the visitor for as long as he cares to stay.

Trunk form of pitahaya

Seri camp at Puerto Libertad. Blankets or tarps suspended from poles afford shade. Little attention is paid to physical comfort.

SIXTEEN

NATURE'S CHILDREN

For the Seris, the sunset trail;
for other tribes, a brighter future

THE REMNANTS of one of the strangest ethnological groups in North America are to be found along the upper part of the Sonoran coast of the Gulf of California. They are the Seri Indians, or, more properly speaking, the pathetically small handful of them that remains.

Originally they were a warlike race, and were the bane of peaceful tribes whose territory bordered theirs. They had the reputation of being unfriendly, and they kept to themselves. In general, the Seris resented the intrusion of the white man, and a long period passed before they would associate with him. They were a nomadic people, constantly on the move in their territory, which comprised the area from slightly below Kino Bay to a little north of Puerto Libertad. They formerly made their headquarters on Tiburón (Shark) Island, a large and long island lying off the Sonoran coast opposite Kino Bay, and extending northward. This is a wild and lonely place, with high mountains rising out of the sea, and very little comparatively flat shore.

Some of the Seris lived on the mainland, and also along the eastern shore of Baja California. In recent years the water supply, which came from springs in the mountains of Tiburón, failed, and the Indians moved to the mainland. They are people of the sea, expert boatmen and fishermen, and they spend much of their time on the water.

From the earliest time to the present the Seris have been a problem to which there is no easy solution. Their aloofness and lack of willingness to cooperate has been a sore trial, both to the Mexicans and to a number of well-meaning Americans who have tried to help them and improve their lot. A number of years ago the Mexican Government provided housing and facilities for them at Ures, a pleasant region on the Sonora River, north and east of Hermosillo. The Seris were moved in and established, but they didn't stay long enough to get acquainted. Singly, and in little groups, they stole away in the darkness of night and trekked across desert and mountains to the Gulf, their homeland. They were a marine people, and they wanted no part of inland country. The move was a psychological mistake.

Later, housing was provided, and a little colony established, at Desemboque, a point on the Gulf coast about midway between Kino Bay and Libertad. Several Americans took a great interest in them, and provided food, clothing, medicine, and other comforts. This is the nominal home of the Seris now, and a few of them live there permanently; but most of them cannot resist the spirit of wanderlust that is an inborn trait of the people, and they are off, to be gone for days or weeks at a time.

From a vigorous, belligerent, and arrogant people, the Seris have changed, in historic times, to a state of utter indifference. They wander aimlessly from one place to another, lack ambition, and have no apparent

194

desire for advancement or improvement of their condition. They are a dying race, and they seem to know and accept it. What each day brings is good enough, be it sun, storm, or hunger. According to a 1958 census, there were about only 250 Seris left, and it is doubtful that the number has increased since.

From the above rather gloomy picture it might be concluded that the Seris are lacking in any kind of talent, but such a conclusion would be hasty and unwarranted. It isn't that they do not have abilities, but rather that they lack the incentive to use them. Besides being skillful in handling boats and nets, in which they catch the huge totuava and other fish, the men are adept in the use of the harpoon with which they take langosta and the giant *caguama* (sea turtle). The women make wonderful baskets, which they weave skillfully from material derived from a species of the torote, a shrub that grows plentifully along the coast. The inner bark provides a red dye, which is used to stain some of the strips used in weaving. These strips are peeled from the wood of the torote, and are kept wet. They are woven around coils of pliable splints of the same plant and are manipulated by the use of a bone awl, which is kept sharp by being rubbed on a stone with abrasive qualities. The baskets are made in many shapes, a flat, concave dish form being a favorite. Some have necks like vases and others are bowl-shaped. Many intricate and beautiful designs are employed.

In recent years, fewer baskets are being made, and these mostly by the older women of the tribe. In spite of a greatly increased demand, and ever-mounting prices, the Seris cannot be induced to produce more. Basically, the trouble lies in their attitude. Money, to them, means not permanent comforts or advancement in their status, but the means of providing a feast, with plenty of mescal, to which they are inordinately devoted. Today is today, and tomorrow will take care of itself. They are true primitives.

We first met the Seris at Puerto Libertad, some ten years ago. A band of about thirty-five Indians was camped on the dunes in a patch of dwarf mesquite brush. For shelter they had scooped out places in the sloping sandbanks, and, using poles, ropes, and blankets, had erected rude tents. There were many old men and women, some younger people, a few children and several babies, besides a small collection of mongrel dogs. It was a scene that might have been enacted centuries before.

In startling contrast, another scene, a few yards away on the beach, transformed one abruptly into the present. There, two long sleek boats were drawn up on the sand. They were painted a bright green, and each was equipped with a powerful outboard motor. In the bottom of the boats lay giant totuava, weighing from 75 to over 100 pounds each. On the shore a Mexican fish merchant had set up a scale and a black-board. As he weighed each fish he chalked up a figure in pesos due the fishermen. An assistant placed the fish on ice in the nearby truck. When the weighing was done, the merchant paid the headman in cash, and departed, to follow a long, tortuous, and rough road, little more than a desert trail, that led to the market in Hermosillo.

It might be supposed from the boats and equipment that the Seris were more prosperous than it seemed; but we were told that the boats were supplied to the Indians on a loan basis, with the provision that fish and other sea products were to be sold only to the merchant. While the Seris have boats of their own, they are not to be compared to the ones mentioned, and are usually propelled by paddles.

We learned that this group of Indians had gone to Libertad to escape an outbreak of measles, which had become epidemic in Desem-

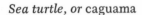

Sea turtle, or caguama

boque. The Seris, like some other tribes, are particularly susceptible to this disease, and several people had died. The group at Libertad had fled, and intended to stay until the trouble was over.

While the Seris speak no English, they are fluent in Spanish. Be-coming acquainted with one fine-looking young fellow, I was invited to go to the camp. The men were dressed in open-front shirts and blue jeans. Each wore a short apron of white material tied around his middle   196

with a tape, and a sheath knife attached to his belt. The hair was worn long, in two braids. The women were garbed in brightly colored squaw dresses that swept the ground.

They were a friendly lot, and we engaged in small talk about the weather, the fishing (we had had no luck with our rods, it being one of those dead spells that sometimes occur on the Gulf), and other trivial matters. I saw an old man squatted on the ground, stretching the skin of a *lobo marino* (seal) that had been taken in one of the deeply set fishnets. Another *anciano* was skillfully cutting long flakes of flesh from a large totuava and packing them in salt, for future use. Camp dogs sniffed and wagged their tails; children smiled coyly and hid behind their mothers' skirts. Here was an exotic picture, and I wanted to have a concrete reminder of it.

Taking aside the young fellow who had introduced me, I asked him about the possibilities of making some color shots with my camera. He said we would have to see the chief, but he thought it could be arranged— for a slight consideration. The chief was a wrinkled old fellow, neither unfriendly nor enthusiastic. He had probably gone through this many times before, and knew just how to act. We agreed on a price of 25 pesos (two dollars, American) which I thought reasonable enough. I was asked to wait for an hour before returning with the camera. This puzzled me at the time, but when I went back the reason became apparent.

I had noticed a girl of about twenty, with fine features and long braids of glossy black hair, when I was first there. She was dressed in a ragged drab-colored shirt and faded old blue jumper; except for her face, she looked like any other of the several younger people there. But upon my return, I was bowled over at the transformation that had taken place. She had put on a brightly hued flowing skirt and a purple blouse. Her hair was neatly combed and partly covered with a gay scarf. But the most startling thing was her makeup. Her face was painted with circles and whorls of red and purple. She had dolled up especially to have her picture taken. I was elated, and went to work.

Then followed one of the worst blunders of which I was ever guilty—an incident about which I can still scarcely bear to think. Going from one group to another, I took several shots. There was one of the old man flaking fish, another of the seal-skin stretcher, and of course I concentrated on the young lady who had so thoughtfully made up just for the occasion. Having finished the film, I rolled it up and put it in a pocket. After having talked for a few minutes and arranged another group, I reached in my pocket for a film and reloaded the camera, then innocently took a series of shots. Of course I didn't know it at the time, but it was the wrong pocket, and the wrong film—the one that had already been exposed! When it was processed later there was a great light streak through the center, with an odd assortment of legs, faces, a montage of mixed and unrecognizable objects and, clear as crystal, one little white dog. It was a real cute dog, too.

While we have bumped into Seris here and there on various trips to the Gulf, we have had little occasion to be in contact with them. But another incident, amusing in some of its aspects, is worth relating. We were camped at Kino Bay, in our favorite spot above a cove overlooking Tiburón Island. On the second day three long Seri boats pulled in and emitted an astonishing number of men, women, and children. We noticed that one of the women lifted several live hens from a boat and dumped them on the shore, allowing them to fend for themselves. The Indians settled down in an arroyo about two hundred yards from our camp and put up the usual blankets on sticks for shelter, built fires, and cooked a meal. They kept looking at us speculatively, but couldn't get up courage to come over. Then the woman who had turned the chickens loose had a bright idea. She noticed that they had strayed some distance from camp and were headed in our direction. Seizing the opportunity she followed and pretended to shoo them back. But by some adroit flank movements she actually drove them closer to our

Seri basket

camp. It was like the fellow who walked into the ball-park gate backward, on the theory that the ticket man would think he was going out. Within hailing distance, we asked her what she wanted. She started enumerating various desirable items, as we had suspected, but we told her firmly, *"Ahorita, no. Mañana, posiblemente."* This was not a flat turndown, and it was understood. She left, driving her flock ahead.

198

In the morning I walked over to the camp and entered into conversation with a chap who seemed to be the headman. A girl and an older woman were making baskets. A finished one lay on the ground, and I inquired the price. It was reasonable, and I bought it. But the basket that the woman was working on promised to be a beauty, and I wanted it. It was only partly completed, and we were leaving shortly after noon on the following day. It was imperative that we go, having a long trip ahead, but I did want that basket. Knowing the Indian's proverbial lack of time sense, I had doubts that the basket would be finished, but I gave it a try. I report the conversation in Spanish, because an English translation loses the flavor.

"*Cuando estará listo?*" I inquired of the headman.

He looked at the basket, but never consulted the maker, who was busily plying the awl in weaving strips of torote. After a moment's consideration he pointed to a place in the southwestern sky.

"*Cuando el sol esta allá,*" he replied.

"*Como las dos de la tarde?*" I answered, "*Bueno. Sin falta.*" I emphasized the last, looking at him intently.

There wasn't a watch in the outfit, but promptly at two o'clock the next day they came—the headman, the woman and girl basket makers, and several others. We bought the baskets; then came the requests. They wanted *camisas viejas* (old shirts), pants, towels—anything we had in the way of clothing. But particularly they asked for *anzuelos*—fishhooks. I dug out a handful of old ones, some rusty, from the tackle box and made the mistake of handing them to one of the men. Immediately a woman poured out a perfect torrent of Seri, glared at him, and held out a demanding hand. He shook his head and looked away. I should, of course, have distributed a few hooks to each of them and everyone would have been happy; but I had assumed that they would be distributed. The thing upset me so that I blurted out, "*Dále unos!*" in probably what was a commanding voice. He looked at me, at her, and then at the handful of fishhooks. After considerable deliberation he selected two very bent and rusty ones, and with an ingracious grunt shoved them at her. She smiled at me gratefully, but he wore a sour look as they walked back to their camp.

Little is known about the ancestors of the Seris, but from the scanty evidence that is occasionally found it has been concluded that they were probably more advanced, culturally, than their descendants especially the few who remain. They are thought by some archaeologists to have lived about five hundred years ago. Along some of the dunes, shards of pottery of remarkable thinness and hardness are found. They vary in color from gray to red, and many of them are polished to a semiglaze. Some examples are as thin as a sixteenth of an inch. This is in marked

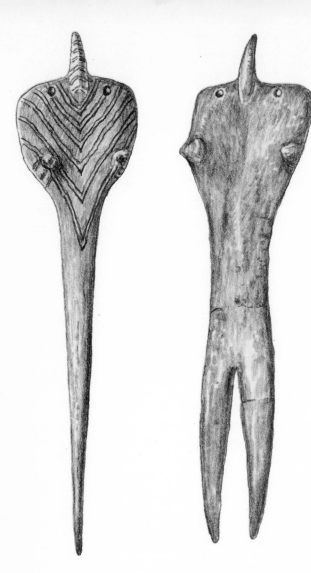

Clay figurines from the Gulf of California area in Sonora. Thought to be of pre-Seri origin, little is known about them.
Drawn from a collection in the Museum of the American Indian, Heye Foundation, New York City, through the courtesy of that Institution.

contrast to most pottery of more northern races. The shards are undecorated. While the present-day Seris are good basket makers, they do not produce pottery, as a general practice. The most remarkable cultural evidence found has been in the form of clay figurines. These were made in the shape of marine creatures, principally stingrays, with long tails, and curious rounded upper sections having human breasts, and terminated with a tapering snoutlike head. Some of the examples were bifurcated, having two appendages. Most of them were decorated with designs of lines and some had stippled areas. The majority have two small holes at the top, like eyes that were probably used for suspension. The effigies were made of clay and then fired to a reddish color. Some badly burned specimens have been found, suggesting the possibility of cremation of the dead—or this may have been the result of overfiring during manufacture.

The figurines are thought to have been fertility symbols, used in religious rites, but nothing definite concerning their use can be stated. A fine collection may be seen at the Museum of the American Indian, in New York City. The accompanying drawings were made from examples 200 in this collection, with the kind permission of my friend Dr. Frederick J. Dockstader, Director of the Museum.

Well-chipped arrowheads of pitchstone, obsidian, and chert have been found in the dune country, indicating that the earlier Indians were probably hunters, in addition to living off the products of the sea. Flat metates and manos made from the native granite suggest the use of meal, possibly made from the dried seeds of the pitahaya and sahuaro. A few stone and clay pipes have been found.

The subject of Indians is a fascinating one, and people with a particular interest in them have ample opportunity to visit several settlements in various parts of the desert, to become acquainted with the inhabitants and perhaps purchase some of their beautifully made products.

The passage of the years since Father Kino's day has brought changes to locations of some of the Indian tribes. The constant raids of Apaches, in the era after Kino's passing, made the southern region of Pimería Alta untenable, and the Pimas moved northward. Today they are located on a reservation in the vicinity of Gila Bend, above the Papago country. The latter people live on a large reservation that includes a small area around San Xavier del Bac. The largest part of the population lives in the region west of the Pozo Verde Mountains, and a little way into Sonora. On the west the boundary reaches almost to Ajo and extends to a little south of Casa Grande on the north, in an irregular pattern.

The town of Sells is the Papago tribal headquarters, and also the center of the basketmaking industry. An annual rodeo is held there early in October, and it attracts many visitors. Baskets and other native products are offered for sale in the shops. Papago baskets are among the finest produced by any of the Indian groups. The workmanship is meticulous, and the baskets are more closely woven than those of the Seris. A great variety of designs is employed, and each has a meaning. Motifs include sahuaro, lightning, clouds, animals, and many other natural symbols. Several dyes are employed, and the black areas are made of strips of the tough and enamel-like outer cover of the devil's-claw (*Martynia*), which is peeled from the long hooks after soaking in water.

The Yaquis still live in their historic territory, in the vicinity of the river named for them, in southern Sonora from below Guaymas to about the Sinaloa line. They are a fine race of people with many talents, and have always been noted for their mechanical ability. As far back as the early part of the century, Carl Lumholtz, in his excellent book *New Trails in Mexico*, refers to this talent. He stated that the average Yaqui Indian could quickly learn to run engines and other devices, repair machinery, and build almost anything. This trait has lasted, and the Yaquis are in demand as workmen on construction projects, whenever they are available. They are also very musical and make several types of instruments, among them a unique harp of their own design. We once heard a performance by a group of Yaqui musicians, and were particularly impressed with the fine clear tones of the harp.

In early times the Yaquis were a warlike race, causing much trouble with neighboring tribes and with the Mexicans. But they took to Christianity with a wholeheartedness that has never left them. Their Easter ceremonies are colorful and are widely attended. Though basically Catholic, the rites include some of the traditional pageantry of the tribe. When the Yaquis settled their differences with the Mexican Government, not so long ago, a small group moved to a locality in the vicinity of Tucson, and the annual Easter ceremony there is a colorful and noteworthy event, attended by many visitors.

The Pimas, greatly reduced in numbers, live on their small reservation and, in addition to some native crafts, work in the fields. They are reliable and steady and are much in demand.

It is heartening to note that, in marked contrast to the Seris, all of the races of Indians—Papagos, Pimas, Yaquis, Maricopas, even the once-fierce Apaches—have improved their position in life and are good and useful citizens. While it is regrettable that they are gradually losing their native traditions, and to a great extent their unique arts and crafts, we must face the fact that the same thing is happening to the peoples of the entire world.

Whether the end results will be to the benefit—or detriment—of the human race only time will tell. "The old order changeth . . . "

La Fiesta

SEVENTEEN

SONORA,
THE BEAUTIFUL LAND

*Our neighbors to the south—their customs,
temperament, and way of life*

"I'D LIKE to go to Mexico for a visit—I've read a lot about it and understand it's a wonderful country—but I hear that it's no place for an American. They say that unless you speak Spanish, and know what it's all about, you'll get robbed blind. Those Mexicans just don't like Americans; all they want is the American's dollars. And I guess they need plenty of them, because they say that the country is all run down, and going to pot fast."

"I'd like to go to Mexico, but—" "They say—" "I hear—"

This is such a familiar and oft-repeated theme that it spins around in one's head like a broken record. It parallels a groove, which harps on misconceptions concerning the desert: "Swarming with poisonous snakes, scorpions, and deadly tarantulas; unbearable heat and drought; beautiful, perhaps, but dangerous to visit."

These statements, of course, come from people who have never been near the land, and base everything on rumors that are founded on ignorance. They prefer to believe these tales, rather than to find out for themselves. Prejudice, and fear of the unknown, prevent many honest and right-minded people from enjoying experiences that could open a whole new world to them.

Concerning the charges, there may be truth in some of the statements. Mexicans certainly don't like Americans—of a certain type. Neither do other Americans like them; nor, for that matter, would even the saints of Heaven, who are reputed to be tolerant of human weakness. These are the boors—brazen, pushy people who attempt to bull their way through all situations, utterly lacking in manners, and devoid of the virtues associated with ladies and gentlemen. Unfortunately, they are the one type that takes to travel, and they may be found in all foreign lands, ignoring local customs, attempting to push the natives

Mesquite corral

around, and generally giving Americans a bad name. Because of its proximity to the United States, Mexico is particularly vulnerable to this vulgar breed of visitor. It is not difficult to see that it takes only a comparatively small number of these obnoxious individuals—fortunately the great majority of people visiting Mexico are ladies and gentlemen —to sour Latin-American relations, rather than improve them. The wonder is that the Mexican people, on the whole, are as kind and tolerant as they are. Having spent considerable time in Mexico, we have witnessed a good deal of behavior on the part of American tourists that was little short of sickening. Loud and noisy women, attired in colored pants, and equally boisterous men, rigged out in gaudy Hawaiian shirts and Bermuda shorts, appearing for dinner in one of the finest hotels in Hermosillo; bossy orders barked out to the waiter in a commanding voice; purposely unguarded remarks about the terrible service, poor food, and pitiful condition of everything in general—these are typical examples. One of the most flagrant incidents illustrative of this lamentable kind of behavior happened to me, an American, just a little while ago.

I was standing on a corner in Nogales, Sonora, waiting for my wife, who was shopping in a *tienda*. Dressed in western pants, open-front shirt, and straw hat, I probably looked like a workman; or at least not like a tourist. Two flashily dressed women approached me, and one of them—without a "pardon me"—stared at me hard and barked out curtly, "Do you understand English?" This sort of rocked me, but I replied that I did.

"Well, then, where's that little park?"

"What park, madam?" I asked.

"Why, it should be right over there, but we can't find it. It's near the gate where we came in, and we want to get out of this place."

They had been walking in the wrong direction, and I advised her, with as much restraint as I could muster, that if they would turn around and walk the other way they would find the park—and the port gate. She glared at me as though I were responsible for their troubles, turned on her heel, took her companion by the arm, and strode away haughtily, without even the hint of a "thank you."

I fervently hope she found the gate, walked through it, and kept right on going. We have troubles enough in our own country with people like that, without imposing them on the Mexicans.

"But how does one get along in Mexico without speaking Spanish?" It is a curious thing that people travel to Europe—to France, Germany, Italy, the Scandinavian countries—without knowing a word of the languages spoken there. They never mention the question of the language barrier. "Everybody goes to Europe; it's the thing to do, you know. But, my dear, *Mexico—!*" Tradition is a hard thing to knock down. Mexico. The land of revolutions, of poverty, of unsanitary conditions (this is never mentioned in connection with France or Italy, possibly because they are "glamorous"), of a fiery, short-tempered race of people. Mexico. There seems to be something sinister in the very word. The gap that exists between the philosophies of the two countries—and there definitely is a gap—is largely caused by a lack of understanding, on the part of tourists, of the nature and customs of the Mexican people. Too often, it is due to a lack of desire to understand. We Americans are an impatient lot. We want things done *right now*, and we want them done in our way. We are so used to driving—in business, in play, even in our social lives—that we can't tolerate people who do things differently. We can't understand why they don't "get right in there and pitch," get the thing done. It never occurs to us that perhaps peoples of other lands—and this applies markedly to Latin America—prefer to take time out to live, a virtue that, I fear, we have sadly neglected.

So, in our eternal rush, we lose patience, and show it. Now, this is exactly the wrong way to get anywhere in Mexico. One does not have to be "south of the border" long to sense that the tempo is decidedly slower, that the whole attitude of the people is calmer and more leisurely. The tourist who wipes the grim look off his face, smiles, and accepts situations as they come—even though they are not always to his liking—is the one who will be accepted, even though he does not speak the language. Mexicans are intuitive to a high degree. They can sense who is a "right guy," to use our slang, and who isn't, and they will go to any length to please such a visitor. He is "*simpático*," a wonderful Spanish word frequently used to denote a kinship of spirit, and if he possesses this quality he holds the key that unlocks the treasure chest of the whole wonderful land. The best advice that any tourist can be given is to leave the "rat race" behind, calm down, and travel leisurely from day to day with an open mind and observing eyes. The tourist who accepts this principle, and goes along with it, learns that the overworked word, *mañana,* is not literally what people think it is. It has come to be associated with the lazy peon, hunched against a patio wall, sound asleep, when he should be working. This symbol of "the siesta" is thought to go on interminably, so that nothing is ever accomplished in Mexico. In fact, the notion is so widespread that the Mexicans themselves regard it as a great joke, and they employ the motif in pottery, ceramics, and decoration—to be sold to tourists. Actually, *mañana* is a word having a significance that we often apply to our own way of life, with profit. It means that not everything necessarily has to be done today. "*Mañana estará un otro día.*" Tomorrow will come, and with it perhaps a new outlook on a problem that today is baffling, simply

because we have driven ourselves too hard. Our neighbors to the south
have one great quality that we, as a nation, too often lack. It is patience
—the virtue of being able to take things as they come, to work steadily
and unhurriedly, and not to get too upset when things don't go just right.
They have an adage in the form of a joke which has a deep meaning:
"*Paciencia, pulga, larga es la noche!*" Patience, flea, the night is long!

People who live in the Southwest—Texas, Arizona, New Mexico,
southern California—have this same feeling for a slower tempo, and
time to enjoy life as they go. For one thing, there is a large population
of people of Mexican ancestry in all these states; but it is not only
that. Westerners have always been noted for their hospitality and tolerance. The stranger notices it at once; it seems to pervade the air, and
he does not have to stay long before becoming infected with it himself.
If he lingers awhile in Arizona before visiting the Sonoran part of the
desert, he will have time to shake off some of the stiffness and conven-
tion that cling to him from custom, and he will not find Mexico nearly so
strange as he had imagined.

The progress that has been—and is being—made in the Republic of
Mexico, within a comparatively recent space of time, is little short of incredible. Cities and towns blossom with fine modern buildings; roads
are being improved and surfaced; education is given top priority, so
that now children in even the most remote areas will not grow up as
illiterates; great progress is being made in a nationwide health and
sanitation program (as an example, malaria has been practically eliminated throughout the Republic), and agriculture has been modernized
to the degree where it compares favorably with other regions.

Hermosillo (loosely translated as "The Little Beautiful") serves well
as a model of what is happening all over Mexico. It is the capital of
Sonora, and is located about 175 miles south of the border at Nogales,
on Route 15. The Sonora River is dammed and forms a large lake to the
east, and its course is through the city, which lies in a beautiful valley,
surrounded by many hills and low mountains. The climate is semitropical
(frosts are practically unknown), and gardens in homes along practically all streets are brilliant with the hues of many exotic plants—
hibiscus, *bugambilia* (Spanish for bougainvillaea), *árbol de fuego, copa
de oro*—besides all northern garden plants that bloom continuously.
Bananas, oranges, limes, avocados, papayas, and other fruits grow as
thriftily as do apples in the north. And the wonderful, thickly foliated,
and handsome *yucateco* trees that furnish shade, and rain-impervious
shelter, never fail to excite the admiration of visitors. These are but a
few of the things that contribute to the charm and beauty of this
lovely little city in the desert. We first visited it about fourteen years ago,
207   shortly after the main highway from Nogales had been surfaced. It was

a city of something over twenty thousand people, lovely then as now, but with a sleepy quality strongly steeped in the flavor of an older Mexico. Many of the streets were unpaved, and buildings in want of repair were evident in many places. Tourist accommodations were insufficient, and aside from a couple of hotels, not of the best quality. With the exception of some new buildings that were just being started, there was nothing to indicate that things wouldn't go on indefinitely as they were. On subsequent visits, a year or two apart, we were struck forcibly with the change that was taking place. New buildings had sprung up, replacing some of the dilapidated ones. Many of the dusty streets had been paved; and the main highway, leading into town, had been widened into a broad dual strip, illuminated at night with rows of tall streetlights, forming an attractive *esplanada.* The Biblioteca, an impressive and beautiful edifice that houses the library and museum, had been finished, as had the new and modern hotel, situated in the square at the center of town. Motels were being built on the outskirts, and modern gas stations, with complete service facilities, were replacing the makeshift ones of former days. The change taking place was like watching the growth of plants in a well-tended garden. Each visit turned up something new. One year an exposition was held; and the motto adopted, which was displayed on signs everywhere, went a long way toward explaining the transformation that was taking place. It read: SONORA ADELANTE! (Sonora forward).

Progress has never stopped, and many new industries have sprung up. With the increase of population, fine homes, constructed in excellent taste, are being built yearly in great numbers in the suburban area. Yet, with it all the Hermosillans have had the good sense to keep the older parts of the city as they were. The narrow streets, lined with solid rows of stuccoed buildings, with their wrought-iron window and door grilles; the enclosed patios that one glimpses while passing by an open door; the flash of color from tropical flowers, parrots and other brilliantly hued birds—these traditional reflections of the Spanish period are still there.

The visitor should see the historic old cathedral—perhaps attend a high mass on a Sunday morning, and listen to the magnificent *a cappella* male chorus. He should browse around in the old and typically Mexican *mercado,* should see the university, the parks, gardens, the *tiendas* and many shops that vend not only the products of Mexico but of many other countries also.

Hermosillo is not just another town; it is something very special, with a flavor all its own. The tourist who takes sufficient time out to sample it will be well rewarded.

The obstacle of the language barrier, which deters many people 208 from visiting Mexico, is not as insurmountable as it might seem. In practically any section nowadays someone speaks English—at least enough to get along, so one need not feel hopelessly stuck if one has no Spanish at all. This is particularly true in urban areas. It seems that, with the great increase in tourism in Mexico, everyone who is interested in business, or has contacts with the public, is eager to learn English. Many of them purchase easy courses, in book form, and study diligently, attend motion pictures in English, and avail themselves of every opportunity to learn and improve. They are to be commended, and it might be hoped that Americans who are really interested in Mexico, and intend to visit it frequently, would take as much interest in learning something about Spanish.

As is true with any language, the matter of pronunciation is a hurdle that trips most learners. We, who have grown up with English, need not be told that it is one of the most inconsistent, puzzling, and at times frustrating tongues ever evolved. No wonder, then, that the Latin often gets himself into amazing, and sometimes funny, scrapes when he wrestles with the mysteries of pronunciation. His tendency to say *ee* for the short *i* so frequently used in English words is one of his greatest stumbling blocks. And, for some strange reason, he invariably reverses the vowel sound where he shouldn't. Thus, he says, "eet ees" for it is, and "titch" for teach. This may lead to some weird effects, to say the least.

Once we were camping on the Gulf, in company with some Mexican friends, on a bluff overlooking a sandy cove. It was a beautiful spot, and Rosita (I'll call her that), quite overcome with the sunset sky and the strip of sun-bathed shore in front of us, exclaimed rapturously, in a mixture of Spanish and English, "Ay *que bonito!* W'at a bee-you-tee-fool bitch!"

The word *too*, used in a comparative sense, is another stickler. A few years ago we had a car that developed a cracked frame, and a Mexican cowhand and handyman on a neighboring ranch volunteered to weld it with his portable outfit. "Preetty bad," he said upon examining the fracture, "eet ees veree lah-kee you deescover heem too soon." Pepe had a real talent for mangling English, so much so that he was the butt of jokes by his countrymen, many of whom had not worked at studying the language nearly so long as he had. Pronouns were his particular bane, and he threw them around indiscriminately. He was the author of a phrase that became a classic, along with other Pepeisms. "I'm like de tequila veree moch. I can dreenk heem all night, an' in de morning I don' got de hang-up."

Now, if all this sounds very funny to us, consider how the Mexicans feel when we start toying with their language. Here again, pronunciation can not only change meaning; it can also create some laugh-producing results. Take, for example, two of the vowels: *a* is always pronounced ah (never ă, as in cat, nor ā, as in fate); *o* is always ō, as in tone. With this rule in mind, it is easy to see how the mispronunciation of a single vowel can change the meaning of a whole sentence. Here is a case:

An American lady hired an attractive young Mexican girl to work as a domestic. The girl spoke no English, and the lady had only a smattering of Spanish; but she was industrious and got down to work, with the aid of a simplified course. One day, just before lunch she asked the girl *"Tiene hombre?"* The girl blushed slightly and averted her eyes. This puzzled the mistress until she later sought help, and got the thing cleared up. She had meant to say, *"Tiene hambre?"*—Are you hungry? (literally translated, Do you have hunger?) But what she really said was, "Do you have a man?"

Most people who live in the border country speak at least a little Spanish; many are fluent in the language. While, as previously stated, it is not a necessary adjunct to traveling in Mexico, the knowledge of a little Spanish—often-used phrases, common categories of words, polite expressions—is literally an open sesame, as one goes along. People with whom the tourist comes in contact appreciate visitors who are willing to attempt at least a little of their language even though the grammar may be mixed up, and the thought not always clear. They are particularly impressed with those who take the pains to cultivate a correct and pleasing pronunciation. Nothing is much more distressing than to hear the language spoken with what has jokingly come to be known as a "New England accent."

One does not stay in Mexico long without becoming impressed with the lighthearted and apparently carefree character of the people. Wherever the visitor goes he hears laughter, animated conversation, a song, or a merrily whistled tune. It seems that no one has a trouble or care; all is sweetness and light. If it were true we should have come close to approaching Eden on earth; but, regardless of country or nationality, we know that this idyllic state cannot exist in this world. The Mexicans have troubles—plenty of them—but they have developed the delightful faculty of keeping them concealed. The deadly seriousness that masks the faces of so many of our people is noticeably lacking in most parts of Mexico, except for a few grouches, who are found everywhere.

Perhaps the greatest single factor contributing to the character of the Mexican people, as a whole, is their universal and never-failing sense of humor. They prefer a cheerful outlook to a gloomy one, and are ever ready to be amused by the simplest things. They are observant of natural things, and will laugh heartily at the antics of a dog burying 210 a bone, or a sparrow struggling to place a big and unruly twig in a nest it is building. Laughter is always close to the surface. It seems to explode spontaneously, on the slightest provocation. They love to twit each other, but they also possess the virtue of being able to laugh at themselves. Humorous nicknames are common, and once bestowed they stick for life.

A man in a small border village was noted for his ineptness and lazy disposition. When hired, he was apt to fall asleep on the shovel handle. Someone dubbed him *"Caballo y medio"* (Horse and a Half). At first he was proud of the title, thinking that it referred to his working ability. But eventually he was badly let down when he came to realize what the people really meant: that he *ate* like a horse and a half.

The *broma* (joke) is as much a part of the Mexican's daily life as are tortillas and frijoles. He is always eager to hear new ones, and often invents ingenious ones of his own, which he springs on his friends. Sometimes he will venture to try one on a tourist, if his intuition tells him that it will go across.

Once in Sonora, on a return trip northward, we came to a Caseta de Inspección, a small station where you are checked for fruits and vegetables, similar to our agricultural inspections between certain states. A pleasant young officer came out, greeted us, and in a serious tone said, "Do you hav' any mar-ee-whana?" "No," I replied, wondering what it was all about. "Do you hav' any 'er-o-een?" he continued, keeping a poker face. "No." "Do you possibly hav' a gude American ceegaret?" he ended up, with a broad grin. We both had a hearty laugh, and I handed him the remainder of the pack in my pocket. With his type of head, that fellow was bound to go places!

Typical of the universal sense of humor is the practice of putting signs on trucks, and labeling small places of business with quaint names. Some of the mottoes are original and whimsical. A sign on a dilapidated old pickup read: *"Me ves—y sufres!"* See me—and you suffer. Others are borrowed Americanisms, literally translated into Spanish. The sign on the front of a panel truck said, *"Acá viene José,"* and the rear sign read, *"Allá va José."* Here comes Joe. There goes Joe. During the height of the flying-saucer excitement, several years ago, a small café owner named his place, "El Disco Volador."

Many trucks carry the names of the owners' sweethearts or wives, as boats are often titled in this country—Conchita, Dolores, Pepita, Consuelo. And religious mottoes are frequently encountered. An experience we have never forgotten occurred on a very narrow stretch of road, covered with deep and loose sand, in northern Sonora. The section was known as the "Angostura" (narrows) and there were few places where cars could pass. We were about midway, and turtling along in second

School Zone

Open Range

Graphic road signs in Mexico

211

Los Lenadores, *or the woodcutters*

gear, when a large truck appeared, coming in our direction. Here was a predicament! To stop might have meant getting stuck, so I crawled along, hoping to find a by-pass. When we were within a couple of hundred yards of the truck, I saw the driver motion me to come on. He then cut the wheel sharply and climbed part way up a sloping bank, freeing the road for us to pass. He smiled broadly as I went by and thanked him. There was just time to note the big fancily lettered sign on the bumper of the truck. It read, *"Que Dios Bendiga Su Camino."* May God Bless Your Road. That driver really believed what he preached!

Food is a topic of never-ending interest to everybody—everywhere. Tradition affects our tastes in diet as much as it does our habit of dress, and our customs in general. One of the first questions asked by the prospective traveler to a foreign country is, "What is the food like?" France is the land of the gourmet, justly renowned for its exquisite dishes, and there are those who, placing the pleasures of the table above all else, make pilgrimages there just to eat and partake of rare wines. 212

The Germans set a magnificent table, groaning with their famous recipes, calculated to tempt even the most stouthearted dieter to break down and add unwanted pounds. In Italy it is pasta in an unending number of delectable forms, plus meats, fish, and seafood cooked in a mysterious and mouth-watering manner. But Mexico? Ah, that is the land of gustatory fire—of throat-searing dishes that bring tears to the eyes and pains to the stomach. Nobody but a native can eat them.

Now, to be perfectly frank, this is true—but only partly so. For generations untold, the Mexican people have used hot condiments as a part of their daily diet—chiles, *jalepeños chiltipiquínes* (little peppers slightly larger than a pea, which are dried and powdered. They are so powerful that women preparing them must protect their fingers with cloth, when crushing them, *to prevent burning the skin*). It is not to be wondered that some old people who have used these fiery condiments over a long period of years have literally burned out their taste buds, and can no longer enjoy plain food.

But it is a mistake to think that this practice is typical of the dietary habits of all Mexico. Many of the people do not use hot adjuncts to their food at all, and the great majority show a preference for the milder forms of condiments.

The degree of food seasoning may roughly be divided into three classes: *bravo*, *picante*, and *blanda*. If your Mexican host wags a finger in warning and says it is *bravo*, you'd better believe him. Even a taste will subject your tongue to a searing that is better imagined than experienced. *Picante* is the term employed for foods that are mildly seasoned—depending on the amount of condiment used. This is usually *chile colorado*, the red pepper with the distinctive flavor present in many Mexican dishes—*chile con carne, tamales, tacos*. When chile is used sparingly in such foods, they are delicious, and no discomfort is experienced in eating them. Restaurants along main routes of travel, that cater to tourists, will prepare dishes with just the amount of chile you wish. If you say, *muy poquito*—a very little—you'll be all right. And here's a hint that we learned long ago, from the Mexicans; drink a bottle of *cerveza* (beer) with the meal. It acts as an aid to digestion. *Blanda* simply means food without condiments, cooked naturally. If you have a squeamish stomach, they are for you.

In the latter category are *guisados* (stews), *asados* (roasts), and steaks and chops, broiled over a charcoal fire. Ask for a filet mignon, cooked this way; or if you care for seafood, broiled cabrilla, eaten with the juice of fresh lime, is delicious. Other seafoods that you mustn't miss are *langosta*—saltwater crayfish, or "rock lobster," with which most people are familiar—and the justly famous *camarones*, shrimps, fresh from the Gulf. The *grandes* are amazingly large, but tender and full of flavor. They are fried in deep fat, or boiled and served cold with various sauces.

Bread in Mexico is delicious. It is usually baked by old-fashioned methods, in the form of French loaves and rolls. But the popularity of tortillas has never waned, and they will be found on every table. Tortillas are made in several sizes, from little ones no bigger than a can cover, to immense discs sometimes fifteen inches in diameter. They vary in thickness and also in ingredients. In most of Mexico corn flour, called *masa*, is used. But the Sonorenses largely prefer wheat flour, and they make their tortillas paper-thin.

Years ago when we were new to Mexico we were invited to a barbecue, near Hermosillo. The meat, refried beans (*refritos*), salad and sauce were served on a plate, and at each setting there was a squared off, folded, pure white object that looked like a linen napkin. My wife and I unfolded them, as a matter of course, and spread them on our laps. We were puzzled by howls of laughter, until it was explained that the things that looked like napkins were tortillas. You break off a small piece, push some meat or beans on it, roll it up, and eat it as you would a sandwich. Though we didn't know it at the time, this was a standard joke often pulled on newcomers.

Much has been written and said about the dangers of acquiring intestinal troubles in Mexico, owing to the prevalence of dysentery and other ailments. The terms "Montezuma's revenge" and *turista* are familiar to travelers. There is no denying that this danger is present; but one may travel all over the country and avoid it by using sensible precautions. Amoebic and bacillary dysentery have been endemic in Mexico, as they have in several European countries, for generations. But they are being eliminated fast by a widespread program of sanitation.

If the tourist eats at accredited places along the main routes of travel, he will rarely encounter any difficulty. Water is perhaps the biggest problem, next to raw salads and vegetables. The latter may be safely eaten at places catering to the tourist trade, and water in all first-class restaurants, motels, and hotels is the type known as *agua purificada*. It has been treated by passing a powerful electric current through it, killing all bacteria, and rendering it sterile. But, in case trouble should develop, there are now several recent remedies, on sale at all drugstores, that will quickly knock it out. People who drink charged water, either plain or with liquor, sometimes get panicked into thinking they have the *turista*, when the trouble is something quite different. There are several kinds of "bubbly" water in Mexico, on sale in bottles, all coming from one district. They are known as *agua mineral*. The situation is somewhat similar to that found at Saratoga Springs, where, mercifully, signs tell you what to avoid—if you care to go along on a   214 normal basis. Some of the Mexican waters are highly mineralized and strongly purgative. Be sure to ask for plain effervescent water, and you will avoid trouble.

The subject of liquids brings us to liquors. Sugarcane is one of the principal agricultural products of Mexico, and much of it is employed in the making of rum. There are several principal brands and two types— light and dark. The former is known as *carta blanca* (white label), and is a light rum, about 70 proof. This is the one generally used for daiquiris. Dark rum runs around 80 proof and is known as *carta de oro*, or *oscuro*. This makes the best Cuba Libre or plain highball, with ice and soda, or plain water.

Gin is termed *ginebra* in Spanish, and several brands are offered for sale. They are of the London Dry type, but some are apt to be a little perfumy, with too much juniper. If you like a very dry gin, ask for *extra seca*. It compares favorably with American brands. Some native whiskies are available, bourbon type, but the visitor will do better to stick to the native liquors, which have a distinctive character. Among these, perhaps the most widely discussed, and controversial, is tequila.

For some reason, not quite clear, this native Mexican liquor long ago acquired the reputation associated with a rattler—treacherous, dangerous stuff that only bandits and gamblers could drink. Because the appellation "fiery tequila" is still widely used by uninformed fiction writers, the myth lives on. It is possible that in the early days, tequila was distilled with a higher alcoholic content than it now contains—so were some whiskies and rums—but it certainly is not true today. The tequila sold in cantinas and liquor stores in Mexico has about the same strength as a mild whiskey; 80 proof, or slightly more.

It is a delightful drink, once one gets used to it. The taste is slightly smoky, a little like Scotch whiskey, but entirely different from any other liquor, except mescal, which comes from the same source. Tequila is made from the heart of the maguey plant, of a certain species, and is distilled mainly in the little town of Tequila, and in other small villages in Jalisco. When the plant has matured, the heart, which resembles a big cabbage, is roasted, and ground up into a mash. This is allowed to ferment, and thereafter the process is much the same as that employed in the making of other distilled liquors.

Tequila may be drunk in a number of ways. The traditional practice is to drink it "neat," and most old-time natives prefer it that way. But they don't just gulp it down. A slice of lime and a shaker of salt accompanies the pony of tequila. The drinker shakes a dab of salt on the back of his hand, licks it, sucks a bit of lime juice, then sips the liquor. The most popular mixed drink is the tequila sour, which now has such

a widespread reputation that many people who have never been to

Mexico know and enjoy it. It is best made with fresh lime juice, sugar, a dash of salt and water, with plenty of ice.

Bacanora is a drink peculiar to Sonora. It is really an aged tequila, and the genuine article is rare and hard to obtain. Several brands of good beer are brewed in Mexico, and a large variety of liqueurs is available. Prices of liquor are extremely low, because there is no heavy federal tax, and each tourist is permitted to bring back a quota every thirty-two days of a gallon, through Arizona ports without duty as of date.

Mexico is famous as the land of the fiesta, and justly so. Patriotic celebrations such as Independence Day, on September 16th, and *Cinco de Mayo* (May 5th) are entered into with a zest that reflects the buoyant spirits of the people. Business practically closes down, not only for the one day, but for several, preceding and following the date. Parades play an important role, in the larger cities, and much time is spent in preparation of extravagant and beautiful floats. Well-trained bands may be heard playing far into the early hours of the morning, and the visitor who wants sleep, in preference to entertainment, is advised to select a motel or hotel well removed from a park that contains a bandstand. Mexican horn players seem never to run out of wind!

The great majority of fiestas are of a religious nature, and every important saint's day is celebrated to some extent. There are many, many saints. San Juan's Day (John the Baptist) is celebrated with great devotion and fervor. Street processions and special services in the churches honor the great saint, whose intercession brings rain to a land that has been parched with many days of drought, following the normal winter rainy season. The date is June 24th, and rain usually does follow shortly. A similar ceremony takes place on October 4th, San Francisco's Day (St. Francis of Assisi), and the Sonoran point of pilgrimage is Magdalena, a little town about sixty miles south of Nogales. Pious souls from many miles around assemble there, some of them having walked great distances, starting several days in advance. Rain, to purify and wash the fields after the summer's crops have been harvested, is asked for; and, coincidental or not, rain frequently comes. Generally it is in the form of one good drenching storm; then there may not be another drop for a month and a half.

Easter, the Feast of the Resurrection, is celebrated with solemnity and deep devotion. All businesses close, and activity of any but a necessary nature ceases, from the morning of Holy Thursday until Easter Sunday morning. Visitors of all creeds never fail to be impressed by the actions—not just the words—of these deeply religious people.

Christmas, the Feast of the Nativity, is a joyous occasion, and fiestas and celebrations begin a week before the actual date. An old traditional custom, which is still in common practice, is the *Posada*. It is based on   216

the Gospel story of the tribulations of Mary and Joseph, trying to find a place to stay, being turned down at the inn, and finally having to seek shelter in a stable. Groups of young people form processions, and, carrying lighted candles, sing Christmas hymns as they slowly walk along the street. Coming to a home, one of them knocks on the door and asks admission, but is refused. This is repeated several times until finally they arrive at a home where they are welcomed. Inside everything is bright and gay, with music and refreshments, and the party is on. Details of the *Posada* are arranged in advance, of course, and each night another family agrees to act as host for the next party; so the fiesta continues right up to Christmas.

Travelers in Mexico are impressed not only with the numbers of churches and chapels, in cities, towns, and in rural areas, but also by the sight of little personal shrines that are to be seen everywhere. They are usually constructed of stone, in the form of an arch, open in front and rounded on back and sides. The small altar is sometimes decorated with a framed picture or statue of the Virgin, or often of the patron saint of the family. Candles are generally placed on each side, and the shrine is constantly kept bedecked with fresh-cut flowers or potted plants. Throughout all Mexico, religion is a real and vital factor in the lives of the people. It is a staunch and constantly evident shield, opposing the false doctrine of Communism.

While baseball is steadily gaining in popularity as a spectator sport, interest in the bullfight, which was inherited from Spain, has never waned. *Aficionados* of "La Corrida" need go no farther than Sonora to witness this spectacle, with its traditional color, pomp and ceremony. Bullfights are held regularly, throughout the season, in the arena at Nogales. Fighting bulls, raised in Sonora and other parts of Mexico, are highly rated, and matadors from Mexico, South America, and sometimes from Spain put on exhibitions that rank right up at the top.

Mexico has been described as a land of sunshine, laughter, and flowers. To this list of the world's gifts must be added another—music. Throughout the Republic there is scarcely a man, woman, or child who cannot sing or whistle an air. Mariachis play an important part in daily living. Little groups of players, from two or three to eight or more, are

heard at all the important dining places and large hotels in the cities and towns. The principal instruments are the guitar (of several sizes, including a large bass type called a *guitarón*), trumpet, clarinet or saxophone, and violin.

Typical Mexican music is stylized to a considerable degree. In most *canciones* and dance numbers, the theme is carried by the clarinet or saxophone and violin. It is supported by the harmonic chords of the guitar (usually several of the instruments) plus runs and obbligatos, and affords a most pleasing background effect. The trumpet plays a very important part in most Mexican compositions. At times it follows the air simply, along with the other instruments, then suddenly bursts out into a dazzling obbligato, which is skillfully woven into the music.

Most *canciones* are simple in harmonic structure. The use of thirds in part-singing is a predominant style. Many are sad and nostalgic. "La Golondrina," a popular air widely known, can moisten your eyes when sung by a good group—especially if you are leaving the country after having had a pleasant visit. In contrast, "Allá en el Rancho Grande" is a rollicking, nonsensical bit of buffoonery, frequently punctuated with high-pitched howls of unrestrained glee. Falsetto is employed a great deal by male voices. It seems to fit into the songs, and doesn't sound effeminate.

Owing to the popularity of Latin-American music in the United States, many Mexican *canciones* and dance compositions are well known. Others, not so familiar, are heard regularly below the Border. Among them are: "Dos Arbolitos," "El Barzón," "La Mula Bronca," "La Burrita," "La Borrachita," "Las Mañanitas," "Adiós Mariquita Linda." Several regional songs are commonly sung: "El Sinaloense," "Que Lindo Es Michoacán," and, particularly applicable to our subject, "El Sonorense."

The above represents a small sample of the popular music heard at all times, anywhere one goes. But there is a great appreciation of classical music in Mexico as well, and the works of the masters are played by fine symphony organizations in the large cities, and are frequently heard on the radio. The Spanish composers—Isaac Albéniz, Manuel DeFalla, María Rodrigo, Cantina Granados—are highly esteemed, as would be expected; and Mexico is vastly proud of its own illustrious composer, Manuel Ponce. His best-known work is the universally loved "Estrellita," but the list of compositions, in many forms, that he has left is impressive and important. He was particularly fond of the classic guitar, and among other works that he wrote for the instrument are twelve Preludes, composed for the great master Andrés Segovia. Several other Mexican composers have distinguished themselves in both the popular and classical fields.

The classic, or true, Spanish guitar (as distinguished from several   218

divergent forms—the jazz, plectrum, and electric instruments) is attracting worldwide attention, and many fine players may be found in Mexico. It is a truly remarkable instrument, limited—within about three and a half octaves—only by the ability of the player. The affection of the Mexican people for the guitar is notable. It is a direct heritage from Spain, and the form and traditional method of making the instrument have been carefully maintained. The guitar center of Mexico is Paracho, a little town in Michoacán, where practically everyone is employed in manufacturing instruments, almost entirely by hand.

Guitars of all qualities and prices may be bought in stores in most cities and towns. Some of them are sold for as little as $12 or $15, others, carefully made instruments known as *tipo Valenciana* (from Valencia, the famous guitar center of Spain) are priced up to $100 or more. As might be expected, cheaper instruments are rougher in finish, and the edges of the frets are seldom polished, leaving sharp projections that snag the fingers. Strangely enough, though, most all Mexican guitars have good tone, when nylon strings are used. Being made in a fairly humid climate, these guitars are affected by dry conditions, such as we have in the desert, and they are inclined to crack. Necks also warp and make the instruments practically unplayable because of high action. I have had two otherwise good guitars act this way, after a few months in the desert. Perhaps if an instrument were kept in a more humid section of the country it might hold up better.

Dancing plays an important role in the lives of the Mexican people, and most of them are adept and very graceful. Ballroom dancing, to the music of mariachis, includes a number of forms of typically traditional steps, such as the *pasodoble*. The rumba and tango are danced with slight variations, and young people are given to fast-tempo dances in which there is much twirling and quick, running steps. The Varsoviana (Put your little foot) has become popular in the United States. This is also true of La Raspa, a rollicking exercise that can knock the breath out of any but the fittest participant.

Folk dances are popular, and trained performers often put on exhibitions that are well patronized. These take many forms, some of them showing Indian, others Spanish influence. The Hat Dance, which is said to be of Tarascan origin, and the Scarf Dance, have attained widespread popularity, and are now often performed by professional dancers of Latin origin in the entertainment centers of the United States.

The Spanish influence in dancing has never been lost, and there is much interest in traditional Old World dances, in some of the more sophisticated centers. This is particularly true of Flamenco, the fast, intricate form of the dance developed by Spanish gypsies.

This sketch of Old Mexico and its people is all too brief; but if it has helped to dispel some false notions, or has aroused in the reader a desire to see for himself this wonderful and unique land, it will have achieved its purpose. To experience the desert, one must visit both Arizona and Sonora.

Pues, amigos, vamos á Méjico? Seguro que si. Cómo no!

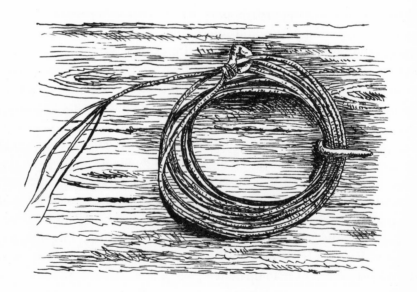

Places of Interest to Desert Visitors

THE ASPECTS OF THE DESERT—fauna, flora, terrain—differ so radically from nonarid lands that the newcomer is often at a loss to know
how to begin his acquaintance with this land of wonders. If he stays
long enough he will encounter many of the things he came out to see
through personal observations, on trips here and there to different
sections. But he will also miss some rare and fascinating things that
even old residents may never have had the privilege of encountering.
One who is truly interested in natural history will do well to spend some
time in visiting museums and monuments that have been instituted
and developed over the years for the education of the public.

Lack of space forbids more than the mention of some of the more
interesting places the visitor should see, if at all possible. If time limited
him to only one, it should, by all means, be the Arizona-Sonora Desert
Living Museum. It is situated a few miles west of Tucson, and is easily
reached on hard road.

Under the able direction of Mr. William H. Woodin and his enthusiastic and capable associates, this institution has gained worldwide re-
nown. It is unique in concept and fascinating in every detail. In a let-
ter, Mr. Woodin wrote:

"One of the chief values of the Museum to those interested in nat-
221 ural history is that here can be seen in one place, alive and carefully

labeled, a large percentage of the more interesting flora and fauna of the Sonoran Desert. An approximate count:

"Invertebrates—	21	different	kinds
Fish	25	"	"
Snakes	34	"	"
Lizards	17	"	"
Amphibians	13	"	"
Birds	53	"	"
Mammals	32	"	"
Plants, about	125	"	"

"Many of these creatures, being highly secretive, might never be seen by the average person."

In Tucson the Museum of the University of Arizona is noteworthy for its fine presentation of the story of the prehistoric inhabitants of the country. While many priceless artifacts and ornaments are displayed, the chief value of the exhibits is educational, affording a graphic insight into the lives and customs of the people who lived in this arid land from earliest times to the coming of the white man.

The university has a large and important collection of bird skins that is available to serious students of desert birdlife who may make use of the facilities upon application.

People interested in underground wonders will want to visit Colossal Cave, situated a few miles east of Tucson in the Santa Catalina Mountains. It is unique in being one of the few really large caves outside the well-known region in New Mexico, which includes Carlsbad and others.

Mention has been made in the text of the Sahuaro National Monument east of Tucson, where one of the finest stands of giant cactus in existence may be found, and the Organpipe National Monument in the southwestern part of Arizona. The former may be seen on a one-day trip in combination with Colossal Cave, and the latter is a natural stopover attraction for those entering Sonora through Lukeville and Sonoyta.

Bibliography

MAMMALS

Burt, William Henry. 1938. Faunal Relationships and Geographic Distribution of Mammals in Sonora, Mexico. The University of Michigan Press, Ann Arbor, Michigan.

Burt, William Henry, and R. P. Grossenheider. 1952. A Field Guide to the Mammals. Houghton Mifflin Co., New York.

Cockrum, E. Lendell. 1960. The Recent Mammals of Arizona: Their Taxonomy and Distribution. The University of Arizona Press, Tucson, Arizona.

Hoffmeister, Donald F., and W. W. Goodpaster. 1954. The Mammals of the Huachuca Mountains, Southeastern Arizona. The University of Illinois Press, Carbondale, Illinois.

Olin, George. 1959. Mammals of the Southwestern Deserts. Southwestern Monuments Association, Globe, Arizona.

Olin, George, and Edward Bierly. 1961. Mammals of the Southwest Mountains and Mesas. Southwestern Monuments Association, Globe, Arizona.

BIRDS

Aiken, Charles E. H. 1937. Birds of the Southwest. Colorado Springs, Colorado.

Bailey, Florence A. 1921. Handbook of Birds of the Western United States. Houghton Mifflin Co., Boston, Massachusetts.

BIBLIOGRAPHY

Blake, Emmet R. 1953. The Birds of Mexico. University of Chicago Press, Chicago, Illinois.

Brandt, Herbert. 1951. Arizona and Its Birdlife. The Bird Research Foundation, Cleveland, Ohio.

Marshall, Joe T., Jr. 1957. Birds of the Pine-Oak Woodland in Southern Arizona and Adjacent Mexico. Cooper Ornithological Society (Pacific Coast Avifauna #32), Berkeley, California.

Peterson, Roger Tory. 1941 (Revised edition, 1961). A Field Guide to Western Birds. Houghton Mifflin Co., Boston, Massachusetts.

Pough, Richard H. 1957. Audubon Western Bird Guide. Doubleday and Co., Garden City, New York.

Smith, Gusse T. 1955. Birds of the Arizona Desert. Double Shoe Publishers, Scottsdale, Arizona.

REPTILES AND AMPHIBIANS

Boys, Floyd, and Hobart M. Smith. 1959. Poisonous Amphibians and Reptiles: Their Recognition and Bite Treatment. Charles C. Thomas Publications, Springfield, Illinois.

Killian, J. 1954. Common Reptiles of Arizona. Arizona Game and Fish Commission, Phoenix, Arizona.

Stebbins, Robert C. 1951. Amphibians of Western North America. The University of California Press, Berkeley, California.

Stebbins, Robert C. 1954. Amphibians and Reptiles of Western North America. McGraw-Hill Co., New York.

FISHES

Jordan, David S., and Barton W. Evermann. 1934. American Food and Game Fishes. Doubleday & Co., Garden City, New York.

LaMonte, Francesca. 1954. North American Game Fishes. Doubleday & Co., Garden City, New York.

Mulch, Ernest E., and W. C. Gamble. 1955. Game Fishes of Arizona. Arizona Game and Fish Commission, Phoenix, Arizona.

Walford, Lionel A. 1937. Marine Game Fishes of the Pacific Coast—Alaska to the Equator. University of California Press. Berkeley, California.

MARINE SHELLS

Keen, A. Myra. 1958. Sea Shells of Tropical West America. Stanford University Press. Stanford, California.

TREES AND PLANTS

Armstrong, Margaret. 1915 (20th edition). Field Book of Western Wild Flowers. G. P. Putnam's Sons, New York.

BIBLIOGRAPHY

Benson, I., and R. Darrow. 1954. Trees and Shrubs of the Southwestern Deserts. University of Arizona Press and University of New Mexico Press, Tucson and Albuquerque.

Dodge, Natt N., and Jeanne R. Janish. 1958. Flowers of the Southwest Deserts. Southwestern Monuments Association, Globe, Arizona.

Hitchcock, A. S. 1950. Manual of the Grasses of the United States. Government Printing Office, Washington, D.C.

Kearney, T. H., R. H. Peebles, and others. 1960 (2nd ed.). Arizona Flora. University of California Press, Berkeley, California.

Standley, P. C. 1923-1926, reissued 1961. Trees and Shrubs of Mexico. Parts 1-3, 5: 1961, Part 4: 1926. Vol. 23, Contributions of the U.S. National Herbarium, U.S. National Museum, Washington, D.C.

THE DESERT AND MISSIONS

Bolton, E. H. 1936. Rim of Christendom. The Macmillan Company, New York. The definitive work on Father Eusebio Francisco Kino and his influence on the history of the Sonoran Desert.

Krutch, Joseph Wood. 1952. The Desert Year. William Sloane Associates, Inc. An inspiring and sensitively written work on the desert. Also other titles by this noted author and scholar.

Lumholtz, Carl. 1912. New Trails in Mexico. Charles Scribner's Sons, New York. Long out of print, but still one of the best accounts of the Sonoran Desert published. Well worth looking up in a library.

INDIANS AND ARCHAEOLOGY

Cummings, Byron. 1953. First Inhabitants of Arizona and the Southwest. Cummings Publication Council, Tucson, Arizona.

Dockstader, Frederick J. 1961. Indian Art in America. New York Graphic Society, New York.

Driver, Harold E. 1961. Indians of North America. University of Chicago Press.

Wormington, H. M. 1961. Prehistoric Indians of North America. Colorado Museum of Natural History, Denver, Colorado.

THE SERIS

Coolidge, Dane and Mary. 1939. Last of the Seris. E. P. Dutton, New York.

Kroeber, A. L. The Seri. Southwest Museum Papers #6, Los Angeles, California.

McGee, J. W. The Seri Indians. Bureau of American Ethnology, Annual Report XVII (1898), Government Printing Office, Washington, D.C. Even though old, still considered the basic study of the Seris.

BIBLIOGRAPHY

ROCKS AND MINERALS

McFall, Russell P. 1951. Gem Hunter's Guide. Science and Mechanics Publishing Co., Chicago, Illinois.

Pearl, Richard M. 1955. How to Know the Minerals and Rocks. McGraw-Hill Co., New York.